THE MAKING OF *A SHROPSHIRE LAD*
A MANUSCRIPT VARIORUM

The Making of
A SHROPSHIRE LAD

A MANUSCRIPT VARIORUM

BY

TOM BURNS HABER

EDITOR OF THE CENTENNIAL EDITION

OF A. E. HOUSMAN'S POETRY

UNIVERSITY OF WASHINGTON PRESS

Seattle and London

Once again, for Grace

Acknowledgments

THE editor wishes to express his thanks to the following institutions whose generosity and interest in the humanities have been of substantial aid in the publication of this book: The American Council of Learned Societies, administrators of a contribution from the United States Steel Foundation; the Ohio State University Development Fund; and the Simon Lazarus Family Foundation.

Contents

THE MAKING OF *A SHROPSHIRE LAD*
A MANUSCRIPT VARIORUM

Introduction

GENERAL CHARACTERISTICS OF THE NOTEBOOKS; DATES; CANCEL-SIGNS

THE Library of Congress collection of A. E. Housman's manuscripts taken from his four poetry notebooks includes the remains of all the poems of *A Shropshire Lad* but three—numbers 41, 54, and 63. Of the sixty other poems, not all of the original material, regrettably, has survived; but as a partial offset to this debit it may be said that, in the erasure and dissection the notebooks underwent before they left England, the manuscripts pertaining to Housman's first volume suffered far less than those of the three other portions of his *Collected Poems*.

The pieces that Housman selected for *A Shropshire Lad* were gathered from areas in Notebooks A and B that also contained drafts and fair copies of poems that were withheld from publication until they saw the light in his *Last Poems* (1922) or the two posthumous collections (1936, 1937). Thus, an examination of the sources of his first volume tends to involve materials representing the other divisions of his poetic canon. This involvement is more fortunate than otherwise, and, in the diplomatic analyses that follow, it will be seen that I have frequently paid attention to the entries that immediately preceded or followed a given poem, showing it to be, perhaps, a solitary experiment, a return to an abandoned theme, or a phase in the onset, culmination, or ebb of a mood. As such examples accumulate they will provide a new and broader comprehension of Housman's development—which is the main objective of this variorum.

Housman's writing was generally clear even in his penciled entry of a poem, though haste or overcrowding sometimes produced script that he may have found hard to decipher. In his Senate House lecture he wryly referred to poetry as a "morbid secretion" and said that he seldom wrote it unless he was "rather out of health."[1] This confession is verified to a

Poetry (Cambridge: at the University Press, 1933), pp. 47-48.

[1] Delivered May 9, 1933, later published under the title *The Name and Nature of*

3

degree by the appearance of a number of manuscripts which in their faintness or erratic letter shapes hint of a malaise such as the poet described as the condition most favorable for the inspirational mood.

Throughout the four notebooks, Housman most often used pencil from first to final draft, except in the "pre-1890" section of the first notebook, where he used black ink in copying and composing most of the lines on the twenty-three pages that survive, in whole or part.

As to the dates of these early manuscripts, simple calligraphic tests make it possible to assign rather narrow limitations for a portion of them. The material itself from A 9 to A 54[2] was heterogeneous, for Housman began writing his serious poetry in a notebook that already contained more than forty pages of classical notes dating from the period of his residence in Oxford—1877-81—or the early years of his London period, after 1882. The versos of the sheets containing these notes, according to Laurence Housman's prefatory note to the Analysis, were later filled with nonsense verse. Of this potpourri, only two and one-half sheets have survived: pages 9-10, 11-12, 17-18 (upper half only).

The writing from recto to verso in these pages may seem to the casual eye to exhibit no variation in letter styles, but there is a difference in the forms of the letter *r*: the form *ɿ* is used regularly on the rectos, *r* on the versos. This latter form is also present throughout the serious poetry, which begins on page 57.

It is the persistence of this *r* form that permits certain inductions and resolves some long-standing questions concerning the dates of the manuscripts from A 57 to A 106, where the first date appears. There is little doubt that Housman adopted the second letter style deliberately, probably in the early or middle eighties, about the time his brilliant series of classical papers began to take shape, and with them his lifelong struggle with myopic printers. After a few disheartening experiences it would have been natural for him to try to achieve unmistakable clarity in his manuscript, and particularly in the form of the letter *r,* for that seemed to be the greatest stumbling block. As late as 1911 he wrote to his publisher, Grant Richards: "At the end of a word [the printers] pretend to think [*r*] is *s,* and in other positions they pretend to think it is *v.* If they would just notice how I write it, and not expect to find *ɿ* it would save trouble."[3]

[2] Following Laurence Housman's Analysis, from *My Brother, A. E. Housman: Personal Recollections together with Thirty Hitherto Unpublished Poems* (New York: Scribner's, 1938), pp. 256-72 (hereafter *Recollections*), I have used the letters A, B, C, D in referring to the notebooks. The following symbols have been used to designate the four sections of Housman's poetry: *ASL, A Shropshire Lad; LP, Last Poems; MP, More Poems; AP, Additional Poems.*

[3] Grant Richards, *Housman: 1897-1936* (New York: Oxford University Press, 1942), p. 103 (hereafter *Memoir*).

I have suggested some date in the early or middle eighties as a *terminus a quo* for the new form of this letter. In support of this, there is a specimen of Housman's writing on page 376 of Richards' *Memoir* (dated 1879) that shows the letter several times and always in the old form; while on page 4 is reproduced another specimen of his hand, dated 1887, in which the letter occurs four times and invariably in the new style. The date 1887, all students of A. E. Housman's poetry know, he used as the title for the opening lyric of *A Shropshire Lad,* which is adumbrated in four lines of an imperfect stanza jotted down on A 66:

> The weapons of the war
> The land they perished for   Lies the defended land
> The soul you died to save

The connection between these four lines and *ASL* 1 is unmistakable: the second became line 24 of the poem, and the third was adapted to become line 16, "Themselves they could not save." A 66 could not have been written earlier than June 22, 1887, the time of the events described in *ASL* 1. Thus the limiting dates of the thirty-nine pages between A 66 and 106, in which three *Shropshire Lad* lyrics were written—numbers 40, 14, and 46—narrow down to approximately three years.

The date September, 1890, is a landmark in Notebook A, possibly in Housman's life as a writer. The larger number of the manuscripts that have survived up to page 106 appear to be copies of earlier compositions: most of them are carefully written in ink and show comparatively few marks of revision. But as we turn to A 106 we cannot resist the feeling that here we are in the presence of something still retaining the warmth of its moment of composition. From this point on Housman's notebook ceases to be a register and becomes a collection of work sheets. Its remaining 136 pages eventually contained, in drafts of varying completeness, sixty-eight poems, thirty-nine of them to be gathered into the printer's copy of *A Shropshire Lad.*

Following A 106 there are fourteen other dated pages surviving in the first notebook—the last, A 237, headed "March 1895"; and in the first 116 pages of his second notebook Housman entered ten more dates, from April, 1895, on B 3, to December, 1895, on B 116.[4] It is difficult to see why he should have considered this or that poem worthy of being dated. Long sections of A and B run on without any sign of date (Laurence in his Analysis apparently recorded all the dated pages; so we now have

[4] This page contains two drafts of "Yonder see the morning blink," a late-comer that must have been dashed off about the time the complete MS of *A Shropshire Lad* was delivered to the publisher, late in 1895. The poem, however, was withdrawn before it reached proof sheets and laid aside until the publication of *Last Poems* (1922), where it appeared as number 11.

a clue even to missing pages that bore dates); provokingly enough, a single date will recur on nearly adjacent pages. For example, "Feb. 1893" occurs three times from A 151 to A 155. Besides noting in his Analysis the dated pages of the notebooks, Laurence published in his *Recollections* a list of all the dated poems in the *Collected Poems.* There are twenty pieces from *A Shropshire Lad* in this list, the final one being the first draft of *ASL* 31 ("On Wenlock Edge . . .") on B 97, a page that has not survived.

One important bit of chronological testimony bearing on these note-book pages occurs in Housman's preface to *Last Poems,* where he states that his great creative period came in the early months of 1895. As the preceding pages have shown, this statement loses some of its validity in the face of plain evidence from the first notebook, in which after page 106 he was composing at a very rapid rate four and one-half years prior to the onset of "the continuous excitement" he said was so productive. A later section of this introduction will show that about one third of *A Shropshire Lad* was on paper before the appearance of the date "Jan. 1895" on A 216, and that after B 36, where Housman wrote "June 1895," sixteen new *Shropshire Lad* lyrics were begun and completed down to the end of the year; and nine others begun before June, 1895, were taken up again and readied for the printer. Thus it will be seen that Housman's poetic development was somewhat less intense and rapid than he would have it believed.[5] His attraction to poetry, like his devotion to scholarship, began in his school days, and when he began transcribing his serious poetry on the fifty-fourth page of his first notebook, he had already served his apprenticeship to rhyme and acquired a facility of expression that mocks maturity. "Parta Quies," quoted in his epitaph,[6] dates from his undergraduate days, and its companion piece "Stay, if you list . . ." *(AP* 12), copied on A 61, is probably as early.

The reliquiae of the notebooks show cancellations and erasures on nearly every page. All but a very few of the erasures, I believe, were made by Laurence Housman, who is in my opinion also responsible for the undula drawn over many single lines. The cancel sign generally used by A. E. Housman was a horizontal line drawn through single words, phrases, and entire lines. His purpose was simply to cancel or to strike through a draft from which he had made a fair copy; whereas Laurence's intention, as he explained to me,[7] was to obliterate. In my notes describing the manu-scripts I have not generally taken account of cancellations I believe to

---

[5] He was believed, and the correction still lags far behind the truth, for as late as May, 1957, Harold Nicolson was writing, "Yet the 'continuous excitement,' which as we know produced the larger part of his lyrics, was experienced by Housman in 1895 . . ." *(The Observer,* May 19, 1957, p. 16).

[6] See Laurence Housman's *Recollections,* p. 123.

[7] In a letter dated January 19, 1951.

have been made by another hand than the author's, as the only attention they deserve is the effort to recover what they were intended to destroy. My policy here will probably leave the reader with the impression that the transcription of the manuscripts as they now exist was a matter of no great difficulty, but anyone viewing them now in the Library of Congress will at once be struck by the fact that Laurence's attempts at obliteration, though not often completely successful, did inject many vexatious problems, some of them beyond solution.

Another cancel sign A. E. Housman used is the symbol X, which he drew through larger portions of his manuscript. Sometimes as many as three of these symbols may overspread an entire page; occasionally the X stands alone in the upper-right corner, again just below the final stanza. In a few instances, as if to make certain his eye would pick it up, he drew a long-shafted arrow pointed in the direction of the X. Another variant consists of the X in the usual corner, with a long wavy line, or undula, trailing along the right margin—perhaps to the bottom of the page. This stigma occurs about twenty times in Notebook A, only twice in B up to page 116. Invariably this device was employed to divide the goats from the sheep, for no poem so marked was admitted to either of the two volumes he himself published.[8]

The most frequent use of the cancel signs is in the tentative rejection of alternative words and phrases. I say *tentative,* for a careful examination of Housman's revisions will leave the impression that every cancellation he made in his manuscript was subject to a reversal of opinion. This reversal might be slow in arriving but it was always imminent, even after the dispatch of printer's copy. As to the alternatives he left open—neither one canceled—in drafts and fair copies, it must not be supposed that the one latest written, above or below the line, had the best chance of survival. There are over seventy situations of this kind in the *Shropshire Lad* manuscripts. In twenty-one cases the original reading went into print; and in sixteen others Housman abandoned both in favor of a third.[9]

[8] The X-undula sign is found on A 58, the verso of the first surviving page of serious poetry. It occurs ten times in the "pre-1890" section of the first notebook; from this section only three pieces were chosen for *A Shropshire Lad.*

[9] A.E.H. must have believed when he granted his brother permission to publish complete and up-to-standard poems remaining in his notebooks that the quantity of eligible manuscripts would be very small. He left his executor no authority to complete unfinished lines or choose between open alternatives although it has been alleged in the public press, without proof, that Laurence had this authority. A. E. Housman's testamentary instructions were, simply, "I permit him but do not enjoin him to select from my verse manuscript writing and to publish any poems which appear to him to be completed and to be not inferior in quality to the average of my published poems. . . ." Laurence's elastic interpretation of these provisos engendered numerous textual faults in his first printings of the posthumous poetry and a long array of corrections in the numerous reissues by the London publisher.

HOUSMAN'S METHODS OF COMPOSITION

The data given in the preceding section will substantiate the opinion that in the notebook remains, ample material exists for a worthwhile manuscript variorum of the poems that went into Housman's first volume. This opinion is not shaken by two deterrent factors: the dissection and obliteration the notebooks have suffered at the hands of the poet's brother, and the absence of a few first or intermediate drafts whose existence is self-evident but which were apparently never a part of the notebooks themselves. Now that, by the use of photographic reproductions, the whole sheets and fragments have been redeemed from the haphazard condition in which Laurence left them—as they still exist, by the way, in the Library of Congress collection—the value of these documents has become more than obvious and calls for a systematic display, poem by poem, of their contents.

It was not often that Housman discussed the composition of his poetry even with his closest friends, and then he tantalizingly hedged his revelations with such obscurity as to arouse more curiosity than he satisfied. His most explicit pronouncement was made late in his life, in his Leslie Stephen lecture, "The Name and Nature of Poetry," delivered in the Senate House at Cambridge University on May 9, 1933. His audience must have been electrified to hear the speaker, after describing his physical reactions to poetry, suddenly announce: "My opinions on poetry are necessarily tinged, perhaps I should say tainted, by the circumstance that I have come into contact with it on two sides...." He continued, "... poetry is a very wide term ... so comprehensive is it that it embraces two books, fortunately not large ones, of my own.... I have seldom written poetry unless I was rather out of health, and the experience, though pleasurable, was generally agitating and exhausting. If only that you may know what to avoid, I will give some account of the process."[10]

Fully aware now of the acute attention of his audience, Housman continued:

Having drunk a pint of beer at luncheon ... I would go out for a walk of two or three hours. As I went along, thinking of nothing in particular, only looking at things around me and following the progress of the seasons, there would flow into my mind, with sudden and unaccountable emotion, sometimes a line or two of verse, sometimes a whole stanza at once, accompanied, not preceded, by a vague notion of the poem which they were destined to form part of. Then there would usually be a lull of an hour or so, then perhaps the spring would bubble up again. I say bubble up, because, so far as I could make out, the source of the suggestions thus proffered to the brain was an abyss which I have already had occasion to mention, the pit of the stomach. When I got home I wrote them down, leaving gaps, and hoping that further inspiration might be forthcoming another day. Sometimes it was, if I took my walks in a receptive

[10] *Name and Nature of Poetry,* pp. 46-47.

and expectant frame of mind; but sometimes the poem had to be taken in hand and completed by the brain, which was apt to be a matter of trouble and anxiety, involving trial and disappointment, and sometimes ending in failure. I happen to remember distinctly the genesis of the piece which stands last in my first volume. Two of the stanzas, I do not say which, came into my head, just as they are printed, while I was crossing the corner of Hampstead Heath between the Spaniard's Inn and the footpath to Temple Fortune. A third stanza came with a little coaxing after tea. One more was needed, but it did not come: I had to turn to and compose it myself, and that was a laborious business. I wrote it thirteen times, and it was more than a twelvemonth before I got it right.[11]

One of the most remarkable features of this description of the poetic process as Housman knew it is the crowding together of idea, language, and emotion into a single undifferentiated creative impulse. His poetry did not originate in an unverbalized mood to which the word later gave communicable form. Idea and language arose together out of the subconscious —"the abyss"—and simultaneously with them came the influx of strong emotion. That is, the first stages of the creative act were not designed, not the result of conscious will but of something deeper. The line, the quatrain, the poem itself arose shaped out of shapelessness; syntax, rhyme, meter all broke surface together and presented themselves at the same moment. A little earlier in his lecture Housman had referred to Wordsworth's well-known definition of poetry as "the spontaneous overflow of powerful feelings" and had implied that Wordsworth's experiences were not unlike his own. But he did not go on to quote the elder poet's corollary about poetry taking its origin in emotion recollected in tranquillity. For with Housman, it would seem, the origin of poetry was not in emotion recollected but in its very onset.

There can be no reason for questioning Housman's account of his experiences, and they have much value for the student of poetry, even though the processes described will always be more clearly felt than told and will be felt differently by each poet. In his Leslie Stephen lecture Housman did not say all that he knew about the writing of poetry, nor all he might have said about his own habits of composition: he merely chose to illuminate his concluding remarks with a glimpse into his workshop, and such insights have a peculiar worth—Housman's the added savor of rarity.

Housman's description of the genesis of his poetry and his recording of it are amply illustrated in page after page of his notebooks. There may be seen the first solitary line that perhaps a few pages later has expanded into a stanza; or it may have had to lie dormant for months or years until the emotion that engendered it was summoned up again to produce the completed lyric. Again there is the near-perfect draft of a poem that came

[11] *Ibid.*, pp. 48-50.

full blown and lost nothing between the footpath and the desk. Often there is the ill-begotten one that came with its stanzas sadly out of order or perhaps with some missing: its rectification by brain might spread over two or three closely written pages. Housman's provocative reference in his lecture to his laboring with the last poem in *A Shropshire Lad* aroused some inquiry among the curious who professed to be able to identify the stanzas first and last written. He may have felt some annoyance in their importunities and took means to forestall them by destroying the manuscript record of *ASL* 63. At any rate, it is one of the three poems of which no traces have survived in the notebooks.[12]

The Notebooks from 1936 to the Present

Frequent reference in the foregoing pages has been made to the handling of the manuscripts after they passed into the hands of Laurence Housman following his brother's death on April 30, 1936. Public interest, Laurence knew, would demand publication of the gleanings he might find among his brother's papers; but when he received the notebooks, he must have recognized after turning a few pages that large portions of them would, by the requirements of A. E. Housman's will, have to be destroyed. The will permitted him to save only manuscripts of poetry already published or of those he himself would publish, and the notebooks did not segregate these materials in a way that made it possible to lay aside many complete drafts that he could legitimately save. For example, a page containing the unique draft of a famous poem might be backed by a full page of scattered fragments, interesting but contraband. Strict obedience required that the whole sheet be destroyed. Page after page required decisions of various kinds, and before coming down to cases Laurence wisely decided while the notebooks were still intact to draw up his Analysis, in which he described the contents of the notebooks. He identified the poems, usually by their first lines, and in his Analysis added many annotations such as "Single lines and fragments," "rough draft," "fair copy," and so on. His review of the *Shropshire Lad* material covered 188 numbered pages of Notebook A and the first 116 pages of B.

Despite some unaccountable omissions and errors of location and page numbering, the Analysis is of immense value in preserving the catalog of Housman's poetic output. As a check list it is indispensable as a means of identifying and correctly locating nearly every piece of manuscript that has survived, besides indicating the nature and amount of missing material.

After he had drawn from the notebooks the pieces composing two

---

[12] Laurence Housman surmises (*Recollections,* p. 255) that his brother destroyed the notebook page containing the draft of *ASL* 63 "in order that his riddle might remain unsolved."

posthumous volumes *(More Poems,* 1936, and *Additional Poems,* in the *Recollections,* 1937) Laurence returned to the manuscripts to take out those that he was formally commanded to destroy. The remainder would be prepared for sale. There were fifty-nine sheets that contained nothing but published verse; obviously he would be fully justified in negotiating these. Then there were approximately 140 sheets containing nothing but workshop sketching and about as many more that bore both published poetry and workshop material on one page or another or sometimes mingled on both pages. The former group of 140 leaves had to be destroyed; but what to do with the other?

Here Laurence adopted a middle course: he salvaged as much as he easily could of the "non-contraband" material by cutting away the other part of the page; and where this separation was too difficult—where, for example, a salvageable draft was backed by contraband manuscript—he erased the latter, which was invariably in pencil, or overscored the lines with an undula and pasted the sheet or the section onto a new mounting sheet, leaving exposed the holograph he wished to preserve. If an ink draft thus treated exhibited variant or rejected passages, he usually effaced these by an undula drawn over them in ink. The fifty-nine notebook sheets that required no cutting or erasure were also affixed to mounting sheets, each leaf tipped on at an upper corner. Together with these two hundred-odd surviving leaves of the notebooks, Laurence set up in the same manner seventeen foolscap sheets of poems A. E. Housman had copied fair while preparing printer's copy for *A Shropshire Lad* and *Last Poems.*[13] As he proceeded in this clipping and pasting, Laurence was filing the mounting sheets in four large envelopes, lettered A, B, C, and D. A fifth envelope, marked E, contained the seventeen foolscap sheets. He did not keep a careful eye on the provenance of the fragments he produced (many of them now bear no page number or other clue to their original location), and the filing of these and indeed of some full notebook pages clearly numbered seems to have been done without much regard for the sequence they had in the notebooks.

While negotiating the sale of his five envelopes and their contents, Laurence made a further sifting of the tattered notebooks and from them picked out fifteen more pieces of manuscript which, with five foolscap sheets of

[13] These seventeen sheets now form volume VI of the Library of Congress collection of the Housman MSS. Three of the poems were once included in the printer's copy of *A Shropshire Lad* and carry Housman's original numerals: "Yonder see the morning blink" (*LP* 11), "In the morning, in the morning" (*LP* 23), and "The Sage to the Young Man" (*MP* 4).

Three other poems are on the same kind of ruled paper and evidently date from the same period: "Easter Hymn" (*MP* 1), "Oh who is that young sinner ... ?" (*AP* 18), and "I promise nothing: friends will part" (*MP* 12). The other ten sheets contain nine poems that were being prepared for *Last Poems.*

humorous verse,[14] were duly mounted, put into two large envelopes, and dispatched to his agent. All of the collection was eventually purchased by Mrs. Matthew John Whittall of Washington, D.C., who in 1940 generously presented it to the Library of Congress. A few years after receiving the collection, the Library authorities, anticipating that the adhesive might in time impair the legibility of the writing, detached the notebook sheets from their mountings, cleaned and remounted them, hinged, in the same order they had exhibited in Laurence's envelopes. In this process 136 new sections of Housman's poetry came to light, many of them early drafts of the lyrics in *A Shropshire Lad.*

THE POEMS IN THEIR ORDER OF COMPOSITION; THEIR SEQUENCE IN
A SHROPSHIRE LAD

There has been much speculation about the order in which the poems of Housman's first volume were composed, the relationship of successive drafts, and their condition when the author was collecting his copy for the printer. These subjects are here reviewed statistically for the first time. The following catalog includes many pages that now exist in two, three, and four fragments; but unless it is evident that a part of the writing on a given page is missing I have made no note of the completeness or incompleteness of that page.

No. 40 ("Into my heart an air that kills") on A 63;[15] unique ink draft with corrections in pencil.

No. 1 ("1887") on A 66; three lines in ink, one in pencil, all heavily canceled in ink, apparently by a later hand. Continued on A 202-3; B 18-19.

No. 14 ("There pass the careless people") on A 82-83; unique ink and pencil draft with corrections in pencil. Probably two stanzas lost with missing sections of both pages.

No. 46 ("Bring, in this timeless grave to throw") on A 84; rough pencil draft, all but four lines canceled; probably two thirds of the MS destroyed. Continued on A 116.

---

[14] "Some of the fragments are, I think, duplicates of what I have already sent you either as fair copies or more complete drafts; and I had probably put them aside as not wanted and forgotten them." Laurence Housman to John Carter, Aug. 31, 1939.

These fragments were in an envelope marked "F" and now constitute volume VII of the Library of Congress collection. The last (seventh) envelope was unlettered; it contained the humorous verse: three poems on the five foolscap sheets and three from the early part of Notebook A, backed with classical notes. This material went into volume VIII of the collection.

[15] This is ten pages after the beginning of the serious poetry, the first complete piece of which is "For these of old the trader" (*MP* 3), on pp. 58-59. The one other antecedent poem is "Stay if you list, O passer by the way" (*AP* 12), on p. 61.

No. 42 ("The Merry Guide") on A 106-7; pencil and ink draft, much corrected, of eleven of the fifteen stanzas. Dated "Sept. 1890."[16] Continued on A 108-9; A 114-15.

No. 42 on A 108-9; second draft, in ink, with corrections in ink and pencil. MS of most of five or six stanzas (6, 7?, 8, 9?, 10?, 11) destroyed. Continued on A 114-15.

No. 42 on A 114-15; third (and final) draft, in ink, with corrections in pencil. Dated "Sept. 1890."

No. 46 ("Bring, in this timeless grave to throw") on A 116; second (and final) draft, in ink, with corrections in ink and pencil. Title "A winter funeral" in pencil.

No. 39 (" 'Tis time, I think, by Wenlock town") on A 125; in pencil, intact. MS of stanzas 2 and 3 destroyed. Continued on A 153, A 155.

No. 21 ("Bredon Hill") on A 132-33; in pencil, corrected. Dated "July 1891." Continued on A 142-43.

No. 52 ("Far in a western brookland") on A 134; in pencil, much canceled. Continued on A 135.

No. 52 on A 135; second (and final) draft, in ink, with light pencil corrections. Dated "1891-2."

No. 21 ("Bredon Hill") on A 142-43; second (and final) draft, in ink, with title and corrections in pencil.

No. 32 ("From far, from eve and morning") on A 144; in pencil, the first quatrain much corrected. Continued on A 145, 158.

No. 32, on A 145; second draft, in ink, with corrections in pencil. MS of stanza 1 destroyed. Continued on A 158.

No. 48 ("Be still, my soul, be still . . .") on A 146-47, in pencil, much corrected. MS of stanza 3 missing. Continued on A 159.

No. 33 ("If truth in hearts that perish") on A 148; pencil draft, with corrections. Continued on A 164-65.

No. 39 (" 'Tis time, I think, by Wenlock town") on A 153; second draft, in pencil, of stanzas 2 and 3 only, corrected. Dated "Feb. 1893." Continued on A 155.

No. 39 on A 155; third (and final) draft, in ink; title "May"; one correction. Dated "Feb. 1893."

No. 32 ("From far, from eve and morning") on A 158; third (and final) draft, in ink; lightly corrected in pencil.

No. 48 ("Be still, my soul, be still . . .") on A 159; second (and final) draft, in ink, with ink cancellations by a later hand and corrections in pencil.

No. 22 ("The street sounds to the soldiers' tread") on A 162; the last line only, in pencil. Continued on B 22-23.

---

[16] This is the first date surviving in the notebooks.

No. 57 ("You smile upon your friend to-day") on A 164; pencil draft of stanza 2, intact; MS of stanza 1 probably destroyed. Continued on B 51-52.

No. 33 ("If truth in hearts that perish") on A 164-65; second (and final) draft, in pencil, with corrections. Alternatives for perhaps two stanzas lost with missing portions of both pages.

No. 10 ("March") on A 170; unique draft, in pencil, with many corrections.

No. 36 ("White in the moon the long road lies") on A 181; unique draft, in pencil, much revised. A draft of stanza 2 destroyed with missing lower section.

No. 8 ("Farewell to barn and stack and tree") on A 191; unique draft, in pencil, with many corrections; title "Severn Shore." Dated "August 1894."

No. 59 ("The Isle of Portland") on A 192; unique draft, in pencil, corrected.

No. 26 ("Along the field as we came by") on A 192; lines 9 and 10 only, in pencil.

No. 61 ("Hughley Steeple") on A 193; unique draft, in pencil, with many corrections.

No. 1 ("1887") on A 202-3; first complete draft, in pencil, with many corrections. Some stanzas lost with missing sections of both pages. Continued on B 18-19.

No. 37 ("As through the wild green hills of Wyre") on A 204; pencil draft of seven scattered lines. Continued on B 57.

No. 3 ("The Recruit") on A 205; pencil draft of stanzas 2 and 3 only. Continued on A 222-25.

No. 60 ("Now hollow fires burn out to black") on A 207; unique pencil draft, with many corrections.

No. 5 ("Oh see how thick the goldcup flowers") on A 208; pencil draft of last three lines of stanza 4 and complete stanza 5 only, lightly corrected. Continued on B 24-25.

No. 53 ("The True Lover") on A 210; pencil draft, much corrected, of stanzas 1, 6, 7, 8. MS of two or three other stanzas destroyed. Continued on A 211, 212-13.

No. 53 on A 212-13; third (and final) draft, in pencil, lightly corrected. Dated "December 1894."

No. 13 ("When I was one-and-twenty") on A 216; title line only, in pencil. Dated "Jan. 1895."[17]

[17] "This [p. 216] is followed by a cut-out page of which only the initial letters of nine lines remain, but showing that it was a rough draft of the same poem." Laurence Housman's note in the Analysis, *Recollections,* pp. 260-61.

No. 28 ("The Welsh Marches") on A 217; unique draft, in pencil. About one half of the MS is missing. Dated "Jan. 1895."

No. 4 ("Reveille") on A 218; pencil draft, much corrected. About one half of the MS is missing. Continued on A 219, B 67.

No. 4 on A 219; second draft, in ink, with corrections in pencil. Dated "Jan. 1895." Continued on B 67.

No. 35 ("On the idle hill of summer") on A 220; line 8 only, in pencil. Continued on B 94, B 101.

No. 55 ("Westward on the high-hilled plains") on A 221, last two lines (15 and 16) only, in pencil. Continued on B 12, B 20-21.

No. 3 ("The Recruit") on A 222-23; first full draft, in pencil, title "The Queen's Shilling"; A 223 much canceled and corrected. MS of perhaps two stanzas (6 and 7) destroyed with missing lower part of A 222. Continued on A 224-25.

No. 3 on A 224-25; second (and final) draft, in ink, lightly corrected in pencil and one stanza canceled. Dated "Jan. 1895." On A 225 an experimental stanza, in pencil, canceled; probably MS of others destroyed.

No. 9 ("On moonlit heath and lonesome bank") on A 226-27; unique pencil draft, portions very heavily corrected. Dated "Feb. 1895."

No. 43 ("The Immortal Part") on A 228-29; pencil draft, with many corrections. Continued on B 72-73.

No. 12 ("When I watch the living meet") on A 230; unique pencil draft, lightly revised.

No. 15 ("Look not in my eyes . . .") on A 232; unique pencil draft, lightly revised. MS of possibly another draft of stanza 1 destroyed.

No. 38 ("The winds out of the west land blow") on A 233; pencil draft of stanzas 1, 2, and 5 only, with corrections. Stanzas 3 and 4 may have been on missing portion of the page.[18] Continued on B 58-59.

No. 56 ("The Day of Battle") on A 236; pencil draft of stanzas 1, 3, and 4 only, lightly corrected. Stanza 2 probably on missing portion of the page. Continued on A 237.

No. 56 on A 237; second (and final) draft, in ink; title and light corrections in pencil. Dated "March 1895."

No. 30 ("Others, I am not the first") on A 238; unique pencil draft, with many corrections.

No. 19 ("To an Athlete Dying Young") on A 240; pencil draft of three stanzas and several scattered lines and couplets. A 241, containing probably the remainder of the draft, was destroyed. Continued on B 10-11.

No. 29 ("The Lent Lily") on B 3; unique pencil draft, lightly revised. Dated "April 1895."

[18] The Analysis records that two lines of *ASL* 38 were written on A 231. The fragment that survives shows no trace of them, but one third of the page is missing.

No. 51 ("Loitering with a vacant eye") on B 8-9;[19] unique draft, in pencil, corrected. Missing portion of B 8 probably contained several lines.

No. 19 ("To an Athlete Dying Young") on B 10-11; second (and final) draft, in pencil, much corrected.

No. 55 ("Westward on the high-hilled plains") on B 12; one line only (number 6) in pencil. Continued on B 20-21.

No. 49 ("Think no more, lad; laugh, be jolly") on B 12; end of line 11 and full last line, and other scattered fragments, in pencil. Continued on B 90.

No. 25 ("This time of year a twelvemonth past") on B 14; in pencil, some lines left incomplete. Perhaps two stanzas on missing lower half of page. Continued on B 15.

No. 25 on B 15; second (and final) draft, in pencil, much corrected. Some lines lost with small lower section.

No. 11 ("On your midnight pallet lying") on B 16; unique draft, in pencil, corrected.

No. 18 ("Oh, when I was in love with you") on B 17; pencil draft, corrected. Dated "May 1895." Continued on B 29.

No. 1 ("1887") on B 18-19; second (and final) draft, in pencil, much corrected. Perhaps two stanzas lost in cut sections from both pages.

No. 55 ("Westward on the high-hilled plains") on B 20; first draft in pencil, revised; cut section from top probably contained early version of stanza 1.

No. 55 on B 21; second (and final) draft, in pencil, with open spaces where lines had been perfected in first draft.

No. 22 ("The street sounds to the soldiers' tread") on B 22-23; two drafts, in pencil, with many canceled lines.

No. 5 ("Oh see how thick the goldcup flowers") on B 24-25; in pencil, much revised. First appearance of stanzas 1 and 2 and the complete stanza 3, the last three lines of which appeared on A 208.

No. 17 ("Twice a week the winter thorough") on B 26-27; unique draft, in pencil, with corrections.

No. 18 ("Oh, when I was in love with you") on B 29; second (and final) draft, in pencil, some lines canceled. A few alternative lines probably lost with the missing upper section.

No. 27 ("Is my team ploughing?") on B 31-32. B 31 is missing; B 32 (now in four sections) contains stanzas 1, 5, 6, and 7; in pencil, much corrected. Continued on B 68-69.

---

[19] The assigning of numerals 8 and 9 to the pages containing this draft is an example of Laurence's frequently erratic numbering: B 7 contains a draft of *LP* 2 ("As I gird on for fighting"); its verso, headed "The Soldier's Grave" and containing one line of the poem, was never numbered, nor was the following recto.

No. 2 ("Loveliest of trees . . .") on B 33-34, unique draft, in pencil, revised.

No. 26 ("Along the field as we came by") on B 36, destroyed. Laurence's Analysis gives the date June ——[1895].

No. 50 ("In valleys of springs of rivers") on B 40; pencil draft, corrected; the "traditional" stanza in quotation marks. MS of stanza 4 probably lost with missing lower section. Continued on next page.

No. 50 on B 41; second (and final) draft, in pencil, corrected.

No. 58 ("When I came last to Ludlow") on B 45; unique draft, in pencil; stanza 1 much revised. Dated "July 1895."

No. 16 ("It nods and curtseys and recovers") on B 46; unique draft, in pencil, many alternatives for stanza 2.

No. 47 ("The Carpenter's Son") on B 49; last two lines only, in pencil. Continued on B 53-54.

No. 57 ("You smile upon your friend to-day") on B 51-52; second (and final) draft, in pencil; first stanza revised on both pages.

No. 47 ("The Carpenter's Son") on B 53-54; unique draft, in pencil, much corrected. Possibly two or three stanzas lost with center portion of B 54. Dated "August 1895."

No. 37 ("As through the wild green hills of Wyre") on B 57; second (and final) entry, in pencil, with many corrections.

No. 38 ("The winds out of the west land blow") on B 58-59; second (and final) draft, in pencil; lightly corrected. Probably some stanzas lost with major portion of B 59.

No. 44 ("Shot? so quick, so clean an ending?") on B 60-61; pencil, much revised. Probably three or four stanzas lost with cut sections of both pages. Continued on B 62-65.

No. 44 on B 62-63; second draft, in pencil, very heavily corrected. Continued on B 64-65.

No. 44 on B 64-65; third (and final) draft, in pencil, lightly revised.

No. 45 ("If it chance your eye offend you") on B 66; unique draft, in pencil, lightly corrected.

No. 4 ("Reveille") on B 67; third (and final) entry, in pencil; stanza 1 only, lightly corrected.

No. 27 ("Is my team ploughing?") on B 68-69; second (and final) draft, in pencil, corrected.

No. 43 ("The Immortal Part") on B 72-73; second (and final) draft, in pencil, corrected.

No. 7 ("When smoke stood up from Ludlow") on B 74-75; unique draft, in pencil, much revised.

No. 20 ("Oh fair enough are sky and plain") on B 77; unique draft, in pencil, lightly revised.

No. 62 ("Terence, this is stupid stuff") on B 84-87; unique draft, in pencil, parts much canceled and rewritten. Probably one third of the MS lost with missing sections of last three pages.

No. 6 ("When the lad for longing sighs") on B 89; unique draft, in pencil, very heavily corrected. Probably several alternative lines lost with cut lower portion.

No. 49 ("Think no more, lad; laugh, be jolly") on B 90; unique draft, in pencil, corrected.

No. 24 ("Say, lad, have you things to do?") on B 92; unique draft, in pencil, heavily corrected.

No. 35 ("On the idle hill of summer") on B 94; unique draft, in pencil; equates printer's copy but for next to last line.

No. 31 ("On Wenlock Edge the wood's in trouble") on B 97-98. The first draft, on B 97, was destroyed; the final draft, on B 98, is in pencil, lightly revised.[20]

No. 23 ("The lads in their hundreds . . .") on B 99; first draft, in pencil, partly canceled, with many corrections. Continued on B 100.

No. 23 on B 100; second (and final) draft, in pencil, with many corrections.

No. 41 ("In my own shire, if I was sad") on B 109-10; unique draft; MS destroyed.[21]

No. 34 ("The New Mistress") on B 114-15; unique draft, in pencil, revised.

From these condensed descriptions it may be seen that some thirty poems of *A Shropshire Lad* are represented by unique drafts; that is to say, Laurence's Analysis lists one draft only, and no others were discovered in the reconstructed notebooks. The finished condition of some of these—for example, the ink draft of the poem ("Into my heart an air that kills," *ASL* 40) on A 63, as well as the drafts (both ink and pencil) of several dating after 1890—strongly suggests that they must have been copied or revised from earlier holographs that were never entered in the notebooks. Again, others of this sizable number must have received much revision later outside of the notebooks, as the manuscripts are so disordered that it seems impossible for printer's copy to have been extracted from them directly.

[20] According to the Analysis, *ASL* 31 occupied two pages, B 97 and 98, dated November, 1895. It might be supposed that, since the sheet containing B 97 was destroyed, little remains of the draft. Erratic numbering of this area of the notebook is again accountable for the confusion: Laurence failed to number B 96 (blank) and may have likewise passed over the next two pages (destroyed), but set the numeral 98 at the head of the next page, a recto.

[21] ". . . rough draft, many lines canceled, dated Nov. 1895." Laurence Housman's Analysis, *Recollections,* p. 264.

These unique drafts are given special attention in the section that follows. In this connection it should also be said that a poem, even in its second or third draft, did not always attain in the notebooks the exact form it would bear in print, for Housman sometimes carried revision into the eleventh hour, occasionally to the very end of it. Examples will be pointed out in the analyses that constitute the next section of this volume.

The catalog just given listed, roughly, a score of drafts in ink, all of them in Notebook A. As a rule Housman used ink only in second or later drafts that might be rewritten in part but not completely recopied. Five of these drafts bear dates (all of these in pencil, probably added some time after the page was written), another indication that the poem was nearing completion.

Also were mentioned in the catalog several examples of the "bubbling up" of lines and larger elements that eventually found their way into fully developed poems. These first fruits of inspiration will be described in connection with their proper poems, but as an adjunct to Housman's lecture the following list is offered. Many more strays of afternoon walks, now tabulated as "Fragments" in the Analysis, doubtless perished in the dismemberment of the notebooks.

1. An incomplete quatrain on A 66 (date before 1890) containing the line "The land they perished for" was the genesis of *ASL* 1. The line became number 24 of the poem, which was first essayed on A 202-3 some time after August, 1894.

2. The line "Soldier, I wish you well," standing by itself on A 162 (spring, 1893), became the last line of *ASL* 22, written on B 22-23, May or June, 1895.

3. On A 192 (August, 1894) are these suggestive lines:

> And she shall lie with earth above
> And you beside another love,

which were in all probability the beginning of *ASL* 26, written on B 36 (destroyed) and which became, with the smallest of changes, lines 9 and 10 of that poem eleven months later:

> But she shall lie with earth above,
> And he beside another love.

4. "Soldiers marching, all to die," penciled on A 220 (January, 1895), became line 8 of *ASL* 35, which was copied on B 94 in September or October of 1895.

5. On the next page of Notebook A (January or February, 1895) was written this isolated couplet:

> And the youth at morning shine
> Makes the vow he will not keep,

which rounded out the last stanza of ASL 55, composed on B 20-21 in

May or June of the same year. Into this poem Housman drew another stray that had flitted into his mind—"Strip to bathe on Severn shore"—which he had transcribed on B 12 only a few weeks, possibly days, before he wrote out the unique draft of the poem.

6. After a walk in April or May, 1895, that must have been visited by lighter moods, Housman jotted down on B 12:

> Beer is good and good are skittles
> 'tis only thinking
> Lays lads underground.

The last line and a half formed the conclusion of the unique draft of *ASL* 49, written on B 90 in the early autumn of the same year.

7. Laurence's Analysis makes mention of these two lines of *ASL* 47, standing alone on B 49, dated July or August, 1895:

> Fare you well, for ill fare I:
> Live, lads, and I will die.

The couplet became the conclusion of the poem composed a few days later on B 53-54.

A curious fact here is that in half of the foregoing examples the concluding lines of the projected poems were the ones that first arose in the well of inspiration. The poem-by-poem analysis that follows will provide other examples showing that some of the earliest lines to appear became the final ones of the poems into which they entered. It is also worth noting that the time between the jotting down of the fragment and the first draft of the poem it engendered varied from a few days to several years. When complete, or nearly complete, drafts are considered, however, we can be certain that almost without exception the time between the first and the last can generally be reckoned in months. The longest period seems to have intervened between the first draft of *ASL* 39 ("'Tis time, I think, by Wenlock town"), on A 125, written late in 1890 or early in 1891, and the second draft, on A 153, dated February, 1893. Though Housman at times delayed sitting down to assemble the scattered materials of a poem, once a draft of it was down on paper he generally lost no time in carrying it on to its final or near-final shape.

The question has been asked: Did Housman arrange the sixty-three poems of his first volume with some thematic sequence in mind?[22] Laur-

---

[22] Nesca A. Robb, in *Four in Exile* (London: Hutchinson, 1948), p. 12, states: "*A Shropshire Lad* is an ordered sequence. One might almost go farther and call it a poem, for the more one studies it, the more intimately do its component parts appear to be related to one another. They are arranged with extreme deliberateness. . . ."

Ian Scott-Kilvert believes that the poems are "grouped in the manner of a sonnet sequence." *A. E. Housman* (London: Longmans, Green, 1955), p. 24.

ence Housman in his *Recollections*[23] cites his brother as saying that he was urged by his publisher to make his book a "romance of enlistment." It is common knowledge that many of the poems have a strong military and patriotic flavor, and it is possible that "1887" and "The Recruit," appearing in the first three poems of the volume, are a vestige of this catchpenny design, which Housman might not have liked at first, although he shared Dr. Johnson's idea of the average Briton's respect for soldiers.

More important than theme sequence, I believe, is his confidence in the twelve pieces he chose to follow the five assigned to the vanguard. Looking again at these five pieces, we see that the military tone of "1887" and "The Recruit" is supported by at least the title of "Reveille" (*ASL* 4) even though the poem itself is not in praise of redcoats; "Loveliest of trees . . ." (*ASL* 2) is a lesson learned from nature, and "Oh see how thick the goldcup flowers" (*ASL* 5) is an idyll of casual love-making. This quintet sounds the keynote of *A Shropshire Lad:* the poems remind us of youth and its swift passing, its pleasures, duties, and inevitable defeats. But Housman's selection of the next twelve poems was guided by quite a different principle, which emerges from the fact that all of these pieces are represented in the notebooks by unique drafts. Some of these were written early—number 14 ("There pass the careless people") is the second *Shropshire Lad* lyric in Notebook A and dates from before 1890. Others of the twelve came late—number 6 ("When the lad for longing sighs") belongs to the autumn of 1895. The notebook drafts of two or three of the others in this group make hard reading now, and some recopies were probably made outside the notebooks, but the important fact is that *ASL* 6 to 17 existed there in the form of single drafts only. The inspiration of the walks that produced them achieved in the very first transcription a finality that made them worthy of being written into printer's copy.

Within these numbers there is one well-defined subdivision. This was indicated by Housman himself when he jotted the note "Another Series" on the sheet of printer's copy containing *ASL* 13 ("When I was one-and-twenty"). He was thinking of numbers 13, 14, 15, and 16 and their theme of lovers' sorrow and disappointment. Only one other small group has a strong homogeneity: numbers 25, 26, and 27, which describe the successful lover confronting his dead rival. Outside of these thematic subdivisions, the hiatuses in the remainder of the book are much more numerous than even the faintest groups of any size. If Housman had been intent on building up prominent themes in the arrangement of his poems, he would not so often have allowed the opposite effect to obtrude; he would not, for example, have put number 34 ("The New Mistress")[24] with its

[23] Laurence Housman, *Recollections,* p. 83.

[24] Miss Robb *(Four in Exile,* pp. 29-30) points out the inappositeness of this poem. Yet there is no doubt that A.E.H. knew exactly how this poem would stand

noisy bravado between 33 ("If truth in hearts that perish") and 35 ("On the idle hill of summer"), which are as like each other in tone as they are unlike the poem that separates them. If a few other groupings seem to stand out, that is only natural in Housman's narrow range.

After *ASL* 17, extensive displacements could be made without disturbing greatly the effect of the book even on a well-acquainted reader. Doubt on this question may be settled by a reperusal of the lyrics in the order in which Housman first gathered them in his printer's copy. Only thirty-four will be found under the numerals they now carry in print. Bearing out my suggestions about his motives for selecting the first seventeen pieces, the longest untouched series in the printer's copy extends from *ASL* 5 to 22 (even in the opening quintet numbers 3 and 4 eventually changed places); but from number 23 on, he made fourteen changes in numerals—of which seven were again altered in proof-sheets.[25] Many other alterations in numerals were necessitated by his withdrawal of five poems and the insertion of three while the book was in the hands of the printer. Even if Housman had cherished the idea of a definite thematic system for the latter three fourths of *A Shropshire Lad,* he probably would have been obliged to abandon it in the face of the disturbing rearrangements which followed his cutting the number of poems to sixty-three.

Summing up my argument—I have given it at length because the question of sequence will reappear in the poem analyses that follow—it is the charm and force of the individual poems in *A Shropshire Lad,* taken in sum, not thematic movements, that constitute the appeal of the book. Such problems as order and climax, the building up of tonal effects, nuance, and resolution did not present themselves significantly to Housman. These things came to him easily if they came at all, a part of the largesse of the afternoon's walk. When brain had to settle down to the task of putting the stanzas of a poem in order, trouble usually arose. On a larger scale, in his gathering of the sixty-three poems of his first book, it would have been contrary to Housman's nature to concern himself with any but the elementary matters of arrangement and grouping of his lyrics. The patriotic

out in its context. After his MS had been dispatched to the printer he sent in "Yonder see the morning blink" (which we now read as *LP* 11) to follow number 33. A few days later he withdrew this poem and substituted "The New Mistress," which was as much out of harmony with *ASL* 33 as its predecessor had been, but certainly not more so. Nevertheless, during his proofreading A.E.H. set his seal of approval on this new sequence, however disturbing it may now appear to some, and drew up his table of contents in the order it has always carried in print.

[25] For example, the printer's copy of "The Immortal Part" originally bore the numeral LIX, which was later altered to XLI. The poem was printed as number 43. "The Day of Battle" was once numbered 61, again 58, finally printed as 56. Other pieces were moved backward and forward over eleven, nine, five, and four places. His first arrangements showed as much thematic order as his last.

note in the opening poem expressed some of his deepest personal convictions, and he probably saw eye-to-eye with his publisher in the choice of "1887" to lead the van. Again, the appropriateness of "I hoed and trenched and weeded" to be the final poem is beyond dispute. Then there are the two small groups of pieces with similar subject matter, but beyond these exceptions there is little objective evidence of thematic design in *A Shropshire Lad.* Housman's intentions may indeed have been the very opposite: his apparent unconcern in the juxtaposition of sadly mismatched poems may have been a trick of studied perversity, calculated to flout the sensibilities of those who prize "linkèd sweetness long drawn out." Writing to his friend and critic, J. W. Mackail, on July 25, 1922, during his gathering of the contents of *Last Poems,* Housman confessed he had inserted "Oh fair enough are sky and plain"—number 20 in his first volume—"only ... for variety." We should not forget that we are tracing here the hand that would write the Prefaces to Lucan and Manilius. Housman the scholar and Housman the poet are one in their scorn of certain accepted ways of doing things. It would have been thoroughly characteristic of him to take a wry satisfaction in the apparent intractability of his poems to being bundled into sections, each with its posy, and thus to show his contempt for a patterned and stylized order that he knew had nothing to do with the making of *A Shropshire Lad.* When answering a French critic's elaborate questionnaire, Housman significantly made no reply to the query about his principle of grouping the poems, although he answered most of the others (Richards' *Memoir,* p. 268). Could he have expressed his unconcern more eloquently?

The Drafts of the Poems

THE drafts of the poems are printed to show as clearly as type will allow the general appearance of the notebook pages as they were when A. E. Housman left them. All of his legible alternative readings are given, and his cancellations are indicated in footnotes. Other alterations in the manuscripts (which are numerous and made by a later hand) are not systematically noted but may be mentioned in the descriptive forewords accompanying the diplomatic reprints of the entries. An entry as defined in this variorum is a single continuous manuscript of a poem or a portion of one; it may contain one or more drafts, complete or incomplete, made at one or more sittings.

If a reading taken from a partly obliterated draft is doubtful, the reading is followed by an interrogation sign and all enclosed within brackets. Lines now completely illegible are indicated by an interrogation sign centered between brackets; an unfinished or missing portion of a line is indicated by brackets only.

Frequently, after beginning a draft, Housman would turn to the page left or right and jot down experimental lines and stanzas. Printer's copy would be written from these parallel interwoven drafts or a later transcription of them. Such drafts have been numbered separately in conformity with the sequence of their notebook pages.

All final entries of poems that approximate fair copy I have collated with the manuscript Housman sent to his publisher and have where possible noted all significant variations introduced between the time the poems left his desk and their appearance in print.

The original version of each draft has been set in 10 point Times Roman type face. First alternatives to Housman's original are set in a smaller size type (9 point); second alternatives in an even smaller size (8 point).

Abbreviations: *canc.* for *canceled; alt.* for *alternative.*

24

1

1887

FROM Clee to heaven the beacon burns,
  The shires have seen it plain,
From north and south the sign returns
  And beacons burn again.

Look left, look right, the hills are bright,
  The dales are light between,
Because 'tis fifty years to-night
  That God has saved the Queen.

Now, when the flame they watch not towers
  About the soil they trod,
Lads, we'll remember friends of ours
  Who shared the work with God.

To skies that knit their heartstrings right,
  To fields that bred them brave,
The saviours come not home to-night:
  Themselves they could not save.

It dawns in Asia, tombstones show
  And Shropshire names are read;
And the Nile spills his overflow
  Beside the Severn's dead.

We pledge in peace by farm and town
  The Queen they served in war,
And fire the beacons up and down
  The land they perished for.

"God save the Queen" we living sing,
  From height to height 'tis heard;
And with the rest your voices ring,
  Lads of the Fifty-third.

Oh, God will save her, fear you not:
  Be you the men you've been,
Get you the sons your fathers got,
  And God will save the Queen.

ASL 1 "1887"

Three entries: A 66; A 202-3; B 18-19.

The first entry consists of four lines written on the lower half of the tenth surviving page of the "pre-1890" poetry. The sheet has been cut and a middle strip about an inch wide is missing. The upper fragment contains seven scattered lines unrelated to the four lines on the bottom section. It would be difficult to connect these lines with the opening poem of *A Shropshire Lad* but for the fact that the second line was written into the first draft of the poem and eventually passed on into printer's copy.

All of four, and possibly seven, years passed before the composition of the first draft. It begins near the top of A 202, in the middle of the line that was to become number 5 of the poem. There is no trace of stanza 1 here or elsewhere in the MSS, although it may have been attempted on some of the missing sections of the lower half of the page. This draft presents all of the remaining seven stanzas (of the sixth, lines 3 and 4 only) in the order they bear in print. The magic name *Khartoum,* written twice on the upper portion of A 202 in a quatrain that has suffered very heavy erasure, is the most prominent residue of a stanza rewritten at least in part on the lower section of that page, taken up again at the bottom of A 203, and possibly carried into B 19 but no farther.

The second draft of *ASL* 1 begins on a fragment surviving from the lower half of B 18. This page was cut into four sections; the upper half is blank. A small middle portion and a strip from the lower margin were destroyed. Faint remains of cut-through letters at the upper margin of the inscribed fragment suggest that some lines of the poem may have occupied the lost center strip of the page. Other truncated letters are evident on the lower edge of the piece, possibly remains of the Khartoum stanza, transcribed along with the two that preceded it from A 202. This and the page following illustrate the frequently erratic numbering Laurence Housman introduced into the notebooks, for both pages—although facing each other—are headed by the numeral 202.

ASL 1 "1887"
Fragments

A 66, lower half   Date: Between June, 1887,
Ink and pencil   and September, 1890

The weapons of the war[1]

The land they perished for.[2] Lies the defended land.[3]
The soul you died to save[4]

---

[1] This line may be a recollection of II Sam. 1:27: "... and the weapons of war perished."

[2] The spacing of this and the line above suggests that they were intended to be rhyming lines of a quatrain.

[3] This line is in pencil. On many pages, especially crowded ones, the original reading of a line is not always possible to determine, as the poet's later choices may occupy various relative positions: above the line, below it, at the beginning or the end; sometimes they are written through part of a line, or canceled, restored, and canceled again. These conditions are illustrated throughout the drafts that follow, where two or more adjacent readings may be exhibited in the same type size. It is to be understood that these lines in whole or part appeared to be, not alternatives, but readings of equal or near-equal priority.

[4] Cf. *Themselves they could not save*, A 203, line 16 of the text.

ASL 1 "1887"
First Draft

A 202, two pieces   Date: Between August and
Pencil   December, 1894

[*Piece 1*]

[   ]   the hills are bright
    The dales are light between,
Because 'tis fifty years tonight
    That God has saved the Queen.

                    Now, that¹ when   watch
        And now² the flame they see³ not towers
                    About   land
                    Upon the soil⁴ they trod
        It makes us think of friends of ours
                    Who
            That⁵ shared the work the⁶ with God.

Oh soldiers [?   ] [tomb ?]   [   ] the bugle of the King's⁷
      You [?   ]   [   ] heard
The [?   ] Khartoum
      And twice [?   ] debar   [   ] the Fifty-third⁸
          On [?   ] Khartoum⁹
              Their bugle sounded far

[*Piece 2*]

        gs,   [   ] heard
        r;   In twice but to debar.
        the King's

        nds to hero-held
        fallen around betrayed Khartoum¹⁰

---

¹ Canc. *that.*   ² Canc. *And now.*   ³ Canc. *see.*

⁴ After writing *land* above *soil,* A.E.H. canceled his substitute by heavily overwriting *shire,* which went into the second draft, on B 18, where in turn it was overwritten by *soil.*

⁵ Canc. *that.*   ⁶ *the* is a slip in hasty writing; canc. by A.E.H.

⁷ *the King's* is the abbreviated name of a military corps.

⁸ The Shropshire Regiment of Infantry.

⁹ This line and the one below are alternatives for the two preceding.

¹⁰ A line under this is cut through. Khartoum, the capital city of the Anglo-Egyptian Sudan, fell and its heroic defender, Charles George Gordon, was slain January 26, 1885, after 317 days of siege. Relief dispatched by a vacillating ministry arrived three days later. Housman, while sharing in the intense public indignation, finally suppressed this reference to "betrayed Khartoum" as it would have been out of key with the affirmative tone of "1887."

ASL 1 "1887"
First Draft continued

A 203, small top section missing
Pencil

And here sat you and I
          spun
To skies that knit[1] their heartstrings right,
    To fields that bred them brave,
The saviours come not home tonight:
    Themselves they could not save.

On Indian graves the morning grows[2]   at Cabul
    And Shropshire names are read;   It dawns in India; tombstones shew,[4]
        his   Asia
And the Nile spills its overflows[3]   [?   ] King's [?   ]
    Beside   And [?   ]
    Around the Severn's dead.   [?   ]

                      The living [?   ] and sing
                      'God save the Queen' the living sing;
And fire the beacons up and down   From hill to hill 'tis heard;
    The land they perished for   And with the rest your voices ring,
                      Lads of the Fifty-third.

                      Oh, God will save her:
                        hear you
[?   ]   Oh, may God save her; fear you not:
                            fear you
[?   ]   God will [?   ] it not:[5]
                        lads[6]
Far [?   ] of the King's   Be you the men you've been,
                    Get you
By [?   ] Khartoum. And get the sons your fathers got,
                      And God will save the Queen.

---

[1] Canc. *knit.*   [2] The line is struck out.

[3] The *-s* in *overflows* was canceled after the line to the right, above, ending in *shew* was written. This cancellation left the rhyme *shew–flow.*

[4] A.E.H. carried this older spelling into his printer's copy, but the first edition has *show.*

[5] This was the first-written line of the quatrain.   [6] Canc. *lads.*

ASL 1 "1887"
Second Draft

B 18, section of lower half   Date: May, 1895
Pencil

      left[1]   right
    right   left   brows
Look west, look east, the hills are bright,
   The dales are light between,
Because 'tis fifty years to-night
   That God has saved the Queen.

                                        flowers
   Now, when the flame they watch not towers
          On hills that once they trod
       About the shire[2] they trod,   Tall on the shire
   we'll
Lads, let's remember
   My heart remembers friends of ours[3]
     Who shared the work with God.

---

[1] Canc. the four antecedents of *left* and *right*.   [2] *soil* was written through *shire*.
[3] This line may have developed thus: A.E.H. canceled *My heart* and wrote the alternative opening *Lads, let's*, striking off the *-s* of *remembers*. He then canceled *let's*, inserted *we'll* above a caret, and copied *remember* above the line.

ASL 1 "1887"
Second Draft continued

B 19, nearly complete
Pencil

> To skies that knit[1] their heartstrings right,
> To fields that bred them brave,
> The saviours come not home to-night:
> Themselves they could not save.

> 'Tis morn in India[2]
> It dawns in Asia, tombstones shew
> And Shropshire names are read;
>   his
> And the Nile spills its[3] overflow
> Beside the Severn's dead.

```
                        field
We [                ?                  ]
           whose coat they wore    And here we toast
   The Queen [          ?        ]   We living toast
   And fire the beacons up and down   We living pledge by farm & town[5]
      And [        ?        ] before.[4]
```

[1] Above *knit* are the remains of a cut-through word, apparently *spun*—carried over from the first draft, A 203.

[2] Above this line occur a broad-arrow and the ending of a transfer-line bringing across from the bottom of B 18 (now missing) an intervening stanza, possibly the Khartoum quatrain.

[3] Canc. *its*.

[4] This stanza was evidently one of those that "had to be taken in hand and completed by the brain"—perhaps in a draft not written into the notebooks. After striking out line 4 and the ending of line 2, A.E.H. sealed his disgust with the stanza by canceling it with a high X.

The earliest-written line of *ASL* 1, *The land they perished for* (A 66), after passing into the first draft of the poem (A 203), is here supplanted by a line ending with *before*. The original line was restored in printer's copy, written six months later.

[5] Below this line is a column of three or more alternatives (now illegible) for the conclusion of this stanza.

the[6]
'God save the Queen' we the living sing;   the song goes round
      height   vale
  From hill to hill 'tis heard;

                                    sound
And with the rest your voices ring,
  Lads of the Fifty-third. Oh, God will save her; fear you not:
              Be you the men you've been,
            Get you the sons your fathers got,
             And God will save the Queen.

[6] Canc. both *the*'s.

2

LOVELIEST of trees, the cherry now
Is hung with bloom along the bough,
And stands about the woodland ride
Wearing white for Eastertide.

Now, of my threescore years and ten,
Twenty will not come again,
And take from seventy springs a score,
It only leaves me fifty more.

And since to look at things in bloom
Fifty springs are little room,
About the woodlands I will go
To see the cherry hung with snow.

ASL 2 "Loveliest of trees . . ."

One entry: B 33-34.

Housman's second notebook was begun in April, 1895, and the contents of its opening pages testify to the close relationship of the season and the poetry it engendered. The degree of his susceptibility to "the progress of the seasons" (to use his own phrase) has never been systematically examined, but his reconstructed notebooks leave no doubt that there is an intimate connection between the subject matter of his nature poems and the dates on which they were written. As an example, the first poem in Notebook B is "The Lent Lily (*ASL* 29), dated April, 1895; page 4 contains "With seed the sowers scatter" (*MP* 32); page 13, "When green buds hang in the elm like dust" (*MP* 9); pages 24-25, "Oh see how thick the goldcup flowers" (*ASL* 5); page 26, "Twice a week the winter thorough" (*ASL* 17), with its reference in stanza 2 to the season of the poem: "in Maytime." *ASL* 2 is the sixth in this roll of springtide pieces, all within the first thirty-four pages of Notebook B.

It appears that the poem was originally only eight lines long, consisting of what we know as stanzas 1 and 3. The draft is contained on the upper two of four narrow strips into which B 33 was cut. Very little of the page was destroyed, not enough to provide room for an intermediate stanza, although the lower margin of the topmost piece shows some truncated words that may have belonged to line 1 of the second quatrain, recopied on piece 2. The quatrain that was to become number 2 was evolved with some difficulty on the page to the right, numbered 34—now existing in two sections—where no fewer than three drafts of it were produced, the last of which was finally carried back to the lower half of B 33 (piece 3). Another product of the B 34 proving ground was the opening couplet of the second quatrain, left incomplete on the preceding page. There was now insufficient room to transcribe it there; so it did not come into its proper place until the collecting of printer's copy at the end of the year. This copy shows only five minor changes, all in punctuation.

ASL 2 "Loveliest of trees . . ."
Unique Draft

B 33, nearly complete; four pieces,   Date: May or June, 1895
   the last one blank
Pencil

[*Piece 1*]

Loveliest of trees, the cherry now
          under
Is hung with bloom along the bough
        along
And stands about the woodlands wide   side[1] ride
    white
Wearing snow[2] for Eastertide.
[?   ] things I love [?   ]

[*Piece 2*]

        So   things
    And[3] since to look at what you love
   to set eyes on
And since to look at things you love[4]
Fifty times is not enough,
About the woodlands I will go
To see the cherry hung with snow.

[*Piece 3*]

Now of my
And since, of[5] threescore years and ten
Twenty will not come again,
And, take from seventy springs a score,
It only leaves me fifty more,

---

[1] After writing *side,* A.E.H. canceled it and then drew an undula through *wide* and
the *-s* of *woodlands.*

[2] Canc. *snow.*

[3] Canc. *And.*   [4] Canc. this line and the alt. above, *to set eyes on.*

[5] Canc. *And since, of.* In writing this stanza Housman first brought over from B 34
the opening couplet of the second stanza and the closing couplet of the third. His
cancellation of *And since, of* and the substitution of *Now of my* made the reading
of this stanza identical with that of the third version on B 34.

ASL 2 "Loveliest of trees . . ."
Unique Draft continued

B 34, small middle strip missing
Pencil

[*Piece 1*]

[now?]
And since my days are days of men,
And only threescore years and ten,
And, take from seventy springs a score,
It only leaves me fifty more,

And since, of threescore years and ten,
Twenty will not come again,
    so
And yet,[1] of all the springs in store,
I shall see but fifty more

[*Piece 2[2]*]

Now of my threescore years and ten
Twenty will not come again,
And take from seventy springs a score
It only leaves me fifty more

So since from seventy springs [?   ]

And since to look at things in bloom
Fifty springs are little room

---

[1] Canc. *yet.*   [2] A.E.H. drew a heavy X through the first five lines on this piece.

3

THE RECRUIT

LEAVE your home behind, lad,
  And reach your friends your hand,
And go, and luck go with you
  While Ludlow tower shall stand.

Oh, come you home of Sunday
  When Ludlow streets are still
And Ludlow bells are calling
  To farm and lane and mill,

Or come you home of Monday
  When Ludlow market hums
And Ludlow chimes are playing
  "The conquering hero comes,"

Come you home a hero,
  Or come not home at all,
The lads you leave will mind you
  Till Ludlow tower shall fall.

And you will list the bugle
  That blows in lands of morn,
And make the foes of England
  Be sorry you were born.

And you till trump of doomsday
  On lands of morn may lie,
And make the hearts of comrades
  Be heavy where you die.

Leave your home behind you,
  Your friends by field and town:
Oh, town and field will mind you
  Till Ludlow tower is down.

ASL 3 "The Recruit"

Two entries: A 205; A 222-25.

Only two stanzas (now numbers 2 and 3) of the poem are contained on A 205, and although the lower half of the page is missing it appears from Laurence Housman's Analysis that no further stanzas of *ASL* 3 were composed there. Housman must have opened this page with the two quatrains full-blown in his mind, for his draft shows no signs of hesitation. There are no corrections or erasures, and the two stanzas there set down went into print with only trifling changes: *of* for *on, bells* for *tower*. The poet probably wrote these eight lines in the full tide of the emotion provoked by the composition of the first draft of "1887," only two pages earlier, and by seven or eight lines of *ASL* 37 ("As through the wild green hills of Wyre") on A 204, which, although not conveying in its completed form anything of the military coloring of "1887," began as a poem of farewell, possibly a soldier's.

Housman opened A 222 by writing boldly the heading " 'Listing" (later changed here to "The Queen's Shilling") and immediately brought over from A 205 the two quatrains composed only a few weeks earlier. The product of "further inspiration . . . forthcoming another day" followed at once in stanzas 4 and 5; the latter was never retouched. Although the lower third of A 222 has been destroyed, we may say with some assurance that Housman completed *ASL* 3 on that page, for drafts of the last two stanzas are legible on the page opposite, which he made a proving ground for portions of the poem eventually copied on the left-hand page. About this time he may have turned back to the top of A 222 and written toward the right-hand margin the first draft of a quatrain which was to become the opening stanza.

A number of minor imperfections were cleared up in the ink draft on A 224-25; but, the late-arrived first stanza resisting all correctives, Housman abandoned it, resolutely striking it out with a high wavy line and numbering the following stanzas 1 to 6. Not until printer's copy do we find any trace of the final casting of the troublesome third line of stanza 1. This, together with the exchange of *lane* and *farm* in the last line of stanza 4 and the choice between two or three open alternatives, had to await later decision.

ASL 3 "The Recruit"
Fragments

A 205, upper half
Pencil, intact

Date: Between August
and December, 1894

Oh come you home on Sunday,
    When Ludlow streets are still,
And Ludlow tower is calling
    To lane and farm and mill.[1]

Or come you home on Monday,
    When Ludlow market hums,
And Ludlow chimes are playing
    'The conquering hero comes.'

---

[1] This line was carried unchanged through the two succeeding drafts. It was prob-ably during the composition of printer's copy that the poet's ear prompted the mutual shift of *farm* and *lane,* thus prolonging the echoic effect—*lane, mill*—that had been introduced into the line when, in the second version on A 222, *tower* was replaced by *bells.*

ASL 3 "The Recruit"
First Draft

A 222, upper two thirds   Date: January, 1895
Pencil, corrected

'Listing[1]
The Queen's Shilling

Oh come you home of Sunday   Leave your home behind, you[2] lad
  When Ludlow streets are still   And reach your friends your hand;
And Ludlow bells are calling   luck to soldiers marching
  To lane and farm and mill,   march with
                         And [   ][3]
                         While Ludlow tower shall stand.

    Or come you home of Monday
      When Ludlow market hums
    And Ludlow chimes are playing
      'The conquering hero comes',

And come you home a sergeant,[4] hero,
  Or come not home at all,
        hearts   [?] you   leave
Here the [lads will   ?] like you[5]   Lads you knew will like you
  Till Ludlow tower shall fall.

    And you will list the bugle
      That blows in lands of morn,
    And make the foes of England
  , Be sorry you were born.
                              wakes you
    [?   ][6] [?   ]

---

[1] Canc. *'Listing.* A.E.H. may have recalled his alternative title when, about ten years later, he opened the third stanza of the poem which became *LP* 8 ("Soldier from the wars returning") with the line "Sweat no more to earn your shilling" (D 22).

[2] The word *you* was struck out, but it reappeared in the draft on A 224.

[3] A.E.H. canceled this line and its two alts. above.

[4] Canc. *sergeant.*

[5] Canc. this line and its alts. above.   [6] Canc. this line and the one to the right.

ASL 3 "The Recruit"
First Draft continued

A 223, complete
Pencil, much revised

> And luck to all your marching
> And here's good luck from Ludlow
> And keep your friends in mind, lad[1]
>
> And if till mayhap till doomsday thunder[2]
>   In lands of morn you lie,
> And make the hearts of comrades
>   Be heavy when you die,
>
> Ears that heard you speaking
>   And hands that held your hand
> Will miss[3] keep the thought to friend them
>   While Ludlow tower shall stand.[4]
>
> And you your head till doomsday
>   On lands of morn may lay
> And make the lads of Ludlow
>   Unhappy
>   Wild sorrow[5] far away.
>
> But leave your friends[6] home behind you
>   And friends by field and town:
> Here [?   ] mind you
>   When Ludlow tower is down.[7]

---

[1] These three lines are tentative substitutes for line 3 of the stanza written in the upper-right corner of A 222. Lines 2 and 3 are struck out.

[2] This line seems to have developed thus: A.E.H. wrote *And if till,* then canceled *till* and went on to complete the line with *mayhap till doomsday.* He came back to cancel *mayhap,* restored *till,* and wrote *thunder* at the end of the line. The line as it stood now may have recurred to him when he wrote on B 41 five months later the last stanza of *ASL* 50: *Where doomsday may thunder and lighten* (line 3).

The remaining lines of the stanza on A 223 were left intact and eventually were preferred over the redraft written below.

[3] Canc. *miss.*

[4] This quatrain was deservedly abandoned, but the last line of it was used to shore up the stanza A.E.H. was trying to construct in the upper-right corner of A 222.

[5] Canc. *wild sorrow.*   [6] Canc. *friends.*

[7] The stanza is canceled by a high wavy line.

ASL 3 "The Recruit"
Second Draft

A 224, complete   Date: January, 1895
Ink; corrections and
    date in pencil

Jan. 1895   lad
                    Leave your home behind you,[1] you,
                        And reach your friends your hand;
                        [?   ][2] each other's [?   ] each with
                    And friends and home will mind you
                        [?   ]
                    While Ludlow tower shall stand.[3]

                                    1
                    Oh, come you home of Sunday
                        When Ludlow streets are still
                    And Ludlow bells are calling
                        To lane and farm and mill,

                                    2
                    Or come you home of Monday
                        When Ludlow market hums
                    And Ludlow chimes are playing
                        'The conquering hero comes',

                                    3
                    Come you home a hero,
                        Or come not home at all,
                    The lads you leave will mind you
                        Till Ludlow tower shall fall.

                                    4
                    And you will list the bugle
                        That blows in lands of morn,
                    And makes the foes of England
                        Be sorry you were born.

[1] Canc. *you* and its alt. *lad.*

[2] Canc. the first portion of this interlineation and the now illegible one below.

[3] A.E.H. launched this quatrain at the top of A 224 even though its rhyme *abab* was out of keeping with the *abcb* of the quatrains already composed. He was evidently determined to employ somewhere the endings *behind you* and *mind you* in lines 1 and 3 here, for he used them again in the stanza numbered 6 on A 225, whence they passed into printer's copy.

ASL 3 "The Recruit"
Second Draft continued

A 225, two pieces; upper section missing
First piece in ink, corrections in pencil;
   second in pencil

[*Piece 1*]
5¹

And you, till trump of² doomsday, wakes you
will
On lands or morn may lie,
And make the hearts of comrades
   Be heavy where you die.

6

Oh So³ Leave your home behind you,
   And friends by field and town;
And⁴ town and field will mind you
   Till Ludlow tower is down.

[*Piece 2*]

Leave your home behind, lad,⁵
   leave your friends behind, lad
Till Ludlow Tower is down.
tower

---

¹ Some truncated letters near this numeral indicate that A.E.H. may have copied at the very top of A 225 the stanza sketched on A 223 beginning *Ears that heard you speaking.*

² Canc. *trump of* after *wakes you* was added.   ³ Canc. *So.*

⁴ A.E.H. drew from *Oh,* above, a transfer-line replacing *And,* which he struck out.

⁵ The first letters of lines 1 and 2 have been cut away. The three lines represent another effort to improve the ailing first and fourth lines of stanza 1.

4

REVEILLE

WAKE: the silver dusk returning
    Up the beach of darkness brims,
And the ship of sunrise burning
    Strands upon the eastern rims.

Wake: the vaulted shadow shatters,
    Trampled to the floor it spanned,
And the tent of night in tatters
    Straws the sky-pavilioned land.

Up, lad, up, 'tis late for lying:
    Hear the drums of morning play;
Hark, the empty highways crying
    "Who'll beyond the hills away?"

Towns and countries woo together,
    Forelands beacon, belfries call;
Never lad that trod on leather
    Lived to feast his heart with all.

Up, lad: thews that lie and cumber
    Sunlit pallets never thrive;
Morns abed and daylight slumber
    Were not meant for man alive.

Clay lies still, but blood's a rover;
    Breath's a ware that will not keep.
Up, lad: when the journey's over
    There'll be time enough to sleep.

ASL 4 "Reveille"

Two entries: A 218-19; B 67.

All but the last of the six stanzas of the poem are represented on A 218, although the last three lines of stanza 2 and the last two of stanza 5 were destroyed when the page was cut and portions thrown away. As with *ASL* 3, the opening stanza of this poem came with difficulty, but for a quite different reason, the problem here being to control the flood of imagery stirring in the mind of the poet as he formulated the opening lines. The pen was hardly less agile than the mind, it seems, and proliferated an un- usually large number of alternative phrases in the draft. The same excess freighted the next stanza, which required special attention six months later, on B 67, which is taken up with no fewer than three copies of the opening couplet, none of which went into printer's copy.

Having thrown off the first draft of the poem, A.E.H. perhaps a few days later made a careful ink copy on the following page, which he dated *Jan. 1895.*[1] For all the seeming finality that ink drafts usually imply, the writing on A 219 is hardly less rewrought than the pencil draft opposite: only ten lines were left intact, and the margins are blurred with alternatives written in pencil, indicating that the labors of revision ran into two or more sessions.

[1] This page shows evidence of some interpolation by a later hand. Through *Dusk,* the first word Housman wrote in the opening line, is crudely written in blue ink (which he did not use in these MSS) the word *Wake,* which, although the first word of the printed version, makes nonsense of the line as it stands here. It may be surmised that whoever tampered with the line, having overwritten *Wake,* later perceived his error but, fearing to make matters worse, let it stand.

ASL 4 "Reveille"
First Draft

A 218, two sections; one third missing   Date: January, 1895
Pencil, much corrected

[Piece 1]

Yonder round the world returning[1]   Dusk in silver tides returning
  Slow the tide of twilight spills   On the brim[3] of darkness spills
And the ship of sunrise burning   Round the coast
        beyond   shore[4]
Heaves behind[2] the eastern hills
  Strands upon

      to Wales
     West away
  Leagues   scatters
  Miles[5] to west the morning shatters

[Piece 2]

Up, man, up [?   ] for lying,[6]
  Heads
    Lads[7] that rouse them with the day
Hear[8] the empty highways crying
  'Who'll beyond the hills away?'

[1] Canc. this line and the next below.   [2] Canc. *Heaves behind* and *beyond*.
[3] Canc. *On the brim*.   [4] Canc. *shore*.
[5] Of these four openings only the word *Miles* was canceled. The alts. are *Leagues to west*, *West away*, and *West to Wales*. This chance assembly of words may have been in Housman's mind when years later he wrote the opening of the poem that was to become *LP* 36 ("West and away the wheels of darkness roll") and line 9 of *LP* 39: "That looked to Wales away."
[6] This line was cut through.   [7] Canc. *Lads*.
[8] A.E.H. inadvertently wrote *Hears,* struck off the *-s*.

La[9]

La

Towns and counties
Land and cloudland[10] woo together,
Forelands Hill-tops[11] beacon, belfries call
Hills send signal, countries call:[12]
Never
Ne'er a[13] lad that trod on leather
Lived to feast his heart with all.

Up, man; thews that lie and cumber
Sunlit pallets never thrive;

[9] Even in his early drafts he usually offset and double spaced his stanzas, but his racing pen could not be halted from twice misplacing the first two letters of this stanza.

[10] Canc. *land and cloudland.*   [11] Canc. *Hill-tops.*

[12] Canc. this line.   [13] Canc. *Ne'er a.*

ASL 4 "Reveille"
Second Draft

A 219, nearly complete
Ink, corrections in pencil

[*Piece 1*]

Reveille.   Jan. 1895
                    To the morning[1] [?   ]
Dusk in silver tides returning
                    bank
          marge   brims
On the coast[2] of darkness spills[3]
Till
And the ship of sunrise burning
                                      rims
Strands upon the eastern hills.

[*Piece 2*]

And the tent of night in tatters[4]
Straws the sky-pavilioned land.

          lad
            my lad
          man
Up, lad,[5] up; 'tis late for lying,
                    Hear the drums of morning play;
          Heads that rouse them with the day[6]
Hark
Hear[7] the empty highways crying
'Who'll beyond the hills away?'

---

   [1] This is the beginning of the first or second line of a stanza that is now illegible. Below are remains of three alternative lines for the opening of stanza 2; the ending of the first may read *the morning scatters*. Under these lines, slanting upward toward the right margin, are remains of three others, possibly alternatives for the conclusion of stanza 1.
   [2] Canc. *coast* and *marge.*   [3] Canc. *spills* and, below, its rhyming word *hills*.
   [4] Over this word are traces of a line that was lost, with others, when a half-inch strip was cut out.
   [5] After *lad* and the two alternatives were canceled, the original word was restored.
   [6] Canc. this line.   [7] Canc. *hear.*

r
Towns and counties[8] woo together,
    Forelands beacon, belfries call;
Never lad that trod on leather
    Lived to feast his heart with all.

man   lad
    then
Up, man:[9] thews that lie and cumber
    Sunlit pallets never thrive;
Morns abed and daylight slumber   Dust lies
    Were not meant for man alive.   Stones lie still but blood's a rover;

        Feet wrought   Rest for night, a lad's a rover;
Legs   Lads were born to play the rover,[10]
Strength's Life's[11] a ware that will not keep:
        lad
    Up, man;[12] when the journey's over
    There'll be time enough to sleep.

[8] The letter *r*, in pencil, is set over a caret. A.E.H. probably misspelled *counties* for *countries,* which had been his word in the phrase *countries call* (A 218) before it was replaced by *belfries.*

[9] As in the second stanza above (note 5), the word first written survived its alts.

[10] This line seems to have evolved thus: After the line *Lads were born to play the rover* was written, *Feet* and *Legs* were substituted, but later struck out; *wrought* was set above *born,* but did not survive.

Over the original line was penciled *Rest for night, a lad's a rover.* A.E.H. partly canceled this substitute and wrote above it *Stones lie still but blood's a rover.* He struck out the first two words and superscribed *Dust lies,* bringing the line to within one word of finality.

[11] Canc. *Life's.*   [12] Canc. *man.*

ASL 4 "Reveille"
Fragment

B 67, complete   Date: August or September, 1895
Pencil

trampling
Wake: the axe of morning shatters[1]
Shadows through [   ]

Wake: the roof of shadow shatters

floor
Splintered[2] on the plain it spanned,
Trampled
And the tent of night in tatters
Straws the sky-pavilioned land

broken
Wake: the breaking shadow scatters
Splinters on the plain it spanned

[1] The unfinished line of this stanza is a reminder, and perhaps was the result, of the same impulsive mood that produced the first draft of this poem. I surmise that, midway in the second line, A.E.H. recalled his second draft of " 'Tis five years since . . ." (*AP* 15) written on B 47-48 only a few weeks before. Here he had described "the blue height of the hollow roof," beneath which "the stark steel splintered." These recollections may have brought into the second stanza the words *roof* and *splintered*.

But the word *trampling*, written over the first line on the page, may have brought with it another train of associations, the imagery of *Adonais*, stanza 52, describing the dome trampled to fragments, which was perfectly in accord with the imagery of the opening of this stanza. A.E.H. substituted *Trampled* for *Splintered* and *floor* for *plain*, leaving the first two lines with the reading they were to take in his printer's copy. However, before it left his hands he altered *roof of* to *vaulted*—which is perhaps another Shelleyan echo.

[2] Canc. *Splintered* and *plain*.

5

Oʜ see how thick the goldcup flowers
    Are lying in field and lane,
With dandelions to tell the hours
    That never are told again.
Oh may I squire you round the meads
    And pick you posies gay?
—'Twill do no harm to take my arm.
    "You may, young man, you may."

Ah, spring was sent for lass and lad,
    'Tis now the blood runs gold,
And man and maid had best be glad
    Before the world is old.
What flowers to-day may flower to-morrow,
    But never as good as new.
—Suppose I wound my arm right round—
    " 'Tis true, young man, 'tis true."

Some lads there are, 'tis shame to say,
    That only court to thieve,
And once they bear the bloom away
    'Tis little enough they leave.
Then keep your heart for men like me
    And safe from trustless chaps.
My love is true and all for you.
    "Perhaps, young man, perhaps."

Oh, look in my eyes then, can you doubt?
    —Why, 'tis a mile from town.
How green the grass is all about!
    We might as well sit down.
—Ah, life, what is it but a flower?
    Why must true lovers sigh?
Be kind, have pity, my own, my pretty,—
    "Good-bye, young man, good-bye."

ASL 5 "Oh see how thick the goldcup flowers"

Two entries: A 208; B 24-25.

The first appearance of this poem in the notebooks is on the lower half of A 208, where Housman wrote the last three lines of the third stanza followed by the fourth, and final, stanza. The upper portion of the full page was never inscribed, and there are no traces of the poem on the immediately adjoining pages. The fragmentary nature of this entry raises some tantalizing questions: Is this a copy of a portion of a draft not entered in the notebooks? or of a draft written earlier in Notebook A and destroyed before Laurence Housman received the manuscripts? Or is this another example of how some parts of a poem, strangely incomplete in themselves and (as we now view them) lacking continuity, "bubbled up" in the poet's imagination and were set down as they had come? Whatever explanations may be proposed, there is an unmistakable finality in these eleven lines: only two were altered significantly in the later entry, and five went to the printer without alteration here or elsewhere.

The second entry, made some months later, if not continued from a draft no longer extant, was the product of the mood that had produced the conclusion of the poem written on A 208. In contrast to the finished appearance of the earlier entry, the MS on B 24-25 has the general air of a first draft. None but a very few lines in it have escaped alteration of some kind, and Housman's excess of zeal was spent on four lines that were destined to pass to printer's copy unchanged from the form they first had on A 208. But it was not until this redaction that the final reading of fifteen of the thirty-two lines of the lyric was determined. Housman's indecision arose from his poem's theme and situation, which are in an area that does not lie easily within his intuitive reach. His dialogue—particularly the lover's part, a strange mixture of mawkishness and assurance—rings false; the accents are strained, as the poet all too clearly perceived, and the plethora of substitutions and alternative readings include some of the most grotesque and banal phrases that ever escaped his pen.

ASL 5 "Oh see how thick the goldcup flowers"
First Draft

A 208, complete   Date: Between August
Pencil   and December, 1894

And not like other chaps:
My love is true and all for you';[1]
'Perhaps, young man, perhaps.'

<pre>
                    and   a
                 so[2] never doubt
                      heart
     Oh yes, 'tis so, my love is pure,—
         Why, 'tis
         'Tis all a mile from town:
                          here about,
     How green the grass is, to be sure,
         We might as well sit down.
     Oh, life, what is it but a flower?[3]
             must
         Why should[4] true lovers sigh?
     Be kind, have
         Do, do[5] take pity, my own, my pretty.—
         'Goodbye, young man, good-bye'.
</pre>

[1] The quotation mark indicates the close of the first part of the dialogue. The sign is not so used in the next stanza nor in the second entry of the poem.

[2] A.E.H. struck out *so* and inserted *a* over a caret.

[3] The song of the two pages in *As You Like It* (V, iii) must have been in the poet's mind from the beginning of this lyric and probably was the genesis of this line. Cf. the third stanza:

The carol they began that hour,
How that a life was but a flower.

[4] Canc. *should.*   [5] Canc. *Do, do.*

ASL 5 "Oh see how thick the goldcup flowers"
Second Draft

B 24, complete   Date: May or June, 1895
Pencil

                              goldcup-flowers
      Oh see how thick the gilcup flowers
                  lying in field
            Are sown in meadow[2] and lane,
With   Oh walk with me to smell the flowers
And dandelions to tell the hours   And look at the leaves uncurled
            never are   For dandelions to count the hours
          That are not told again.   Are lying about the world[1]

                              meads
      Oh may I squire you round the [?   ][3]
                              meadows

                  pick
            And pull[4] you posies gay?
      —'Twill do no harm to take my arm.
            'You may, young man, you may'.

      Ah
      The[5]
      Oh, spring was sent for lass and lad,
            And makes the lover bold   'Tis then the blood
            In many a book 'tis told;   runs gold,
            maid   youth
      And he and she had best be glad
            Before the world is old.

    [1] These four lines were an echo from the conclusion of an eight-line poem written
on B 13 a few weeks earlier:
                        by hedgerow
            Forth I must to the wild wood bowers
                  To look at the leaves uncurled
            And stand in the fields where cuckoo-flowers
                  Are lying about the world.

This quatrain now forms the conclusion of *MP* 9 ("When green buds hang in the elm
like dust").
    [2] Canc. *sown in meadow.*   [3] Canc. two words now illegible.
    [4] Canc. *pull.*   [5] Canc. *Oh* and *The.*

And he and she had best be glad
       maid be vext
 Before[6] Why should a maid be vext?
Suppose I wound my arm right round—
 'What next, young man, what next?'[7]
 ' 'Tis true, young man, 'tis true'.

  blooms   bloom
What flowers today may flower tomorrow,
 But never as good as new.

---

[6] A.E.H. did not complete this line but jotted down its alternative, struck it out, then rewrote, above, *maid be vext*. Eventually he canceled all of the stanza between the words *old* and *vext*. The substitute lines are at the bottom of the page. Here the rhyme-word *new* appeared, accounting for the cancellation of the line first set as the conclusion of the stanza and the choice of *'Tis true,* etc. There are two or three illegible lines in the right margin, opposite.

[7] The line (now canceled) had ended with an interrogation point, but A.E.H. dramatized the maiden's alarm by changing the sign to an exclamation point.

ASL 5 "Oh see how thick the goldcup flowers"
Second Draft continued

B 25, complete
Pencil

                                                          And, once they bear the bloom away,
                                                            'Tis little enough they leave.
                chaps[1]   say
Some lads there are, 'tis shame to tell,
    That do but court to thieve,
        once they steal the prize[2] bloom   and
And steal the lovely flower[3] away   The stalk may stand to grieve
        sorrow is all they leave.   And little enough they leave
    And leave the maid to grieve   honour
You maids Then only trust   lads of
Oh, girls should trust to lads like me   Then keep your heart for men
        safe from faithless[4]
    And not to treacherous chaps: trustless
        love   'tis
My heart is true and all for you.
    'Perhaps, young man, perhaps.'

Oh,
Here,[5] look
            see in   then;
Oh, look in[6] my eyes and can you doubt?
    —Why, 'tis a mile from town.
                all
How green the grass is here[7] about!
                lie[8]
We might as well sit down.

[1] Canc. *chaps* and *tell*.   [2] Canc. *prize*.   [3] Canc. *flower*.
[4] This alt. is accommodated to the line, upper right, *Then keep your heart.* . . .
[5] Canc. *Here*.   [6] Canc. *Oh, look in* and *and*.   [7] Canc. *here*.
[8] This more suggestive verb may have been recalled from the pages' song, already
mentioned:

              Between the acres of the rye,
              These pretty country folk would lie.

Ah,

Oh, life, what is it but a flower?

Oh, life, what is it but a flower?[9]   Heigho, for life is but a flower,

a true lad

Why must true lovers sigh?

Be kind, have pity, my own, my pretty.—

  'Good-bye, young man, good-bye.'

---

[9] This line and the alt. written out after it were canceled, together with *Oh,* beginning the line above.

A comparison of this much-rewritten page with the corresponding stanzas of printer's copy shows that only seven of the sixteen lines involved were transcribed from B 25 as A.E.H. left them. Of nine alternatives remaining open, six were resolved by choosing the latest reading; for the other three the original reading was preferred. For one other line a version appears in printer's copy that was not present on B 25. Thus it is evident from this comparison (and it will be shown again) that A.E.H. often left much to be done between his final notebook draft and the redaction prepared for print, and that he by no means automatically preferred his latest alternatives.

6

WHEN the lad for longing sighs,
   Mute and dull of cheer and pale,
If at death's own door he lies,
   Maiden, you can heal his ail.

Lovers' ills are all to buy:
   The wan look, the hollow tone,
The hung head, the sunken eye,
   You can have them for your own.

Buy them, buy them: eve and morn
   Lovers' ills are all to sell.
Then you can lie down forlorn;
   But the lover will be well.

ASL 6 "When the lad for longing sighs"

One entry: B 89.

The creative energy which Housman said produced his first volume in the early months of 1895 actually lasted throughout August, which in quantity was his most productive month. After that came a slump which is plainly recorded in the outward appearance of the second notebook down to the end of the year. The writing in the vicinity of B 89 is in many pages cramped and erratic, and between B 80 (headed "September 1895") and B 116 ("Dec. '95") only seven sheets have survived uncut and eight were destroyed completely. These heavy casualties suggest that Laurence must have found in these pages a large quantity of fragmentary sketching he could not allow himself to preserve. Within the thirty-six pages mentioned Housman found only seven poems worthy of a place in the MSS of *A Shropshire Lad,* and two of these drafts were evidently copies of holographs that were never entered in the notebooks.

The sole entry for *ASL* 6 survives on the upper half of a page that resembles its neighbors in its blurred and heavily corrected writing, many lines of which are now illegible. This condition may be partly due to the effect of the adhesive Laurence applied to this side of the notebook sheet. Of the twelve lines of the poem, all are represented but the last, which was probably written on the missing lower section of the page. Lines 2 and 3 of the opening stanza were not perfected in the draft (line 2 is hardly adumbrated), but all of the remaining lines—except the next-to-last, where a word is in doubt but almost certainly is *down*—were worked out to the shape they took in print, though much remained to do in the way of rescuing some words from cancel-lines, bringing in others from marginal jottings, and making selections among many alternatives.

ASL 6 "When the lad for longing sighs"
Unique Draft

B 89, upper two thirds   Date: September or
Pencil, heavily corrected   October, 1895

              lad for longing
                  starving
      When the pleading lover[1] sighs,
          his looks are wan and [?   ]
      When the [look of him ?] is pale[2]
                    nigh to death   Though at death's own door[4]
      When the lad looks like to die,[3]   Though at point of death
      Maiden, you can heal his ail.   When against death's door he lies,

          Lovers' ills are all to buy:
                  cheek[5]
      The wan look, the hollow tone,
          dull look   hung head
      The slack[6] [   ], the sunken eye
      You can have them for your own.[7]

          He will sell thee[8]
                  have them
      You can buy them: eve and morn
          You can [?   ] them
                  heal him
          Lovers' ills are all to buy   Lovers' ills are all to sell
      Buy them, buy them;
                              have
          Cheap enough a maid can buy
      What the lover longs to sell
          Then you can lie [down ?] forlorn
      You can lay you down and die

[1] Canc. *pleading lover* and *starving*.
[2] Canc. this line.   [3] Canc. this line.
[4] Canc. this line and the two below.
[5] Canc. *cheek*.   [6] Canc. *slack* and the alt. *dull look*.

[7] Apparently it was this stanza, which required the least reworking, that set the rhyme pattern for *ASL* 6: *abab*. The lines of the preceding stanza had left the choice open between *abab* and *abcb* before the three lines in the margin were canceled.

[8] The final word here may be *them*. All of the remaining lines on the page are canceled either by heavy horizontal strokes or light pencil lines.

7

WHEN smoke stood up from Ludlow,
  And mist blew off from Teme,
And blithe afield to ploughing
  Against the morning beam
  I strode beside my team,

The blackbird in the coppice
  Looked out to see me stride,
And hearkened as I whistled
  The trampling team beside,
  And fluted and replied:

"Lie down, lie down, young yeoman;
  What use to rise and rise?
Rise man a thousand mornings
  Yet down at last he lies,
  And then the man is wise."

I heard the tune he sang me,
  And spied his yellow bill;
I picked a stone and aimed it
  And threw it with a will:
  Then the bird was still.

Then my soul within me
  Took up the blackbird's strain,
And still beside the horses
  Along the dewy lane
  It sang the song again:

"Lie down, lie down, young yeoman;
  The sun moves always west;
The road one treads to labour
  Will lead one home to rest,
  And that will be the best."

ASL 7 "When smoke stood up from Ludlow"

One entry: B 74-75.

The manuscript indicates in its deliberateness and the regularity of its spacing that the majority of the lines of this poem arose from the well of inspiration fully formed. Sixteen of the thirty lines of *ASL* 7 were perfected in this draft, two more required the change of but one word, and seven others attained finality in the parallel list of alternatives and corrections that compose the right-hand columns of B 74 and 75. On the latter page only three words, one a mere inadvertence, were struck out.

It is probable that the inspiration of this poem was a continuation of the mood that produced *ASL* 27 ("Is my team ploughing?"), one of Housman's most admired lyrics, which he had completed on B 68-69 only a few days earlier.

ASL 7 "When smoke stood up from Ludlow"
Unique Draft

B 74, complete   Date: August or September, 1895
Pencil, much revised

As down the lanes to ploughing   As down the lanes to ploughing
   I strode beside the team   Against the morning beam
And whistled [   ]   I strode [   ]
[   ]
   Against the morning beam[1]   And whistled to the team

            in
The blackbird from the coppice
   Looked out to see me stride
     flew
                       hearkened as I whistled
And perched to hear me whistle[2]   And when he heard me whistle[3]
   trampling   The trampling[4] team beside,
   The jingling team beside,   And fluted whistled
   And whistled and replied: He whistled[5] and replied

'Lie down, lie down, young yeoman;
      use to rise and
What ails a man to rise?[6]
   Rise man a thousand mornings,
Rise he a thousand mornings   He'd rise a thousand mornings,
   Yet down at last he lies,   eve
At evening down he lies,[7]   But down at last he lies,
And then the man is wise.'

---

[1] Though this stanza is incomplete, its display suggests that its rather unusual pattern was in the poet's mind at the writing of line 1.

[2] Canc. this line and the rest of the stanza.   [3] Canc. all but *And.*

[4] The word *trampling* is probably carried over from the draft of *ASL* 26, on B 68.

[5] A.E.H. canceled *He whistled,* superscribing *And fluted,* which gave way to *whistled,* recopied.

[6] Canc. all but *What.*   [7] Canc. this line.

So the blackbird fluted[8]   sang me
    Along his yellow bill.   I heard the tune he fluted[9]
    picked   swung it   And spied his yellow bill:
I spied[10] a stone and cast it
    threw sent
    And flung[11] it with a will:
    Then the bird was still.[12]

---

[8] Canc. this line and the next.   [9] Canc. *fluted.*   [10] Canc. *spied, cast it.*
[11] Canc. *flung, threw.*

[12] Housman's meticulous care in word choice is shown in the revision of the last stanza on B 74. Having written *And spied his yellow bill* in the right-hand column, he had to look about for a word to replace *spied,* already used in the third line, left. So he canceled it there and went on to reject *cast* in the same line and write over it *swung.* Then he perceived that this word would produce an unwanted rhyme with *flung* in the line following; so *flung* was struck out and *sent* put in its place but did not stay. In sum, of the seven words A.E.H. tested in these three positions, only one—*picked*—went on into printer's copy, though one of the rejects—*threw*—was restored there.

ASL 7 "When smoke stood up from Ludlow"
Unique Draft continued

B 75, complete
Pencil, lightly revised

Then my soul within me
   Kept up the echo long,
            my
And still the[1] beside the horses
   It sang the blackbird's song
   The dewy lanes along.

              Then in my heart the echo
                Took up the blackbird's strain

                         steamy
                Along the dewy[2] lane

                       tune
                It sang the song again

'Lie down, lie down, young yeoman;
   The sun moves always west;
Who drives afield to labour
          yet
   Will aye come home to rest,
   And that will be the best.'

                The men
                And men that rise to labour

                Will aye lie down to rest,

As blithe afield to labour
   Through dewy lanes asteam
          my
I strode beside the waggon
   Against the morning beam
   And whistled to the team,[3]

                Against the morning beam

                Through dewy lanes asteam

[1] *the* was canceled before the next word was written.

[2] Canc. *dewy* and *song,* below.

[3] The revision of this stanza, number 1, was not wasted effort, for out of the phrase *blithe afield* in line 1 was evolved line 3 as we now have it. What determined the later recasting of the two opening lines? It may have been that *Teme,* bringing *Ludlow* with it, declared itself as a homonym for *team,* and the imagery in *dewy lanes asteam* suggested the other changes. It may be remembered that A.E.H., in turning to place names to produce this stanza, was following a natural bent: twenty-nine pieces in his *Complete Poems*—one out of six—contain place names within the first four lines.

8

"FAREWELL to barn and stack and tree,
    Farewell to Severn shore.
Terence, look your last at me,
    For I come home no more.

"The sun burns on the half-mown hill,
    By now the blood is dried;
And Maurice amongst the hay lies still
    And my knife is in his side.

"My mother thinks us long away;
    'Tis time the field were mown.
She had two sons at rising day,
    To-night she'll be alone.

"And here's a bloody hand to shake,
    And oh, man, here's good-bye;
We'll sweat no more on scythe and rake,
    My bloody hands and I.

"I wish you strength to bring you pride,
    And a love to keep you clean,
And I wish you luck, come Lammastide,
    At racing on the green.

"Long for me the rick will wait,
    And long will wait the fold,
And long will stand the empty plate,
    And dinner will be cold."

ASL 8 "Farewell to barn and stack and tree"

One entry: A 191.

Early drafts of two poems thus far examined have illustrated Housman's uncertainty in arriving at the stanza order he desired: an intermediate stanza was written for *ASL* 2 after stanzas 1 and 3 had been drafted; and the opening stanza of *ASL* 3 was composed and put in place after the other six were written. The manuscript of *ASL* 8 resembles that of *ASL* 3 in that the first quatrain as we now have it appears to have been an afterthought, crowded as it is in the extreme upper-right corner of the page. The stanza we now read as number 5 also required a change in sequence; in the draft it was originally number 4.

The third stanza set down on A 191 was canceled out of hand; it contains the motive for the fratricide. One reason for the suppression of this quatrain may have arisen from the poet's dislike of the infelicitous expression in the second line: *us two to strive.*

The manuscript of the stanza beginning *And here's a bloody hand* reveals the difficulties raised in the composition of line 3, which went through five versions before he arrived at the form we now read. After this crux was passed, it is apparent that the next, and final, stanza of the poem came without hesitation; it passed intact into printer's copy.

This unique draft shows no trace of the single quotation marks Housman used at the beginning and end of his poem when transcribing his printer's copy. There he omitted them at the head of stanzas 2, 3, 4, 5, and 6, but an editorial pencil doubled the two already in the MS and went on to add the others.

ASL 8 "Farewell to barn and stack and tree"
Unique Draft

A 191, complete   Date: August, 1894
Pencil, much corrected

Severn Shore.[1]

                          stack
           Farewell to barn and rick[4] and tree,
  on the half-mown   Farewell
The sun burns hot upon the[2] hills;   Goodbye[5] to Severn shore.
    And By   Terence,[6] look your last at me,
And By now[3] the blood is dried: For I come home no more.
And Maurice amongst the hay lies still,
  And my knife is in his side.

us
My mother thinks me[7] long away;
  'Tis time the field were mown.
I leave her heavy moan:[8]
             rising
She had two sons at break of[9] day,
  Tonight she'll be alone.

Let Lucy sorrow that she was born
  To set us two to strive:
If she loves the lad she loved at morn
  She loves no lad alive.[10]

[1] These two underlined words, written just below the margin, were probably the last touch given to the poem. Housman's fondness for alliteration may have induced him to elevate to this position the two words he had just written into line 2 of the quatrain at the right. Even though they kept this eminence no farther, they were not forgotten, for eight months later A.E.H. wrote them in a fragment on B 12—*Strip to bathe on Severn shore*—a line which eventually found its poem on B 20 and was printed as line 6 of *ASL* 55 ("Westward on the high-hilled plains").

[2] Canc. *hot upon the.* The *-s* in *hills* was canceled when line 3 was written.

[3] The three starts in front of *now* were canceled before *By* was set over a caret.

[4] Canc. *rick.*   [5] Canc. *Goodbye.*

[6] This is the first appearance in the notebooks of Terence Hearsay, the mythical correspondent of some of the poems.

[7] Canc. *me.*   [8] Canc. this line.   [9] Canc. *break of.*

[10] Each line of the quatrain is struck out.

bring
I wish you strength to win[11] you pride,
And a love to keep you clean,

fairing-tide
And I wish you luck, come Whitsuntide,[12]

Lammastide,
At racing on the green.[13]

And
So[14] here's a bloody hand to shake,
  And oh, man Oh Terence, here's
    And bid your friend good-bye;[15]
  At home I've
For him [?] no more work to make,[16]
    These[17]   s
My bloody hands[18] and I.

We'll sweat no more[19]
We've sweat our last on scythe and rake
Tonight We'll sweat no more on scythe
                & rake
Today an end of work we make,
For no more work at home we make,

Long for me the rick will wait,
  And long will wait the fold,
And long will stand the empty plate,
  And dinner will be cold.   August 1894

[11] Canc. *win.*

[12] The two alts. for this word were struck out. (*Lammastide* is the season of Lammas, a harvest festival celebrated on the first of August; *fairing-tide* is the time when a rural fair is held.)

[13] A.E.H. threw a loop about this stanza and, not lifting his pencil, carried the trace straight down to the last stanza, stopping just above the word *rick.*

[14] Canc. *So.*

[15] All but the last word of this line was struck out, and all but *here's* of the alt.

[16] Canc. this line and its alternative phrase.   [17] Canc. *These.*

[18] A.E.H., having written *hands,* struck out the -*s,* later added it above the line.

[19] These lines were written in the ascending order. All the marginalia were canceled except the four words in the top line and the last four words in the next.

9

ON moonlit heath and lonesome bank
    The sheep beside me graze;
And yon the gallows used to clank
    Fast by the four cross ways.

A careless shepherd once would keep
    The flocks by moonlight there,[1]
And high amongst the glimmering sheep
    The dead man stood on air.

They hang us now in Shrewsbury jail:
    The whistles blow forlorn,
And trains all night groan on the rail
    To men that die at morn.

There sleeps in Shrewsbury jail to-night,
    Or wakes, as may betide,
A better lad, if things went right,
    Than most that sleep outside.

And naked to the hangman's noose
    The morning clocks will ring
A neck God made for other use
    Than strangling in a string.

And sharp the link of life will snap,
    And dead on air will stand
Heels that held up as straight a chap
    As treads upon the land.

So here I'll watch the night and wait
    To see the morning shine,
When he will hear the stroke of eight
    And not the stroke of nine;

And wish my friend as sound a sleep
    As lads' I did not know,
That shepherded the moonlit sheep
    A hundred years ago.

---

[1] Hanging in chains was called keeping sheep by moonlight [Housman's note].

ASL 9 "On moonlit heath and lonesome bank"

One entry: A 226-27.

Housman apparently began his draft of this poem on A 227 and filled the entire page with the first seven stanzas; then turning back to the top of A 226 he made another essay at stanza 7 and below it wrote a nearly perfect draft of the eighth, and final, quatrain.

When he sat down to compose this lyric, the overture of the product of his afternoon walk must have been nearly complete in his thought, for the first three stanzas flowed smoothly, the second attaining finality here except for a choice left open in two places between *the* and *his*. But the remainder, down to the final stanza, came with difficulty; and when Housman finally turned away from his embattled pages, nearly one half of the lines of the poem as we know it were still submerged in the chaos of the lower portion of A 227. Below the second stanza the page divides into two columns: in the left, quatrains more or less complete that were to be wrought into numbers 3, 4, 5, 6, and 7; in the right, two alternative lines of stanza 3, two drafts of stanza 5, and a new attempt at the sixth. All told, there must have been at least thirty-five lines legible at one time on the lower half of this page. The manuscript is compressed and desperately precise, as if the poet were loath to turn the sheet and renew the struggle elsewhere for fear that his gains, such as they were, might be lost unless he kept them under his eye. No other page in the notebooks is more explicit in its revelation of how the poet's art constructs the bridge between idea and language.

The draft shows no trace of the printed note to line 6, "Hanging in chains was called keeping sheep by moonlight," added by Housman at the bottom of the first page of the copy he prepared for the printer.

ASL 9 "On moonlit heath and lonesome bank"
Unique Draft

A 226, two pieces, small middle   Date: February, 1895
   section missing
Pencil, lightly corrected

[*Piece 1*]

And there's no more to do
Here by the gallows foot,[1] my lad,
   I'll wake the night for you.   And hear the stroke of eight[2]

        safe
And wish my friend as sound a sleep
And then my friend's as safe asleep
          sure asleep

  As lads[3] I did not know
That shepherded the moonlit sheep
  A hundred years ago.

[*Piece 2*][4]

        Than most that sleep outside.[5]

---

[1] Canc. *Here by the gallows foot.*

[2] This significant line, here considered as the closing line of the stanza, was carried over from the bottom of A 227. (Cf. the title "Eight O'Clock," *LP* 15.)

[3] The possessive *lads'* was needed when this line was imagined as following directly the one above beginning *And wish.* . . . After writing the alternative *And then my friend's.* . . , A.E.H. struck out the apostrophe after *lads'*.

[4] This piece is nearly filled by eight lines (later printed as *MP* 26) apparently written before the draft of A 227 was begun.

[5] Below this line, which became number 16 of the poem, are the remains of at least two more, erased beyond legibility, that seem to belong to *ASL* 9. Probably more alternatives were lost with the cut-out midsection.

ASL 9 "On moonlit heath and lonesome bank"
Unique Draft continued

A 227, complete
Pencil

Feb. 1895

On silent heath and lonesome bank
  The sheep in moonshine graze,
    And here the[1] And here the
[Where once ?] gallows used to clank
  Beside the four cross ways.
         Close to

      A careless shepherd once would keep
      The
      His flocks by moonlight there,
          the
      And high amongst his glimmering sheep
      The dead man stood on air.

They hang us now in Shrewsbury jail;   Where whistles blow to warn[4]
  The whistles blow forlorn: wheels[5]   groan
The whistle whistles from the rail[2]   And brakes all night scream on the rail
      hang[3]   trains
  To men that die at morn.

      readying   helpless
Tonight [is waiting ?] for the noose[6] And naked to the hangman's noose
  While [?   ] drive,   blue of morn
A neck I'd liefer hang to loose[7]   In [?   ] will go
    half the   A neck [   ]
  Than most men's[8] necks alive.   lightly
                      I know   breath [?   ]
                       And life and [?   ] part
                        and soul will cleave apart

   [1] Having superscribed *And here the* over the opening of line 3 (canc. down to *gallows*), A.E.H. struck out his alternative but later restored it over a caret.
   [2] Canc. this line.   [3] Canc. *hang*.   [4] Canc. this line.
   [5] Canc. *wheels, brakes, scream.*
   [6] This and the following line are struck out. The words *noose* and *neck* precipitated allusions that could not be successfully dealt with in this stanza (number 4) and overflowed into the two drafts of the fifth quatrain in the column opposite. Of the original version of the fourth stanza, so far as it can be read, A.E.H. preserved only the word *tonight* and the formula *than most*.
   [7] Canc. *loose*. A now illegible alt. was set over a caret.
   [8] Canc. *most men's* and *alive. I know* at the end of this line provides the rhyme for the line to the right, *In blue of morn will go.*

blithe light
And quick to nine the minutes post[9]
　When still[10]
　And dead on air will stand
In shoes　　　　　　black
The feet[11] I'd liefer [　?　] than most
　That walk upon the land.

And flesh [　　?　　] part from ghost[12]
Strike eight, and soul and flesh will part.
　　　help up　　　　as true a
Feet that have borne[13] a truer heart
　　　[　　?　　][14]　a truer
[　　　　?　　　　] land[15]
Than most that tread on land.

　　　here I'll　　　tonight
So I will watch the night and wait
　　For his short day to shine
To see the morning shine,
When
And[16] he will hear the stroke of eight
And not the stroke of nine.

　　　helpless
And naked to the hangman's noose[17]
　In blue of morn will go
　　　　liefer die to loose
A neck I'd keep for kinder use
　　　string it up for
Than break it for a show.[18]
　　　have it swing for show
　　　　hang

　A neck God made for better use
　　Than swinging there for show.

A fellow fit for better use
　Than swinging there for show

[9] Canc. this line and the alts. *blithe* and *light,* above.　　[10] Canc. *When still.*

[11] Canc. *feet* and the word below *black.*

[12] *ghost* was intended to rhyme with *post* or *most* in the stanza to the left.

[13] Canc. *have borne* and the alt. above, *as true a.*

[14] Canc. this illegible alt.　　[15] Canc. this line.　　[16] Canc. *And.*

[17] Here begins the redraft of stanza 5, first attempted in the third line of this column.

[18] In this line and others below there may be an echo from Tennyson's "Rizpah," line 35: "They hang'd him in chains for a show."

10

MARCH

THE Sun at noon to higher air,
Unharnessing the silver Pair
That late before his chariot swam,
Rides on the gold wool of the Ram.

So braver notes the storm-cock sings
To start the rusted wheel of things,
And brutes in field and brutes in pen
Leap that the world goes round again.

The boys are up the woods with day
To fetch the daffodils away,
And home at noonday from the hills
They bring no dearth of daffodils.

Afield for palms the girls repair,
And sure enough the palms are there,
And each will find by hedge or pond
Her waving silver-tufted wand.

In farm and field through all the shire
The eye beholds the heart's desire;
Ah, let not only mine be vain,
For lovers should be loved again.

ASL 10 "March"

One entry: A 170.

Though Laurence Housman's Analysis correctly designates this entry a "rough draft," eight lines of the twenty composing the poem were never retouched, and all the rest but one, the seventeenth, were brought to finality in this single entry. The most troublesome lines were the first two. Housman line-canceled his original draft of them, wrote out an alternative couplet to the right, overscored that with a high wavy pencil stroke, and set over it another substitute, which suffered the same fate. The symbol *stet,* once hopefully written above the word *Sun* to ensure the survival of some part of the opening line, itself disappeared beneath a scrawl of cancel-lines. Not until he assembled the copy for his book did Housman bring into this poem the wording of the opening couplet as we now read it. At this time he restored the first of his two substitutes, changing only *each noon* to *at noon.*

As it often happened, he had difficulty in fixing the order of the stanzas of this poem: The one beginning *Afield for palms* ... (now number 4) was originally the second; but in reviewing his notebook page he decided that this quatrain should change places with the one immediately below, and, enclosing it in brackets, he marked it with the numeral 3. However, in preparing final copy, he returned it to fourth place. The basic fault in this lyric, though, was not to be mended by these shifts; its inferiority, despite a few admirable phrases, is still apparent in its lack of unity, its faltering sequence, and its inconclusive ending. Though the date of composition cannot be fixed exactly, it is indicated by the title of the poem and the date "Feb. 1893" appearing only fifteen pages earlier. Since his mother's death on the twenty-sixth day of March, 1871—Housman's twelfth birthday—this month had brought back its burden of poignant memories, and it is probable that they entered disturbingly into the composition of *ASL* 10, recalling perhaps a poem (now printed as *MP* 25, "Yon flakes that fret the eastern sky") copied in the pre-1890 section of his first notebook, in which he commemorated his natal day and his present life, with its "heavier cause to mourn."

ASL 10 "March"
Unique Draft

A 170, complete   Date: Spring, 1893
Pencil, much corrected

                                    The sun, that from the [?   ] pales
1   stet   March   Unharnessing [?   ]
                                              at noon
The Sun, that from the Fishes' pales,[1]   The Sun each noon to higher air,
Unharnessing the silver [?   ]   Unharnessing
That late before his chariot swam,   And [?   ] the silver Pair
Rides on the gold wool of the Ram.   And leaving dark
                                                    dim

              3 [Afield for palms the girls repair,
                  And sure enough the palms are there,
                            ledge[2]
                  And each will find by hedge or pond
                  Her waving silver-tufted wand.][3]

2   braver still[4] notes
So now of nights the storm-cock sings
    start
To move[5] the rusted wheel of things,
  And trout in brook and herd on plain
And beasts are glad on all the plain[6]   And brutes in field & brutes in pen
  Leap   that
To feel[7] the world go round again.

---

[1] Canc. the opening couplet and the two alts. to the right.
[2] Canc. *ledge*.
[3] These brackets and the numerals heading each stanza are in the manuscript.
[4] Canc. *still*.   [5] Canc. *move*.   [6] Canc. this line.
[7] Canc. *to feel; -es* was added to *go* when *Leap that* was chosen to head the line.

streams⁸ woods

4   The boys are up the hills with day
     To fetch the daffodils away,
at by noonday⁹
     And home at evening from the hills
     They bring no dearth of daffodils.

through
By farm and town in all the shire¹⁰
cote
5   in pen and byre
In wood and field, and all the shire¹¹
The eye beholds the heart's desire,
And why should only mine be vain,¹²   Ah, let not only mine be vain;
Who ask but to be loved again?   For lovers should be loved again

---

⁸ Canc. *streams* and *hills*.

⁹ A.E.H. struck out *at evening* and superscribed *by noonday,* later substituting *at* for *by.*

¹⁰ Below this line are two illegible lines, the second struck through.

¹¹ Canc. *and all the shire.*

¹² Canc. this line; its substitute was written to the right. After writing this alternative, A.E.H. canceled an interrogation mark he had set at the end of the closing line, to the left.

11

ON your midnight pallet lying,
    Listen, and undo the door:
Lads that waste the light in sighing
    In the dark should sigh no more;
Night should ease a lover's sorrow;
Therefore, since I go to-morrow,
    Pity me before.

In the land to which I travel,
    The far dwelling, let me say—
Once, if here the couch is gravel,
    In a kinder bed I lay,
And the breast the darnel smothers
Rested once upon another's
    When it was not clay.

ASL 11 "On your midnight pallet lying"

One entry: B 16.

All but five lines of this fourteen-line poem show an alteration of some kind, but when Housman got up from this page of his notebook he left every line but one identical with the final copy he would make seven months later. One peculiarity of the B 16 draft is the frequency of punctuation changes. Seldom are these very numerous or important in the drafts, and for that reason they are not often described in these analyses. But the accumulation of these changes in *ASL* 11—in the unique draft of the poem, in the printer's copy, and in the proofsheets—is worth tabulating as an example of the poet's practice on the subject. In the preface to the first edition of *Last Poems* he remarked, "It is best that what I have written should be printed while I am here to see it through the press and control its spelling and punctuation." His revisions on B 16 include the following changes:

line 1—comma added to end of line in proofsheets;

line 2—semicolon changed to period (to colon in printer's copy);

line 4—semicolon changed to comma but restored;

line 5—comma and dash changed to semicolon and dash (to semicolon in printer's copy);

line 9—comma changed to colon (to dash in printer's copy);

line 11—semicolon changed to comma.

ASL 11 "On your midnight pallet lying"
Unique Draft

B 16, nearly complete   Date: April or May, 1895
Pencil, second stanza much revised

midnight pallet
On your bed at midnight lying
   Listen, and undo the door.
Lads that waste the light in sighing
   In the dark should sigh no more;
        end
   should sain[1] a lover's sorrow;—
Night is not for lovers' sorrow,
So, because I part tomorrow,[2]   Therefore since I go tomorrow
   Pity me before.

In the land to which I travel,
   The far country[3] dwelling,
   When I come there, let me say:
Once, if here the couch is gravel,
      kinder
   In a softer[4] bed I lay,

And   heart   tombstone   darnel
Once the breast the cerecloth covers[5] knotgrass smothers

   Beat one night upon a lover's   another's
Breathed against a happy lover's[6]   Rested once upon a lover's
   When it was not clay.

---

[1] *sain* is one of several archaic words in Housman's poetry. Though he eventually rejected this use of it and again decided against it after writing *saining* four times into a late copy of *LP* 30 (now preserved on the foolscap sheet no. 149), he did keep the word in his final draft on *ASL* 14, line 13: *There flowers no balm to sain him.* (This line, it is worth noting, is quoted in the *NED* under *sain*.)

[2] Canc. this line.   [3] Canc. *country*.   [4] Canc. *softer*.

[5] The end of this line evolved thus: After writing *cerecloth covers,* Housman canceled the first word and wrote over it *tombstone,* which in turn gave way to *knotgrass,* set over a caret. He struck out this word and superscribed *darnel,* following with *smothers.* This left open the alts. *darnel smothers* and *darnel covers*—which stood until printer's copy was taken. The words *Once,* in the original line, and *heart,* written above it, were also struck out.

[6] This line, with its alt. above, was line-canceled.

12

WHEN I watch the living meet,
   And the moving pageant file
Warm and breathing through the street
   Where I lodge a little while,

If the heats of hate and lust
   In the house of flesh are strong,
Let me mind the house of dust
   Where my sojourn shall be long.

In the nation that is not
   Nothing stands that stood before;
There revenges are forgot,
   And the hater hates no more;

Lovers lying two and two
   Ask not whom they sleep beside,
And the bridegroom all night through
   Never turns him to the bride.

ASL 12 "When I watch the living meet"

One entry: A 230.

This unique draft, like that for *ASL* 11, contains a poem that must have been complete in theme and nearly complete in language before a word of it was put on paper. Of the sixteen lines of *ASL* 12, just over half were never retouched at all, only one was radically altered, and before Housman completed his transcript he had brought five other lines to the form in which we now read them in the text. As a further proof of the rightness of the original shaping of this lyric, three other lines for which second thought had provided alternatives were written into printer's copy in the version they had in this entry before revision.

The mood of this poem is of a kind with that which dominates the final pages of Notebook A, which were written in the spring (probably in March) of 1895; it produced *ASL* 9 ("On moonlit heath and lonesome bank") and *ASL* 43 ("The Immortal Part") on the pages just preceding and carried on into *ASL* 15 ("Look not in my eyes . . .") and *ASL* 38 ("The winds out of the west land blow") on A 232-33.

ASL 12 "When I watch the living meet"
Unique Draft

A 230, complete   Date: February or March, 1895
Pencil

>   living
> When I watch the townsmen meet[1]
>   moving
> And the endless[2] pageant file
> Warm and breathing through the street
>   Where I lodge a little while,
>
>   If[3]
> When
>   If the heats of hate and lust
>   my
>   In this[4] house of flesh are strong,
>   Let me
> Then I[5] mind the house of dust
>   will
>   Where my sojourn shall[6] be long.

[1] A.E.H. could hardly have failed to perceive that stanza 1, even before he had completed his first draft of it, was unluckily laden with the atmosphere of the opening lines of "Tam O'Shanter." The substitution of *living* for *townsmen*, announcing the balance between the passers-by and the dead, thus served a double purpose.

[2] Canc. *endless*.

[3] He canceled *If* and wrote above it *When*, which was also canceled, and *If* was restored.

[4] The second word in this line was originally *the*. After heavily penciling *this* through it, A.E.H. canceled his substitute and rewrote above, *my*.

[5] Canc. *Then I*.   [6] Canc. *shall*.

In the nation that is not[7]
              wrongs
None remember what they bore,[8]   Nothing stands that stood before;[9]
There revenges are forgot
  And the hater hates no more.

   Lovers lying two and two
    Ask not whom they sleep beside,
  And the bridegroom[10] all night through
    Never turns him to the bride.

[7] This line was borrowed from a poem (later printed as *MP* 2, "When Israel out of Egypt came") written some years previously on A 77.

[8] Canc. this line and the alt. *wrongs*.

[9] Though this substitute line allowed the poet to exploit his favorite word *stand*, which in some form occurs six times in the first eleven poems of *A Shropshire Lad*, it was at the same time a substitute of the impersonal for the personal, and by breaking the sequence *wrongs . . . revenges . . . hater hates* may be said to have weakened the strong effect in the stanza as first conceived.

[10] To note a small peculiarity in the manuscript: After inadvertently writing *bridge* here, A.E.H. carefully inserted an *e* between *d* and *g*, altered the final *e* to a none-too-clear *r*, and went on to add the last three letters of his wanted word. Oddly enough, he made the identical error and correction in the copy he prepared for the printer.

13

WHEN I was one-and-twenty
   I heard a wise man say,
"Give crowns and pounds and guineas
   But not your heart away;
Give pearls away and rubies
   But keep your fancy free."
But I was one-and-twenty,
   No use to talk to me.

When I was one-and-twenty
   I heard him say again,
"The heart out of the bosom
   Was never given in vain;
'Tis paid with sighs a plenty
   And sold for endless rue."
And I am two-and-twenty,
   And oh, 'tis true, 'tis true.

ASL 13 "When I was one-and-twenty"

One entry: A 216.

The draft of *ASL* 13 is one of the two destroyed by Housman himself. The only trace of the poem in the notebooks is the first line of it, standing alone on the lower half of A 216 beneath the date "Jan. 1895." He drew a long pen stroke beneath the line and two strokes beneath the date. Laurence's Analysis records that the following sheet in the notebook had been cut out, but the recto showed on its margin enough of nine lines to indicate they belonged to "When I was one-and-twenty."

The scantiness of the entry suggests that it may have been intended as a memorandum for the completion of the draft that was to occupy the next page; or the title-line and the date may have been dashed off in order to mark the location of the poem on A 216 after the page carrying the draft had been cut out. In any event it is reasonably certain that the destruction of the sheet following A 216 was aimed not at the draft of *ASL* 13 but at the writing on the other side of the sheet.

In the upper-right corner of the page of printer's copy containing the poem Housman wrote lightly in pencil "Another series"—probably to designate the group of pieces from number 13 to 17, which have to do with heart- or soul-sickness, the theme expressed in *ASL* 13.

14

THERE pass the careless people
   That call their souls their own:
Here by the road I loiter,
   How idle and alone.

Ah, past the plunge of plummet,
   In seas I cannot sound,
My heart and soul and senses,
   World without end, are drowned.

His folly has not fellow
   Beneath the blue of day
That gives to man or woman
   His heart and soul away.

There flowers no balm to sain him
   From east of earth to west
That's lost for everlasting
   The heart out of his breast.

Here by the labouring highway
   With empty hands I stroll:
Sea-deep, till doomsday morning,
   Lie lost my heart and soul.

ASL 14 "There pass the careless people"

One entry: A 82-83.

This is the second *Shropshire Lad* poem written in the "pre-1890" section of Housman's first notebook. In general appearance the draft resembles that of "Into my heart an air that kills" *(ASL* 40) on A 63: both are in ink (except for one quatrain of *ASL* 14), and the pencil corrections, made probably when the contents of *A Shropshire Lad* were being chosen, show a similarity in style.

Stanzas 2, 3, and 4 are preserved on a middle section of A 82, which may have received a complete draft of the five-stanza poem. The fifth and first quatrains, the latter in pencil, are on a 2¾ inch strip cut from A 83. A brace-and-transfer line leading from stanza 1 carries it off the page in the direction of A 82; a line terminating at the upper margin of the surviving fragment of this page seems to mark the destination of this penciled stanza. The remains of a similar device running off the lower cut margin of A 82 indicate either that its missing bottom strip at one time contained a quatrain Housman transferred to A 83 or that A 82 was to receive one written originally on its facing page.

These transfer lines are witness to the poet's effort to get his stanzas into better order. Only stanza 1, the last written, is headed by an uncontested numeral. The stanza beneath the numeral 2 was once number 3; stanza 3, 1; stanza 4, 2; stanza 5, 4. All of this shifting was labor lost, however, for the last four quatrains went into final copy in the order they first had on A 82-83. It would seem that the problem of second thought here was the construction of the needed first stanza, stating firmly the *mise en scène* of the poem. Once this was achieved, the closely knit texture of the continuing four stanzas as originally set down formed a natural sequence.

ASL 14 "There pass the careless people"
Unique Draft

A 82, middle two thirds   Date: before September, 1890
Ink, corrections in pencil

3 2.[1]

Oh   the
Ah No,[2] past all plunge of plummet,
In seas I cannot sound,
My heart and soul and senses,
World without end, are drowned.

1 3.

His folly has not fellow
In all the ken of day[3]
That gives to man or woman
His heart and soul away.

2 4.

There flowers no balm to sain him
From east of earth to west
That's lost for everlasting
The heart out of his breast.

---

[1] The first of these two numerals, as in each of the pairs shown below, was canceled by a wavy line.

[2] A.E.H. struck out *No,* wrote *Ah* before it; then superscribed *Oh* but canceled it. Canc. *all.*

[3] Canc. this line. Its substitute, *Beneath the blue of day,* was jotted down on B 101, along with five other corrigenda, late in 1895 after A.E.H. had sent off his MSS, where the line had read *From Thule to Cathay.* The line from B 101 was inserted during proofreading.

ASL 14 "There pass the careless people"
Unique Draft continued

A 83, strip from top or middle
First stanza ink; second, pencil

5 4[1]

Here by the
  Along   [swarming?]
Beside the[2] labouring highway
  With empty hands I stroll:
Sea-deep, till doomsday morning,
  Lie lost my heart and soul.

1.

There pass the careless people
  That call their souls their own:
Here by the road I loiter,
  How idle and alone.

---

[1] Canc. this numeral.
[2] Canc. *Beside the*. The word above *labouring* may also have been canceled.

15

Look not in my eyes, for fear
    They mirror true the sight I see,
And there you find your face too clear
    And love it and be lost like me.
One the long nights through must lie
    Spent in star-defeated sighs,
But why should you as well as I
    Perish? gaze not in my eyes.

A Grecian lad, as I hear tell,
    One that many loved in vain,
Looked into a forest well
    And never looked away again.
There, when the turf in springtime
        flowers,
    With downward eye and gazes sad,
Stands amid the glancing showers
    A jonquil, not a Grecian lad.

ASL 15 "Look not in my eyes . . ."

One entry: A 232.

The two stanzas of this poem fill the lower two thirds of A 232, the upper part of which has been destroyed. Near the cut margin the last line of the opening stanza—"Perish? gaze not in my eyes"—can just be deciphered, suggesting that the complete stanza was probably composed at the head of the page. The second version, written fair in the lower-left corner of the page, shows the alteration of only a single word and was taken into printer's copy with only two other changes, in punctuation.

The second stanza probably exhibits the kind of revision the first draft of the other stanza received and provides a clue as to why Laurence could not even by heavy erasure bring it up (or down) to his standard for salvage: Only three lines of stanza 2 escaped retouching and a number of alternatives and substitutes were interlined, some of them now illegible. However, the original reading held up well against these tentative improvements and went into print with the change of only one word—one that was not challenged in the draft but was introduced by Housman into his next, and final, copy.

ASL 15 "Look not in my eyes . . ."
Unique Draft

A 232, lower two thirds   Date: February or March, 1895
Pencil

Perish? gaze not in my eyes.

The   fables
 A Grecian lad, as I hear tell,
   like you beloved Who like you [?   ] in vain,
 One that many loved in vain,
  once in the woodland
 Looked into a forest well[1]
 And never looked away again.
There
 Now, when the turf in springtime flowers,
 With downward eye and bearing[2] sad
   among [?   ][3]
 Stands amid the glancing showers
 A jonquil, not a Grecian lad.

Look not in my eyes, for fear
 They mirror true the sight I see,
And there you find your face too clear
 And love it and be lost like me.
One the long nights through must lie
 Spent in star-defeated sighs;
But why should you as well as I
   gaze
 Perish? look[4] not in my eyes.

---

[1] A.E.H. apparently began his reshaping of this line by striking out only the word *a* and writing *the* above it. Then he filled out the alternative as shown but later rejected it.

[2] He wrote *bearing* in printer's copy, then penciled over it *gazes*. Eventually this word was retraced in ink and *bearing* canceled.

[3] Canc. this alternative beginning *among*.   [4] Canc. *look*.

16

IT nods and curtseys and recovers
　　When the wind blows above,
The nettle on the graves of lovers
　　That hanged themselves for love.

The nettle nods, the wind blows over,
　　The man, he does not move,
The lover of the grave, the lover
　　That hanged himself for love.

ASL 16 "It nods and curtseys and recovers"

One entry: B 46.

It is evident from the full-page draft of this eight-line poem that it flowed easily and no difficulties arose until revision was undertaken. An alternative word was set above line 2 but was struck out. Then the pencil hesitated over line 7 and finally moved through all but the last two words. The substitute written below the stanza did not please, and the lower half of the page became a testing-field for the needed line. One after the other Housman ran off five alternatives, of which he canceled all but the first and fifth; then, as if to summon context to his aid, he copied the opening two lines of the stanza and wrote into its proper position his eighth version of the recalcitrant seventh line. This did not please either, but finally toward the right margin he wrote the substitute that went into print—as repetitive and unadorned a line as could possibly be written.

All in all, this lyric is an excellent example of Housman's power of concentration. The meaning of the poem is conveyed by the words *nods, wind, blows, nettle, grave, lover, hanged,* each of which, save one, occurs in both stanzas. It was his return of the seventh line to the overriding language pattern that saved the poem from the false imagery of the alternatives strewn by the way and made of it a right, close-lipped declaration.

ASL 16 "It nods and curtseys and recovers"
Unique Draft

B 46, complete   Date: July or August, 1895
Pencil

It nods and curtseys and recovers
                    sighs[1]
When the wind blows above,
The nettle on the graves of lovers
    That hanged themselves for love.

The nettle nods, the wind blows over;
    The men, they do not move:
A lad for [sleeping ?] is the lover[2]
        hangs[3]
    That hanged himself for love.

                                a
There are worse sleepers than the lover
Not even love disturbs the lover[4]
The lad that sighs is not the lover
Sleep has enamoured so the lover
The lad to sigh is not the lover[5]

                            blows
The nettle nods, the wind sighs[6] over;
    The [?   ] not move:[7]   The man, he does not move,
            [?   ][8]
No longer sighing is the lover   The lover of the grave, the lover
            [9] [   ]
    That hanged himself for love.

---

[1] Canc. *sighs.*

[2] Through the beginning of this line was written an alt. which made the reading approximate *The lover of the spring's the lover.* All but the last two words of the double line are struck out with two or three horizontal lines.

[3] Canc. *hangs.*   [4] Canc. this line and the one following.

[5] This accumulation of so many complete lines as tentative substitutes for a single line is not often paralleled in the notebooks. Cf. p. 122.

[6] Canc. *sighs.*   [7] Canc. this line and the one below, *No longer. . . .*

[8] Canc. this alt. for *sighing* and the one below the line.

[9] The first two letters of *hanged* were rewritten here.

17

TWICE a week the winter thorough
    Here stood I to keep the goal:
Football then was fighting sorrow
    For the young man's soul.

Now in Maytime to the wicket
    Out I march with bat and pad:
See the son of grief at cricket
    Trying to be glad.

Try I will; no harm in trying:
    Wonder 'tis how little mirth
Keeps the bones of man from lying
    On the bed of earth.

ASL 17 "Twice a week the winter thorough"

One entry: B 26-27.

It is apparent in the draft that the labor of revision in this three-stanza poem centered upon the opening stanza. After making numerous inter-lineations and rewriting line 2 in the right margin twice, Housman, still dissatisfied, continued on the following page, B 27, his efforts to bring about the refractory line. Before he closed his notebook he had before him among the alternatives the line that was to go into print, although it is doubtful that he recognized it this early in the none-too-assured writing and the maze of cancel-strokes.

A fortunate correction was made earlier, on B 26, in the third line of stanza 2 when the phrase *sons of men* was supplanted by *son of grief*. This change, it may not be too much to surmise, effected the alteration in the opening of the next, and final, quatrain where *Try I will* took the place of *Try, my lads*. These two substitutions hark back to the *I* of stanza 1 and, by making the whole poem an utterance of the youthful player, produce a sense of unity that was lacking in the original version.

ASL 17 "Twice a week the winter thorough"
Unique Draft

B 26, complete   Date: May or June, 1895
Pencil

Twice a week the winter thorough   Afternoons
            trampled   [?   ] kept the goal
  besieged   threatened   [?]
I [bestrode ?] the guarded goal:[1]   I bestrode the trampled goal
      made the fight with   guard before
Football then was [warring ?][2] sorrow I stood [?   ] the goal
    then was fighting
     the
For the[3] young man's soul.

Now in Maytime to the wicket
  Out I march with bat and pad:
        [?] grief
See the sons[4] of men at cricket
  Trying to be glad.

  Try I will
Try, my lads;[5] no harm in trying:
  Wonder 'tis how little mirth
Keeps the bones of man from lying
  On the bed of earth.

[1] A.E.H. drew a high undula through all but the last word of this line.

[2] Canc. the middle three words of this line and the alt., above.

[3] After canceling *the*, A.E.H. rewrote the word as shown; then heavily penciled *a* through it.

[4] He struck off the last letter of *sons*, canceled *men* and its alternative, and set *grief* above a caret.

[5] Canc. *Try, my lads.*

ASL 17 "Twice a week the winter thorough"
Unique Draft continued

B 27, complete
Pencil

>   stood I
>   I stood to keep[1]
>   Here in field
>   Mud or frost,[2] I kept the goal:

[1] Canc. *stood to keep* and the *I*, above.
[2] Canc. *Mud or frost*.

18

Oh, when I was in love with you,
    Then I was clean and brave,
And miles around the wonder grew
    How well did I behave.

And now the fancy passes by,
    And nothing will remain,
And miles around they'll say that I
    Am quite myself again.

ASL 18 "Oh, when I was in love with you"

Two entries: B 17; B 29.

Though Laurence Housman's Analysis makes only one reference to this poem, placing it on B 17, a second draft exists, written only a few days later on B 29 (or 30). These two pages Laurence designated "Fragments and single lines," but it may be that he failed to identify the eight-line poem, obscured as it was with heavy cancellations. It exists on a three-inch fragment cut from a midsection of a page, the verso being blank; and, since the help of the Analysis is lacking, my assignment of the numerals 29 and 30 to the notebook sheet is conjectural. My reason for so doing is, mainly, that the writing of the draft is remarkably like that on B 28; furthermore, the material on twenty adjacent pages preceding and following is accounted for in the Analysis.

Stanza 1 of this *jeu d'esprit,* begun near the top of B 17 beneath the date May, 1895, flowed smoothly, the opening of only one line (number 3) being disputed—*And miles around* contending with the first-written *In town and field.* This contest, with others in the second stanza, was resumed in the second draft.

The second stanza shows much revision in both drafts, only line 2 passing unchallenged throughout. Alternatives for lines 1 and 4, apparently settled on B 17, sprang up again in the second writing. The third line, which seems to have been the last to come to rights, was brought around by one of Housman's frequent ways of breaking deadlocks: the repetition of a phrase from an earlier line. This left the poem, but for a small variation in one word, in the form it carried into print.

ASL 18 "Oh, when I was in love with you"
First Draft

B 17, two pieces, the lower blank   Date: May, 1895
Pencil

> Oh, when I was in love with you,
>   Then I was clean and brave;
>   And miles around
> In town and field[1] the wonder grew
>   farm
>   How well did I behave.
>
>   But   [?   ] flash is by   fancy passes by
>   And now the shallow fount is dry,[2]
>   And nothing will remain;
>   farm   say
>   And town and field will see[3] that I
>   The wonder it will end, and I
>   Am quite myself again.
>   Shall be myself again

---

[1] Housman generally distrusted phrases and meters of which he was too fond, and his suspicions must have been instantly aroused upon rereading this line, for on A 225 he had rung the changes on *field and town* in his last stanza of *ASL* 3; *farm and town* had crept into an alternative line of *ASL* 10 on A 170. The phrase *And miles around,* though it owes little to originality, was a fortunate introduction here, for it was the making of the troublesome seventh line in the next draft.

[2] Canc. *shallow fount is dry* and its alt., above. (Another alt., below *shallow*, is now illegible.)

[3] Canc. *see.*

ASL 18 "Oh, when I was in love with you"
Second Draft

B 29, upper section   Date: May or June, 1895
Pencil

        Oh, when I was in love with you,
          Then I was clean and brave,
          In town and field[1]
        And miles around the wonder grew
          How well did I behave.

    And   wonder
        But[2] now the fancy passes by,
          And nothing will remain,
      The wonder, it will end, and I[3] And miles around they say that I
          Shall be myself again.   Am quite myself again.

[1] Canc. *In town and field.*

[2] Canc. *But* and *wonder;* the latter must have been struck out once A.E.H. had glanced over his finished draft, when he would have noted in line 7 the repetition of *wonder.*

[3] Canc. this line and the line below.

19

TO AN ATHLETE DYING YOUNG

THE time you won your town the race
We chaired you through the market-place;
Man and boy stood cheering by,
And home we brought you shoulder-high.

To-day, the road all runners come,
Shoulder-high we bring you home,
And set you at your threshold down,
Townsman of a stiller town.

Smart lad, to slip betimes away
From fields where glory does not stay
And early though the laurel grows
It withers quicker than the rose.

Eyes the shady night has shut
Cannot see the record cut,
And silence sounds no worse than cheers
After earth has stopped the ears:

Now you will not swell the rout
Of lads that wore their honours out,
Runners whom renown outran
And the name died before the man.

So set, before its echoes fade,
The fleet foot on the sill of shade,
And hold to the low lintel up
The still-defended challenge-cup.

And round that early-laurelled head
Will flock to gaze the strengthless dead,
And find unwithered on its curls
The garland briefer than a girl's.

ASL 19 "To an Athlete Dying Young"

Two entries: A 240; B 10-11.

Nowhere in the four notebooks does one obtain a better view of Housman's workshop method than in the two drafts of this poem. One can see his racing pen in motion over A 240 jotting down stanzas, couplets, single lines, seizing the separate fragments as they took shape in language. There we may now read, in this order, substantial forms of stanzas 1, 6, 3, and 7; the closing couplet of stanza 5, and the opening couplet of stanza 4. Here much was done, but much remained to do, for only seven lines on A 240 were carried intact into the second draft; however the theme of the poem was firmly established in the first and final quatrains. The theme itself is akin to that of "The Day of Battle" (*ASL* 56), written in two drafts on A 236-37, where the youth, now a soldier, was admonished to stand fast and . . . *take the bullet in your brain.*

It is likely that the poem advanced measurably toward completeness on the next (now missing) page, for the entry on B 10-11 has the look of a page rewrought with the measured confidence of one who had sat down to deal with an approximately full-scale draft. Each quatrain is now complete and in its proper position although nearly every one shows traces of cancellation and rewriting. Below the last line of his final stanza, Housman immediately turned to two stanzas left unresolved on the preceding page and rewrote the fourth and the opening couplet of the fifth. Neither revision was altogether satisfactory, and a number of cruxes here and in other stanzas were left for later reckoning when printer's copy was in the making, eight months later. The guiding principles at work on B 10-11 were Housman's preference for colloquial forms (*Smart lad* instead of *Wise lad*), alliteration (*fields where glory* instead of *fields where victory*), and his right choice of imagery (*Eyes the cloudy night has shut* instead of *Eyes the night has filled with smoke*).

ASL 19 "To an Athlete Dying Young"
First Draft

A 240, complete   Date: March, 1895
Pencil, much corrected

                    your
The day you won the[1] town the race
                  through
They[2] We chaired you in the market-place,
[Where market ?] folk
And [here ?] the crowd[3] stood cheering by,
And   home
Home[4] we brought you shoulder-high.

                                                    before it [?   ]
                                                    unbeaten, unafraid
    So now with ribboned breast invade   before the laurels fade
        Unbeaten yet,   So, now, with laurels undecayed,[6]
    First in the race, the sill of shade,   So set, before its[7] echoes fade,
                    low   Set foot upon[8] the sill of shade
    And hold to the dark[5] lintel up   The fleet foot on
    The still-defended challenge-cup.

                                              Wise lad, to steal betimes away
                                              From fields where victory will not stay

                                              And [?   ] braids
A garland briefer than a girl's   A garland briefer than a maid's.
    [?   ][9]   Now the eye that night has shut
        And never see your record cut

---

[1] Canc. *the*.   [2] Canc. *They* and *in*.
[3] Canc. the line down to *stood* and the alt., above.
[4] Canc. *Home*.   [5] Canc. *dark*.
[6] Canc. this line and the first two of the alts., reading upward.
[7] In writing this line A.E.H. probably had *cheering* (stanza 1) in mind as the vague antecedent of *its*. When this stanza became number 6 in the poem, *it* had to be read with *fleet foot* in the line following.
[8] Canc. *Set foot upon*.
[9] There are only faint traces of a line here, the predecessor of the one written out after it.

         that young and laurelled
And round your early-laurelled head
       come and gaze
Will throng to gaze the strengthless dead,
      find unwithered on
And yet unfaded round its curls
Your
The The[10] garland briefer than a girl's.

Of runners whom renown outran
  Or[11]
And the name died before the man.

---

[10] After *The* and *Your* were canceled, *The* was restored at the head of the line.
[11] Canc. *Or.*

ASL 19 "To an Athlete Dying Young"
Second Draft

B 10, complete   Date: April, 1895
Pencil

    time
The day[1] you won your town the race
We chaired you through the market-place;
Man and boy stood cheering by,
And home we brought you shoulder-high.

    Today, the road all runners come,
    Shoulder-high we bring you home,
    And set you at your threshold down,
    Townsman of a stiller town.

Well done,
Wise lad, to slip betimes away   Smart lad,
              glory
From fields where victory will[2] not stay
And glory for the runner braids[3]   And early though the laurel grows
A chaplet briefer than a maid's.   lasts no longer[4] better a
                                   It withers sooner than the[5] rose.

    The   man   cloudy
    He[6] whose eye the night has shut   Eyes the shady night has shut
    Never sees his record cut,[7]   Will never see
             sounds no worse than   Never see the record cut[10]
    And silence is the same as[8] cheers
               his[9]
    After earth has stopped the ears.

---

  [1] Canc. *day*.

  [2] In printer's copy A.E.H. wrote the first two letters of *will*, struck them out, and continued with *does*.

  [3] Canc. this line and the one below.   [4] Canc. *longer*.

  [5] Canc. *the*.   [6] Canc. *He*.   [7] Canc. this line.

  [8] Canc. *is the same as*.   [9] Canc. *his*.   [10] Canc. this line and the alt., above.

have   swelled

And[11] Now you will not join the throng   No fear you now should join

shall swell   the throng

stayed spell

Of lads that lived a day[12] too long,

Runners whom renown outran

And the name died before the man.

---

[11] Canc. *And, have,* and *swelled.*   [12] Canc. *day.*

ASL 19 "To an Athlete Dying Young"
Second Draft continued

B 11, complete
Pencil

> So set, before its echoes fade,
> The fleet foot on the sill of shade,
> And hold to the low lintel up
> The still-defended challenge-cup.

>   that
>   your
> And round that[1] early-laurelled head
> Will flock to gaze the strengthless dead
> And find unwithered on its curls
> The garland briefer than a girl's.

>   Eyes the cloudy
> Now the eye that[2] night has shut
> Will never see the record cut,
> And silence sounds no worse than cheers
>   After
> Now that[3] earth has stopped the ears.

>   Eyes the night has filled with smoke
> Cannot[4] see the record cut   Will not
>   Never[5] see the record broke,

>   Now you'll never[6]
> No fear you now should swell the rout
> Of lads that wore their honours out,

---

[1] A.E.H. struck out *that* and *your,* restored *that.*

[2] Canc. *Now the eye that.*   [3] Canc. *Now that.*

[4] *Cannot* is heavily underscored—perhaps to approve the line and express the poet's rejection of the faltering couplet to the right. After writing it he probably felt he was making a mistake in abandoning the phrase *the record cut,* which he had already written three times. This, an idiom remembered from boyhood, is perfectly suited to the poem and was, fortunately, retained. However, the meaning of *record cut* ("running time lowered") may escape the nonsporting or casual reader. (See Housman's explanation of the phrase in *The Yale Review* [December, 1936], p. 284.)

[5] Canc. *Never.*   [6] Canc. this alt.

20

Oн fair enough are sky and plain,
  But I know fairer far:
Those are as beautiful again
  That in the water are;

The pools and rivers wash so clean
  The trees and clouds and air,
The like on earth was never seen,
  And oh that I were there.

These are the thoughts I often think
  As I stand gazing down
In act upon the cressy brink
  To strip and dive and drown;

But in the golden-sanded brooks
  And azure meres I spy
A silly lad that longs and looks
  And wishes he were I.

ASL 20 "Oh fair enough are sky and plain"

One entry: B 77.

This poem must have been produced during one of those fortunate sessions when Housman sat down to his notebook with the work of inspiration so far advanced that little remained for second thought to perfect. After the sixteen lines had been written down, the wording of only five of them required alteration, and most of the changes were minor. When made, they brought the poem to within one word of the form it carried into print.

A more significant change, which occurred in the writing of printer's copy, was the transposition of the first two stanzas. As they stand on B 77, they give the effect of a descending order; by reversing this, a satisfactory introduction to the main theme is produced: the first six lines of the poem as we read it in print describe the domain of the earth-reflecting waters, and lines 7 and 8 express the youth's desire to enter it.

Claims of literary influence must be made with caution; but it is now felt that Housman's poetry shows more traces of derived elements than was at one time believed, and it is possible that *ASL* 20, in its theme and language, as well as in its line movement, may owe something to "Boats Sail on the Rivers," by Christina Rossetti (*Sing-Song,* 1872), whose poetry Housman admired.

ASL 20 "Oh fair enough are sky and plain"
Unique Draft

B 77, complete   Date: August or September, 1895
Pencil

           pools
The meres[1] and rivers wash so clean
    The trees and clouds and air.
The like on earth was never seen,
    And oh that I were there.

               sky
    Oh fair enough are hill[2] and plain
      I know   fairer
    But there are[3] lovelier far:
    Those are as beautiful again
          in the
    That under[4] water are.

These are the thoughts I often think
    As I stand gazing down
In act upon the rushy[5] brink
    To strip and dive and drown.

    But in the golden-sanded brooks
        azure meres
    And silver pools[6] I spy
    A silly lad that longs and looks
    And wishes he were I.

---

[1] Canc. *meres.*   [2] Canc. *hill.*   [3] Canc. *there are.*   [4] Canc. *under.*
[5] This word was transcribed into printer's copy, but A.E.H. later wrote above it in pencil *cressy,* which was eventually traced over in ink and *rushy* line-canceled.
[6] Canc. *silver pools.*

21

BREDON[1] HILL

IN summertime on Bredon
   The bells they sound so clear;
Round both the shires they ring them
   In steeples far and near,
   A happy noise to hear.

Here of a Sunday morning
   My love and I would lie,
And see the coloured counties,
   And hear the larks so high
   About us in the sky.

The bells would ring to call her
   In valleys miles away:
"Come all to church, good people;
   Good people, come and pray."
   But here my love would stay.

And I would turn and answer
   Among the springing thyme,
"Oh, peal upon our wedding,
   And we will hear the chime,
   And come to church in time."

But when the snows at Christmas
   On Bredon top were strown,
My love rose up so early
   And stole out unbeknown
   And went to church alone.

They tolled the one bell only,
   Groom there was none to see,
The mourners followed after,
   And so to church went she,
   And would not wait for me.

The bells they sound on Bredon,
   And still the steeples hum.
"Come all to church, good people,"—
   Oh, noisy bells, be dumb;
   I hear you, I will come.

[1] Pronounced Breedon [Housman's note].

ASL 21 "Bredon Hill"

Two entries: A 132-33; A 142-43.

The first draft laid down the essential features of the poem: all of the seven stanzas are present and in their final order. All but one of the four stanzas on the first page of this draft required some revision, but when that was done there was little left to do between this portion of the poem and the form it took in printer's copy. The three remaining stanzas, on A 133, were left amid considerable disorder. Unresolved alternatives and lines canceled with no substitutes in view are numerous, and Housman sealed his disgust with the draft as it was left by marking it with a heavy X and a broad arrow drawn below the last line.

The second draft, written several months later, is in ink and headed by the underscored title *Bredon Hill*. The only extensive revision occurred in stanza 6, where the allusions to the tolling bell, which had proved difficult in the first draft, were still troublesome. After much experimenting with this original idea and others, Housman finally wrote into this manuscript every word that was to go into printer's copy, although some had to be picked out of open alternatives. There is no trace in the notebook drafts of the note which was added in printer's copy, and which appears in printed forms of the poem.

ASL 21 "Bredon Hill"
First Draft

A 132, complete   Date: July, 1891
Pencil

    In summertime on Bredon
      On Bredon [?   ] Sundays[1]
      The bells they sound so clear;
  Round
      In[2] all the shires they ring them,
      In steeples far and near,
      A happy noise to hear.

Here of a Sunday morning
   My love and I would lie,
And see the land of England
   And [?   ] high,   And see the sunny counties
   My love [?   ] I.   And hear the larks so high
                                            About us in the sky

    The bells would ring to call her
      In valleys miles away:
    "Come all to church, good people,
      Good people, come and pray."
      But here my love would stay.

                  All their[4]
       turn and
And she and[3] I would answer,
   Among the springing thyme,
     well
"Chime[5] upon our wedding;
   And we will hear the chime,
   And come to church in time."

---

[1] A.E.H. struck through this line after writing its alt. above.

[2] Canc. *In.*   [3] Canc. *she and; turn and* added over a caret.

[4] It is not clear whether these two words were a false start on stanza 4 or the beginning of an alternative for the line above.

[5] *Ring* was written through *Chime; well* added over a caret.

ASL 21 "Bredon Hill"
First Draft continued

A 133, complete   Date: July, 1891
Pencil

But on a winter morning   But when the snows on Bredon
   When all the roads were stone,   At Christmastide were strewn
My love rose up so early,
   And stole out unbeknown,
   And went to church alone.

  All   chimes
There in the tower hung silent   The wedding peals were silent[1]
   The chime I thought would be;   That will not ever be;
  tolled   They[3] tolled but one bell only,
They rang[2] but one bell only
   For more there might not bc:

                                            And so to church went she,
The mourners followed after   And would not wait for me.

      sound on Bredon
The bells they ring so pleasant[4]
    still
   And then[5] the steeples hum,
"Come all to church, good people,"[6]
Oh [?   ] calling:[7]
   I hear you, I will come.   O noisy bells, be dumb;
                                               Good pcople, all and some."[8]

                                                          July 1891

[1] This line, with the alt. *chimes*, and the following line were struck out. (The chimes, also mentioned in a discarded line in the second draft, were the three bells rung for weddings.)

[2] Canc. *rang.*   [3] The last letter of *They* was penciled over to form *There*.

[4] Canc. *so pleasant.*   [5] Canc. *then.*

[6] The quotation marks indicated that the message of the bell was contained in this line and the two remaining lines were the lover's reply. But when the penultimate line *Good people, all and some* was also given to the bell, A.E.H. canceled the sign after *people* and placed it after *some*. Final adjustments of the dialogue had to await the second drafting.

[7] This line is struck out with a line extended to cancel *O noisy bells, be dumb.*

[8] A.E.H. wrote this same archaic expression into a quatrain on C 28, beginning

      Since men are born to toil,
        All, and not only some. . . .

(Cf. Chaucer's Prologue of the Pardoner's Tale, line 8: "And then my bulles shewe I, alle and somme.")

ASL 21 "Bredon Hill"
Second Draft

A 142, complete
Ink; corrections and
   title in pencil

Date: 1892 or early 1893[1]

Bredon Hill[2]
In summertime on Bredon
   The bells they sound so clear;
Through both
Round all[3] the shires they ring them
   In steeples far and near,
   A happy noise to hear.

Here of a Sunday morning
   My love and I would lie,   coloured[4]
           pleasant checkered patterned
And see the sunny counties
   And hear the larks so high
   About us in the sky.

The bells would ring to call her
   In valleys miles away:
"Come all to church, good people,
   "Good people, come and pray."
   But here my love would stay.

---

[1] The nearest anterior date is 1891-92, on A 135; the nearest following, Feb. 1893, on A 151.

[2] The title is lightly underscored in pencil.

[3] The word *all* was brought over from A 132 but was canceled here. The preferred word *both* probably is intended to refer to Gloucestershire and Housman's native Worcestershire.

[4] Canc. all of the adjectives but *coloured.* Asked by his brother how this line developed, A.E.H. said, "When I wrote the poem I put down, just to fill up for the time, a quite ordinary adjective, which didn't satisfy me; others followed. Then with the poem in my head, I went to bed and dreamed, and in my dream I hit on the word 'painted'; when I woke up I saw that 'painted' wouldn't do, but it gave me 'coloured' as the right word." *(Recollections,* p. 102.) Laurence goes on to say how he found the list of adjectives shown above, but errs in referring to the draft as the "first draft of the poem."

And I would turn and answer
  Among the springing thyme,
    peal
"O ring upon our wedding,
  And we will hear the chime,
  And come to church in time."

ASL 21 "Bredon Hill"
Second Draft continued

A 143, complete[1]   Date: 1892 or early 1893
Ink, corrections in pencil

at Christmas
But when the snows on Bredon
On Bredon's top
At Christmastide were strown
My love rose up so early,
And stole out unbeknown,
And went to church alone.

the   Groom there was none to see,
They tolled but[2] one bell only,   And groom was none to see
   And silent hung the three;   And few came out to see
For more there might not be; Over the winter the [   ]
The mourners followed after, No wedding chimes had we,[3]
   And so to church went she,
   And would not wait for me.

The bells they sound on Bredon
And still the steeples hum.
"Come all to church, good people"—
Oh, noisy bells, be dumb;
I hear you, I will come.

[1] The sheet has been cut through in the middle but nothing appears to be missing. It is probable that Laurence's intention in dividing it was to take out the much-corrected sixth stanza, but he contented himself with heavily erasing the alternatives and tracing over the original second line in ink.

[2] Canc. *but*.

[3] Canc. the line *For more there might not be* and all the alts. but *No wedding chimes had we* and the one last written above, *Groom there was none to see,* which is the sixth alternative line—a number unique in the notebooks. (Cf. p. 97.) The alts. above *No wedding chimes had we* are written toward the margin in the shape of a fan, striking the right margin at a point even with the third line of the stanza above. It was this spread of the marginal writing that prevented an even excision of the sheet and thus preserved this middle stanza.

22

THE street sounds to the soldiers' tread,
 And out we troop to see:
A single redcoat turns his head,
 He turns and looks at me.

My man, from sky to sky's so far,
 We never crossed before;
Such leagues apart the world's ends are,
 We're like to meet no more;

What thoughts at heart have you and I
 We cannot stop to tell;
But dead or living, drunk or dry,
 Soldier, I wish you well.

ASL 22 "The street sounds to the soldiers' tread"

One entry: B 22-23.

It is possible that this poem is another product of the emotions that produced the second draft of "1887," which precedes it by only four pages. The early portion of Notebook B was written rapidly during the spring of 1895, Housman's most productive year, and the scripts show remarkable similarity from B 3 to B 47, where the first ink draft is found.

The unique entry of *ASL* 22 may be said to comprise two drafts, probably done at a single sitting. Of the first, the opening stanza underwent the largest amount of revision, the second line having been abandoned in a maze of cancellations and open alternatives. When Housman began the second draft, on B 23, he wrote for stanza 1 nothing but the wanted second line. Of the eight lines that followed, five were altered in the transit from the preceding page, but when revision on B 23 was complete, only the difference between *lad* and *man* stood between this draft and the copy read by the printer.

ASL 22 "The street sounds to the soldiers' tread"
Unique Draft

B 22, complete   Date: May or June, 1895
Pencil

            road[1] sounds to
  The street rings to the soldiers' tread   come
    We [?   ] to see:[2]   We all [?] out to see
     A single redcoat turns his head The folk come out to see:
  One soldier in the ranks of red,[3]
        turns   looks
  He turned[4] and looked at me.

  My lad, so far is sky from sky[5]
    We never met before;
       apart
  So wide the world's ways are
    We're[6] like to meet no more.[7]

  Two strangers in the streets go by[8]
    And[9] there's no news to tell;
  But dead or living, drunk or dry,
    Soldier, I wish you well.

[1] Canc. *road* and *rings to.*   [2] Canc. this line.
[3] Canc. this line.   [4] Canc. *turned* and *looked.*
[5] Having written this line, A.E.H. put an *'s* after the last word, threw a loop about *from sky's,* and drew it back to a position just after *lad;* he then canceled *is.* This produced the badly garbled line: *My lad, from sky's so far [to] sky.* However, he knew, even before he set down the third line, that the last word of the opening line would be *far,* to rhyme with *are* in line 3. His racing pen dropped the word *apart* from this line; it was set in above a caret.
[6] A.E.H. began this line with the letter *A*—probably with *And* in mind—but wrote through it *We're.* His sketchy treatment of this stanza and the next gives weight to the surmise that he intended to write the second draft of his poem immediately.
[7] This stanza, like the next, is struck through with a high caret.
[8] Canc. this line and the one below.
[9] This line began with *We. And* was written through it.

ASL 22 "The street sounds to the soldiers' tread"
Unique Draft continued

B 23, complete
Pencil

And out we troop to see:

                    lad
                    man
My lad,[1] from sky to sky's so far
                  crossed
We never met[2] before;
Such leagues
So wide apart the world's ends are
We're like to meet no more;

---

[1] Canc. *lad* and *man*. This particular indecision (sometimes *boy* is a third con-
testant) is recorded many times in the notebooks. The word *lad* was brought over
from B 22, and it appears to have won here; but it did not hold its place in printer's
copy.

[2] Canc. *met*.

What thoughts at heart
Thoughts in the heart³ have you and I
We cannot stop to tell;
But dead or living, drunk or dry,
Soldier, I wish you well.⁴

³ Canc. *Thoughts in the heart.*
⁴ This line, written by itself on A 162 in the spring of 1893, may have been the genesis of *ASL* 22. Immediately beneath it A.E.H. wrote a quatrain that he may have intended to be his comment on the salutation of the redcoat:

remembers,
And one [?   ] and one forgets,
But 'tis not found again,
Not though they hale in crimsoned nets
The sunset from the main.

The quatrain has several points of association with *ASL* 22 as we know it: rhyme and meter are in agreement; the first two lines suggest the unspoken thoughts—"not found again"—of the soldier and the viewer; and the wide spatial allusion in line 4 of the quatrain—"sunset from the main"—matches the scope of stanza 2 of the lyric— *from sky to sky's so far, so wide apart the world's ends are.*

The quatrain, however, was printed by Laurence Housman as the third (and last) stanza of "Give me a land of boughs in leaf" (*MP* 8). Now the Analysis lists for A 162-63 " 'Give me a land of boughs in leaf,' the last line of 'The street sounds to the soldiers' tread,' and fragments." On the uncut page A 162, however, no other stanzas of *MP* 8 were written. It is possible, since more than one half of A 163 has been destroyed, that the page once had room for the other stanzas of the poem printed as *MP* 8. (They do not exist elsewhere in the notebooks.) But it is also possible that Laurence may have been in error when he brought together the three stanzas to form a single poem. There is no continuity between stanzas 2 and 3 of *MP* 8 and very little between the first and second. In printing "When Adam walked in Eden young" (*AP* 3), Laurence assembled three stanzas from A 188 that A.E.H. probably never intended to compose a single poem, and it is likely that he committed a similar fault in his printing of *MP* 8.

Note on printer's copy: In the upper-right corner of the sheet there appears, probably in the typesetter's hand, the single word: *Excellent.* This spontaneous and highly unofficial encomium is the earliest recorded criticism of *A Shropshire Lad.*

23

THE lads in their hundreds to Ludlow come in for the fair,
   There's men from the barn and the forge and the mill and the fold,
The lads for the girls and the lads for the liquor are there,
   And there with the rest are the lads that will never be old.

There's chaps from the town and the field and the till and the cart,
   And many to count are the stalwart, and many the brave,
And many the handsome of face and the handsome of heart,
   And few that will carry their looks or their truth to the grave.

I wish one could know them, I wish there were tokens to tell
   The fortunate fellows that now you can never discern;
And then one could talk with them friendly and wish them farewell
   And watch them depart on the way that they will not return.

But now you may stare as you like and there's nothing to scan;
   And brushing your elbow unguessed-at and not to be told
They carry back bright to the coiner the mintage of man,
   The lads that will die in their glory and never be old.

ASL 23 "The lads in their hundreds to Ludlow . . ."

Two entries: A 206; B 99-100.

Laurence Housman's Analysis of Notebook A has this note for page 206: " 'The lads in their hundreds to Ludlow' (two lines.)" The lower half of this page has not survived and the fragment contains only a few traces of illegible writing enclosed in an awkwardly drawn circle.

If Laurence's note is correct, *ASL* 23, like the poem just reviewed, belongs to that group of pieces developed after—and, it may be believed, as a result of—a line or two written on a notebook page months or years before the production of a substantial draft. In the case of *ASL* 23, eleven months, possibly fifteen, elapsed between A 206 and B 99.

"The lads in their hundreds to Ludlow . . ." again resembles its immediate predecessor in that the two drafts of it occupy facing pages and may have been composed at one sitting. Only the first two stanzas written on B 99 are complete; of the third, Housman set down only the first two words of line 1, the last five of line 2, and the two concluding lines. The opening line of the final stanza he also left unfinished. Between this line and the stanza above he carefully left a stanza's space—indicating that he had in mind a poem of five quatrains. Some time later, beginning at the upper left of B 99, he drew two high wavy lines diagonally down to the end of stanza 3.

When Housman transferred the four stanzas to the following page, he again left room for a stanza between 3 and 4. There are no traces of this elusive quatrain, but whatever its substance was, it haunted his mind and probably added to his difficulties in bringing off the late-written final stanza. However, much was advanced in the second version: the blank spaces left in stanza 3 were filled in, many open alternatives were resolved, and the fourth stanza was radically altered; line 3 of stanza 1 and the opening line of the next were completely rewrought. In brief, half the lines on B 100 show revision of some kind, and as many lines required more revision before going into the copy sent to the printer.

The fourth stanza was evidently the most troublesome. The other three went from B 100 to printer's copy at a single sitting, but there is evidence that the fourth had to wait. On the foolscap page it exhibits a different style of writing—smaller and more precise than the heavier hand in the three above it. In the final stanza there are no remarkable differences between this version and the one abandoned on B 100; the main task lay in making choices between a number of nearly equivalent phrases. The stroke that counted most had been performed between the two notebook drafts when *They carry back bright to the coiner the mintage of men* superseded *They carry unspoilt into safety the honour of man.*

ASL 23 "The lads in their hundreds to Ludlow . . ."
First Draft

B 99, complete   Date: November, 1895
Pencil

         in their hundreds   Ludlow
The lads from the country to Wenlock¹ come in for the fair,
            pleasant
And there are the welcome to hear and the good to behold
   ready to help and the safe to   believe in
The steady to trust and the ready to help you are there
              crowd
        in the midst
And there with the rest² are the lads that will never be old.

    shoulder
   mix with their fellows
They stand in the market, and nothing to tell them apart:
   And many to count are the stalwart and many the brave,
And many the handsome of face and the handsome of heart
           in the crowd that will carry their grace to the grave
    And few that will carry their looks or their truth to the grave.³
    And which are the few that will carry their grace to the grave?

I wish [   ]
   [   ] that I never shall learn
              give
And then one could talk to them friendly and wish⁴ them farewell
   ' bring them a mile   luck
   And bid them good speed⁵ on the way that they will not return.

            know
But no, they have nothing to tell⁶ them by [   ]
     the streets through the midst of us,
   As crossing unknown through the market place,⁷ not to be told,
          safety
They carry unspoilt into darkness⁸ the honour of man,
   The lads that will die in their glory and never be old.

¹ Canc. *Wenlock*. This word was probably an echo from the first line of "On Wenlock Edge the wood's in trouble" (*ASL* 31), written on the other side of this sheet.
² Canc. *with the rest*.
³ After writing this line A.E.H. experimented with the one below it and finally wrote the alternative above, leaving all uncanceled. The original version passed into the second draft and thence into print, another instance of the poet's final election of the *first* form of a line—and a warning that his last-written notebook version cannot invariably be taken as his choice in determining the text of his posthumous poems.
⁴ Canc. *wish*.   ⁵ Canc. *bid them good speed* and *luck*.
⁶ Canc. *tell*.   ⁷ Canc. *unknown through the market place*.   ⁸ Canc. *darkness*.

ASL 23 "The lads in their hundreds to Ludlow . . ."
Second Draft

B 100, complete
Pencil

The lads in their hundreds to Ludlow come in for the fair,
smart
And there are the straight and the sprack[1] and the good to behold,
The lads for the girls and the lads for the liquor are there,
And there with the rest are the lads that will never be old.

	town	farm	
	farm	town	
There's chaps	town	farm	till

They come[2] from the fold and the grange and the plough and the cart,
And many to count are the kindly, and many the brave,
And many the handsome of face and the handsome of heart,
And few that will carry their looks or their truth to the grave.

foreheads[3]
I wish they were sealed on their   there should have been[4]
guess   there were[5] tokens[6]
I wish one could know them; I wish they had tickets to tell
you
The fortunate fellows that now one[7] can never discern;
And then one could talk to them friendly and wish them farewell
And bring them a mile on the way that they will not return.

---

[1] This is one of several dialectal words in *A Shropshire Lad:* "brisk, lively."

[2] Canc. *They come; fold* and its alts. *town* and *farm; grange* and its alts. *farm* and *town;* and *plough.*

[3] The phrase *sealed on their foreheads* is an echo of Rev. 7:3: ". . . till we shall have sealed the servants of our God on their foreheads."

[4] Below this alt. there is a line-canceled phrase, now illegible.

[5] *I wish there were* is canceled by an upward-curving line.

[6] The preference for *tokens* over *tickets* was perhaps inspired by a recollection of a passage in Juvenal's Tenth Satire (11. 196-98) describing a concourse of young men. Housman, in his schoolboy reading, may have construed the word *discrimina* in the passage as "tokens"; certainly the parallel *discrimina–tokens* was congenial to him, for in 1913, in an article "Ciceroniana," published in the *Journal of Philology,* XXXII, 261-69, he quoted the passage from Juvenal and rendered *discrimina* by the word *tokens.*

[7] Canc. *one.*

<pre>
          I   make   I
But now you⁸ can never be certain, do all that you can,
                        unspoken-to
                        unguessed-at
                        unthought-of
And brushing my shoulder unlooked-at and not to be told,

          I shall   I
But now you can never be sure of them, try as you can;
     They pass at my
     And passing your   knocking it   jostle it
        As brushing one's⁹ elbow and passing one, not to be told,
     And
They carry back bright to the coiner the mintage of man,
     The lads that will die in their glory and never be old.
</pre>

---

⁸ Canc. *you.* Having apparently abandoned his idea of writing a new stanza in this reserved space, A.E.H. used it to try out alternatives for the opening lines of his final quatrain.

⁹ Canc. *As brushing one's, passing one,* and the alt. *knocking it.* There may have been another alt. (now illegible) over *passing one.* The alt. *jostle it* was intended to be read with *They pass at my elbow,* at the head of the line.

24

Say, lad, have you things to do?
  Quick then, while your day's at prime.
Quick, and if 'tis work for two,
  Here am I, man: now's your time.

Send me now, and I shall go;
  Call me, I shall hear you call;
Use me ere they lay me low
  Where a man's no use at all;

Ere the wholesome flesh decay,
  And the willing nerve be numb,
And the lips lack breath to say,
  "No, my lad, I cannot come."

ASL 24 "Say, lad, have you things to do?"

One entry: B 92.

As with *ASL* 23, the final stanzas of this poem were left unfinished even after extensive revision had been expended upon them. The general appearance of the draft on B 92 is disorderly but there is order in it, for one half of the lines went into print in the form in which they were first set down. The revision of others left the first stanza only two words short of finality, and nothing remained to be done for the second quatrain after its second and third lines had been rewrought.

After composing and correcting the three stanzas of the lyric, Housman wrote a new version of line 3 of the second, beginning with the word *Quick,* already used twice in stanza 1. This did not please, and he returned the line to the reading he had determined for it in the stanza revised above. He also set in their proper places the remaining five lines of the poem, but was unable to bring about the opening line of his final stanza (an achievement of a session unrecorded in the notebooks).

This poem, once number 23 in printer's copy, became number 24 when *ASL* 30 was shifted to become the twenty-third poem. There had been another headed 24, which we now read as *ASL* 33. These shifts were made before the copy for the next poem was written, for the number over it, XXV, was never altered.

ASL 24 "Say, lad, have you things to do?"
Unique Draft

B 92, complete   Date: September or
Pencil, much revised   October, 1895

Say, lad, have you things to do?
                     the
            now   day's
Do them quick while life's at prime:[1]
                                                'tis
                  buckle to   Quick; & if there's[3] work for two,
What's a friend for? [?   ]:[2]
Here am I, man; now's your time.

Send me now, and I shall go;
                while I hear you
Call me, I shall come at call;[4]
                    I shall hear you call;
     Use me ere
Wait not till[5] they lay me low
     Where a man's no use at all;

Till Ere   ready   nerve
Ere[6] the [?   ] nerve decay,   trusty nerves
                                       Ere the [?   ] betray
       nimble   is
And the willing foot be[7] numb,
And the lips lack breath to say
'No, my lad, I cannot come'.

[1] The line seems to have developed as follows: A.E.H. first wrote
                    Do them quick   life's at prime:
leaving hardly enough space for *while* to be crowded in after *quick*. He then canceled
life's and set *day's* over a caret, giving the reading
                    Do them quick while day's at prime:
Striking a line through *quick*, he superscribed *now*, making
                    Do them now while day's at prime:
But a capital Q restored *quick; the* was set in after *while,* to give
                    Quick, now, while the day's at prime:
Finally he canceled *now*, its substitute *then* probably in mind but not written.
[2] Canc. this line and the alt., above. The last word in the line (heavily erased) may
be *you.*
[3] Canc. *there's.*   [4] Canc. *I shall come at call* and the alt., above.
[5] Canc. *Wait not till.*   [6] Canc. *Ere* and *Till.*   [7] Canc. *be* and *is.*

　　　　Use me, ere
　　Quick, before[8] they lay me low
　　　　Where a man's no use at all;
　　　　　　Quick, before the
　　　Where the [　　?　　][9] nerves betray,
　　　　And the willing foot is numb,
　　　And the lips lack breath to say
　　　　　　'No, my lad, I cannot come'.

---

[8] Canc. *Quick, before.*　　　[9] Canc. the line up to *nerves.*

25

THIS time of year a twelvemonth past,
    When Fred and I would meet,
We needs must jangle, till at last
    We fought and I was beat.

So then the summer fields about,
    Till rainy days began,
Rose Harland on her Sundays out
    Walked with the better man.

The better man she walks with still,
    Though now 'tis not with Fred:
A lad that lives and has his will
    Is worth a dozen dead.

Fred keeps the house all kinds of weather,
    And clay's the house he keeps;
When Rose and I walk out together
    Stock-still lies Fred and sleeps.

ASL 25 "This time of year a twelvemonth past"

One entry: B 14-15.

The upper half of B 14 contains an adumbration of the first stanza of *ASL* 25, a substantial outline of the second, and the opening line of the third. The page has been cut—probably to destroy some fragments on the reverse side—just below this line, where one may still find remains of some truncated letters that support the assumption that the poem was continued on the lower half of B 14.

Housman's characteristic indecision about the selection of proper names comes to the front in the two drafts of the poem: the rival in the first draft is named Ted Harland, the girl is Jane. But in the second he is named Ted in stanza 1 and, later, Fred Laughton; as for the heroine, she is, variously, Jane Crossley, Rose Archer, Rose Andrews. None of these names—except Jane—went into the next, and final, version. The question of nomenclature was, however, the only matter of language left unsettled after revision of the full four stanzas on B 15.

The order of the stanzas is 1, 2, 4, 3. However, the reason for imperfect sequence is found in this case to lie in the rapid, inspired composition. After writing the last line of the second quatrain, Housman suddenly dropped his pencil a full stanza's space, doubtless seized with the inspiration of his fourth stanza, and immediately ran off the four lines of it. Having done so, he added an alternative above the first line, thus closing up part of the space where he had intended to insert the the third stanza— which had to find room near the bottom of the page. There is evidence that he attempted to crowd another draft of stanza 4 between *a dozen dead* and the margin, for along the cut edge (about one inch of the sheet is missing) are smudges of erased writing, of which only *the weather* is legible.

ASL 25 "This time of year a twelvemonth past"
First Draft

B 14, upper half   Date: April or May, 1895
Pencil

'tis a twelvemonth past,
Ted Harland, fourteen months ago
When he and I would meet
Would start some quarrel, till at last
To settle which should walk with Jane
We fought and I was beat.[1]

So all that year [   ]
Till rainy days began,
[   ]
Walked with the better man.[2]

The better man she walks with still,[3]

[1] The untouched materials of this quatrain and their later use offer an interesting example of Housman's poetic method. Here the rhyme of the poem was, originally, *abcb*, until the alternative for the ending of line 1 adjusted it to the words *past, meet, last, beat*. The fourth line on B 14, *To settle which should walk with Jane*, was not set in as an afterthought but was given full space, as if A.E.H. might have felt it was important enough to make the rest of the stanza conform to it. (This would have required considerable reshaping to bring about syntactic harmony.) Apparently he wanted his opening stanza to announce the reason for the quarrel, but there was too much to do here; that had to wait for the second quatrain.

[2] The incompleteness of this stanza may be due to the fact that A.E.H. wanted the first or the third line to contain the name of the girl. He did not stop here to choose it and the rhyming words of the quatrain.

[3] The page is cut through just below this line, which is canceled not with the undulas traced over all the lines above it but with a careful horizontal line (not made by A.E.H.), indicating that the cancellation was done after the cutting of the notebook page.

ASL 25 "This time of year a twelvemonth past"
Second Draft

B 15, nearly complete
Pencil

<blockquote>

This time of year a twelvemonth past
   When Ted and I would meet
       still would jangle till
We always jangled, and¹ at last
   needs must
   We fought and I was beat.

      then the   fields about
   So all last² summer, Sundays out,
     Till rainy days began
Rose Andrews   Rose Archer on her Sundays out
Jane Crossley in the fields about³
    Walked with the better man

Fred   the house all kinds of weather
  He keeps his bed now days are warm,⁴
       house
   And clay's the bed⁵ he keeps;
        out together
  When Rose and I walk arm in arm⁶
   Stock still   Fred
   Fred Loughton⁷ lies and sleeps.

The better man she walks with still,
   Though now 'tis not with Ted:
A lad that lives and has his will
     worth a dozen
   Is better than the⁸ dead.
               [?   ] the weather

</blockquote>

¹ Canc. *always jangled, and.*

² Canc. *all last* and *Sundays out,* together with the comma preceding *Sundays.*

³ Canc. *in the fields about.*

⁴ Canc. *his bed now days are warm.*   ⁵ Canc. *bed.*   ⁶ Canc. *arm in arm.*

⁷ Canc. *Fred Loughton. Fred* was set over a caret.

⁸ Canc. *better than the.* The substitute represents one of Housman's most characteristic verbal shifts: a banal phrase, *better than the dead,* giving way to an apt colloquialism with an alliterative lilt.

26

ALONG the field as we came by
A year ago, my love and I,
The aspen over stile and stone
Was talking to itself alone.
"Oh who are these that kiss and pass?
A country lover and his lass;
Two lovers looking to be wed;
And time shall put them both to bed,
But she shall lie with earth above,
And he beside another love."

And sure enough beneath the tree
There walks another love with me,
And overhead the aspen heaves
Its rainy-sounding silver leaves;
And I spell nothing in their stir,
But now perhaps they speak to her,
And plain for her to understand
They talk about a time at hand
When I shall sleep with clover clad,
And she beside another lad.

ASL 26 "Along the field as we came by"

Two entries: A 192; [B 36].

The notebook material of this twenty-line poem is sadly deficient, only two lines of it having survived. These consist of one couplet

> *And she shall lie with earth above*
> *And you beside another love.*[1]

written carefully in pencil near the bottom of A 192 in the late summer or early autumn of 1894. Except for two minor differences (*And,* in line 1, changed to *But;* and *you* changed to *he*), the couplet is the conclusion of the first stanza of the poem as we know it.

A full draft of *ASL* 26 may have been composed on B 36, for Laurence Housman's Analysis describes that page as containing " 'Along the field as we came by,' dated June [1895])." But the entire sheet was destroyed—the second of six[2] complete sheets from Notebooks A and B containing *Shropshire Lad* material that Laurence destroyed after making his Analysis. The loss of B 36 adds to the value of the scanty reliquiae of *ASL* 26, which belong to that small and interesting group of germinal pieces, some of which have already been noted, that first declared themselves in the notebooks in the form of significant isolated fragments.

---

[1] A 192 is headed by the unique draft of *ASL* 59 ("The Isle of Portland"), written below its title. The lower half of the page contains ten scattered lines, the last four being the quatrain beginning "When Adam first the apple ate," first printed in my *Manuscript Poems of A. E. Housman,* p. 48. It is not beyond the bounds of probability that the couplet itself is a reflex of *ASL* 8 ("Farewell to barn and stack and tree"), written on the page preceding. There Terence listens to the fratricide's story; the couplet on A 192 may be his prophecy: "Lucy will destroy herself in remorse and you will find another love."

[2] The other five are A 241-42, latter part of the second draft of *ASL* 19 ("To an Athlete Dying Young"); B 31-[31a], part of the first draft of *ASL* 27 ("Is my team ploughing?"); B 97-[97a], first draft of *ASL* 31 ("On Wenlock Edge the wood's in trouble"); B 109-10, unique draft of *ASL* 41 ("In my own shire, if I was sad"); and A 117-18, corrected second draft of *ASL* 46 ("Bring, in this timeless grave to throw").

27

"Is my team ploughing,
     That I was used to drive
And hear the harness jingle
     When I was man alive?"

Ay, the horses trample,
     The harness jingles now;
No change though you lie under
     The land you used to plough.

"Is football playing
     Along the river shore,
With lads to chase the leather,
     Now I stand up no more?"

Ay, the ball is flying,
     The lads play heart and soul;
The goal stands up, the keeper
     Stands up to keep the goal.

"Is my girl happy,
     That I thought hard to leave,
And has she tired of weeping
     As she lies down at eve?"

Ay, she lies down lightly,
     She lies not down to weep:
Your girl is well contented.
     Be still, my lad, and sleep.

"Is my friend hearty,
     Now I am thin and pine,
And has he found to sleep in
     A better bed than mine?"

Yes, lad, I lie easy,
     I lie as lads would choose;
I cheer a dead man's sweetheart,
     Never ask me whose.

ASL 27 "Is my team ploughing?"

Two entries: B [31]-32; B 68-69.

Some stanzas of the first entry written on B 31 and its verso B 31a have perished with the notebook sheet. B 32 exists in three, possibly four, inch-wide strips, one of which, a piece trimmed to the dimensions of a postage stamp, may have belonged to B 31 or 31a[1] and may preserve the very earliest lines of the draft. It contains the opening stanza of the poem; the verso is blank. (For convenience' sake I have regarded the four fragments as belonging to B 32.) The numeral 32, written by Laurence on one fragment, identifies it as the upper section, but the original sequence of the others, which preserve stanzas 6 and 7 and the first two lines of 8, is open to question.

The much-corrected writing on the remains of B 32 indicates that Housman's first essay at the poem was fraught with difficulty; however, the work of another day, although two or three months removed, must have recaptured all the impetus of the first moments of inspiration. The two stanzas that had proved unmanageable in the first draft—numbers 5 and 6—were the only ones that called for extensive rewriting; these and the six other quatrains of the poem were brought to the status of printer's copy on B 68 and 69. The painstaking care manifested in these entries testifies to Housman's absorption in this poem, which years later he thought might be his best. (Richards' *Memoir,* p. 8.)

[1] This page designation is necessitated by the fact that Laurence, after numbering a recto page that had a blank verso, did not generally number the verso but used its number for the next page. Thus are accounted for the many even-numbered rectos appearing throughout the notebooks as they now exist in the Library of Congress collection.

ASL 27 "Is my team ploughing?"
First Draft

B 32, small strips missing   Date: May or June, 1895
Pencil

[*Piece 1*]

girl happy
'Is my love contented,
        thought hard
That I was sad to leave
    is her heart
And lies she down contented   And do her tears fall fewer[2]
    Wept[1]
Late in the fading eve?'   At to-shut of the eve?

[*Piece 2*]

        think to   seldom thinks
Be sure[3] she does not weep;   She [turns ?] no more to weep;
Your girl is well contented,   She long left off to weep
    Be
Lie still, my lad, and sleep.

[*Piece 3*]

Is[4] my friend hearty
    To see the daylight shine,[5]   Now I am thin and pine,
And
    Has he found to sleep in
        A better bed than mine?'
                lie
        Yes, lad, I sleep[6] easy,
                lie
        I sleep as lads would choose[7]

---

[1] A.E.H. considered this word after writing the first of the two substitute lines in the right margin: *And do her tears fall fewer / Wept in the fading eve?*

[2] This appears to be the only line in piece 1 not struck through with a cancel-line.

[3] A.E.H. canceled *Be sure,* made the initial of *she* a capital, and set in *think to* over a caret.

[4] The scissors-cut removed the '*I* of '*Is,* together with the first letter of the added word *And* in line 3 below.

[5] Canc. this line.   [6] Canc. *sleep.*

[7] This line is cut through, but the word *lie* clearly shows as the alt. for *sleep,* which may have been canceled.

[Piece 4]

the[8]
'Is my team ploughing,
    That I was used to drive
And hear the harness jingle
    When I was man alive?'

---

[8] Canc. *the.*

ASL 27 "Is my team ploughing?"
Second Draft

B 68, complete   Date: August or September, 1895
Pencil

'Is my team ploughing
    That I was used to drive
And hear the harness jingle
    When I was man alive?'

Ay, the horses trample,
    The harness jingles now;
No change though you lie under
    The land you used to plough.

'Is football playing
Along Against Against Along[1]
    Beside the river shore
With lads to chase the leather
    Now I stand up no more?'

Ay, the ball is flying,
    The lads play heart and soul;
The goal stands up, the keeper
    Stands up to keep the goal.

---

[1] This *Along* is the only uncanceled word of the five alternatives. They seem to have been written in this order: *Beside, Against, Along, Against, Along.*

ASL 27 "Is my team ploughing?"
Second Draft continued

B 69, complete
Pencil

'Is my girl happy
    That I thought hard to leave,
And has she ceased from crying[2]
And [?   ]
    At to-fall of the eve?'[3]

   she lies down lightly
     tears are fewer
Ay, her heart [?] griefs forgetting[4]
    She lies not down to weep;
    She lies not down to weep;[5]
Your girl is well contented.
    Be still, my lad, and sleep.

'Is my friend hearty
    Now I am thin and pine,
And has he found to sleep in
    A better bed than mine?'

Yes, lad, I lie easy,
    I lie as lads would choose,
I cheer a dead man's sweetheart,
    Never ask me whose.

                  tired of weeping
          And has she ceased her crying[1]
          When she lies down at eve?
          As

                    cry
          And does she weep no longer
            And turns she [?] to slumber
      And [?] she [   ]
      And [?   ]

          She does not wake to weep
          She lies [?   ] weep

[1] Canceling *When,* A.E.H. enclosed these two lines in a scroll and drew them down to their proper place in the stanza below, left.

[2] Canc. this line and the next below.

[3] Canc. this line and the alt. written out after it.

[4] Except for *Ay,* all of this line and the alt. *tears are fewer* was canceled. The alt. phrase *griefs forgetting* was a tentative substitute for *heart* and the now illegible word that followed it.

[5] After striking out this line and the two alts. at the right, A.E.H. restored his original version of the line.

28

THE WELSH MARCHES

HIGH the vanes of Shrewsbury gleam
Islanded in Severn stream;
The bridges from the steepled crest
Cross the water east and west.

The flag of morn in conqueror's state
Enters at the English gate:
The vanquished eve, as night prevails,
Bleeds upon the road to Wales.

Ages since the vanquished bled
Round my mother's marriage-bed;
There the ravens feasted far
About the open house of war:

When Severn down to Buildwas ran
Coloured with the death of man,
Couched upon her brother's grave
The Saxon got me on the slave.

The sound of fight is silent long
That began the ancient wrong;
Long the voice of tears is still
That wept of old the endless ill.

In my heart it has not died,
The war that sleeps on Severn side;
They cease not fighting, east and west,
On the marches of my breast.

Here the truceless armies yet
Trample, rolled in blood and sweat;
They kill and kill and never die;
And I think that each is I.

None will part us, none undo
The knot that makes one flesh of two,
Sick with hatred, sick with pain,
Strangling—When shall we be slain?

When shall I be dead and rid
Of the wrong my father did?
How long, how long, till spade and hearse
Put to sleep my mother's curse?

ASL 28 "The Welsh Marches"

One entry: A 217.

The notebook remains of this poem were, according to Laurence Housman's Analysis, fragmentary, and he is responsible for the loss of a portion of the only page containing the sole entry of the poem. His note in the Analysis for A 217 reads, " 'High the vanes of Shrewsbury gleam [the opening line of *ASL* 28] (three verses, dated Jan. 1895)." Twelve lines are still to be read on the two dismembered pieces of A 217—they constitute only one half of the total page—and it seems obvious, when the evidence from the remains is carefully read, that the missing portions of the page contained more lines of the same poem.

Just above the cut margin of the second piece may be read the word *Cain,* slanting upward as if it had been inserted as an alternative word over a continuing line of the poem. The appropriateness of this name to the theme of *ASL* 28—the struggle between divided halves of a soul—is undeniable. Further, running through the same piece toward the approximate point where a subsequent stanza would begin are faint traces of a transfer-line, of the kind already described in my notes on the manuscript pages, which Housman frequently employed to carry a stanza from its original site to another. This peculiarity of piece 2 of A 217 strengthens the probability that this page once contained more than three quatrains of *ASL* 28, for the beginning of the transfer-line does not appear on the other piece, above.

The next-to-last of the nine stanzas of the poem appears to have been the one composed first. It was begun near the upper margin of the page, beneath the date Jan. 1895. It and the two other surviving quatrains bear marks of correction, the first being extensively revised and brought to the reading of the stanza as we find it in the text. It would seem unnatural for Housman to expend such thoroughgoing revision on a poem only one-third finished. Certainly no other example of such careful retouching of scattered fragments is to be found in the notebooks.

ASL 28 "The Welsh Marches"
Unique Draft

A 217, about half the page missing   Date: January, 1895
Pencil

[*Piece 1*]

Jan. 1895

 None   part   none
Who will loose us, who'll undo[1]
               chain   locks   This knot that makes one flesh
The mortal [?   ] that [?   ] us two?   of two.
Sick with hatred, sick with pain,
Strangling: when shall we be slain?

[*Piece 2*]

Long ago the vanquished bled
Round my mother's marriage-bed,
   And
Where kite[2]
Kite and raven feasted far
About the open house of war.

          When Severn down to Bewdley[3] ran
          Coloured with the death of man,
          Stretched   brothers'
          Couched upon her [?   ] grave
          The Saxon[4] got me on[5] the slave.

[1] The revision of lines 1 and 2 seems to have been as follows: After writing them as shown in the question formula, A.E.H. experimented with *None* as the opening word, wrote it again over *who'll,* and dropped the interrogation point at the end of line 2. He then drew a heavy capital over the initial of the second word in line 1, again making the first couplet interrogative: *Will none. . . ?* No part of the writing seems to have been canceled until the substitute for line 2 was written; then he lined out his original version of it.

[2] *Where kite* was set above *Kite* and all topped by *And. Kite* was line-canceled.

[3] *Bewdley* is the name of a town in Worcestershire, on the Severn River. In printer's copy it yielded to *Buildwas*—preferred perhaps as a Shropshire place name. A.E.H. made the same kind of change after beginning his first draft of *ASL* 39 ("'Tis time, I think, by Wenlock town"), on A 125 with the line *'Tis time, I think, by Stourbridge town.*

[4] A capital initial was written through *s* in *saxon.*

[5] The word *Cain* appears below this place, just above the cut margin of the piece.

Note on printer's copy: The ending of line 3, . . . *her steepled crest,* was changed during the handling of proof to . . . *the steepled crest.* The word *brothers'* in the draft (line 15) appears in printer's copy and in the text as *brother's.*

29

THE LENT LILY

'TIS spring; come out to ramble
   The hilly brakes around,
For under thorn and bramble
   About the hollow ground
   The primroses are found.

And there's the windflower chilly
   With all the winds at play,
And there's the Lenten lily
   That has not long to stay
   And dies on Easter day.

And since till girls go maying
   You find the primrose still,
And find the windflower playing
   With every wind at will,
   But not the daffodil,

Bring baskets now, and sally
   Upon the spring's array,
And bear from hill and valley
   The daffodil away
   That dies on Easter day.

ASL 29 "The Lent Lily"

One entry: B 3.

The manuscript of this draft, small and precise, with the four stanzas spaced with unusual care, is one of the finest specimens in the notebooks even though the upper portion of the page is now blurred with cancellations and erasures. All but one of these remedial touches were spent upon line 4 of the opening stanza. The original reading of this line and its first revision cannot now be read, but Housman's first alternative line, written toward the right margin, was certainly *About the littered ground.* Seeking a substitute for *littered* or a better word for the opening of the line as he had first composed it, he experimented with *Bejewelling* and *Emblazoning;* and these words precipitated a flood of alternatives which outnumber even the contenders for the modifier of *counties* in the eighth line of "Bredon Hill," on A 142.

In fatigue or disgust, Housman finally drew a heavy pencil through his original version of the line, extended it to strike out the alternative, and left to another day the choice among the profusion he had created. Eventually, however, the long array of glittering alternatives above his canceled line gave way to a slightly altered reading of it—*littered* replaced by *hollow*—and a few minor changes in the three stanzas below produced in printer's copy the form of the text.

ASL 29 "The Lent Lily"
Unique Draft

B 3, complete   Date: April, 1895
Pencil

April 1895

The Lent lily

'Tis Spring; come out to ramble   Apparelling
The hilly brakes around,   Enamelling Bedizening
      thorn   Illumining Embroidering
For under bush and bramble   Bejewelling Emblazoning
     [?   ]¹ the ground   About the littered² ground
   In [?   ] the ground
The primroses are found.

     And there's the windflower chilly
       With all the winds at play,
     And there's the Lenten lily
       That has not long to stay
       And dies on Easter day.

   And since, when girls go maying,
     They find the primrose still,
  And find the windflower playing
         that³
     With every wind at will,
     But not the daffodil,

     Bring baskets now, and sally
       Upon the spring's array,
   And bear from hill and valley
       The daffodil away
       That dies on Easter day.

¹ The first letter in this now illegible word or phrase was *B*, and the ending *-ing*. A.E.H. may have written here one of the alternatives later tried out in the margin to the right.

² This use of *littered* may have been in Housman's mind when six months later he composed his first draft of *ASL* 41 ("In my own shire, if I was sad"). Line 15 reads *Or littering far the fields of May*. This is the only appearance of the word in the text of the poems.

³ The word *that* would have made a considerable difference in the meaning of the line. It was not taken into printer's copy, however.

30

OTHERS, I am not the first,
Have willed more mischief than they durst:
If in the breathless night I too
Shiver now, 'tis nothing new.

More than I, if truth were told,
Have stood and sweated hot and cold,
And through their reins in ice and fire
Fear contended with desire.

Agued once like me were they,
But I like them shall win my way
Lastly to the bed of mould
Where there's neither heat nor cold.

But from my grave across my brow
Plays no wind of healing now,
And fire and ice within me fight
Beneath the suffocating night.

ASL 30 "Others, I am not the first"

One entry: A 238.

The notebook sheet containing A 238 is complete except for a tiny slip cut from the upper portion in order to remove the line first written as number 8 in an ink draft of *ASL* 56 ("The Day of Battle"), on A 237. Fortunately, the scissors-stroke passed just below the eighth line of the poem opposite, *ASL* 30, and although Housman had altered the line, the alteration amounted to no more than the replacement of a single word —still visible—that brought the line to the reading of the text; so we may conclude that all of the notebook material for this poem has survived.

The display of the first twelve lines leaves the impression that the beginning of the poem was composed not in stanzas but in unseparated rhyming couplets. (Actually, lines 3 and 4 were first set down without rhyme.) The draft shows no characteristic space or offset between lines 4 and 5, and line 9 begins with the same marginal room allotted to the lines above it. Only the last four lines of the draft were spaced and set over, to give the appearance of constituting a stanza.

This holograph, described in the Analysis as a "rough draft," was brought near the status of perfect copy on A 238; the only work remaining was to decide the stanza pattern and to arbitrate among several open alternatives. On the other hand, there are few notebook drafts that show more extensive revision affecting every stanza. Only five of the sixteen lines came through intact, and a majority were subjected to drastic changes in vocabulary and syntax.

ASL 30 "Others, I am not the first"
Unique Draft

A 238, nearly complete   Date: March or April, 1895
Pencil

[*Piece 1*]

Others, I am not the first,
    meant[1]
Have willed more mischief than they durst:
      breathless
      sultry smothering
  If in the stifling[2] night I too   They in stifling midnights too
    now, 'tis nothing new
Shiver in the stifling night.[3]   Shivered: this is nothing new.

      graves tonight
Men whose very graves[4] are old   More than I, if truth were told,
Have stood and sweated hot and cold,
    through their reins in ice and fire
And in their marrow, ice to fire,
      contended
Fear did battle[5] with desire.

[1] Canc. *meant.*

[2] Above *stifling,* A.E.H. wrote *sultry,* which was written through by *breathless;* after it he added *smothering* and left all uncanceled.

[3] This line, which was thrown down in evident haste, leaving both rhyme and syntax of the stanza unresolved, may have been considered as an alternative; or, more likely, lines 3 and 4 were merely intended to express the material which revision would bring into shape. The first effort in this direction was probably the couplet in the right margin. However, this, together with all but the first word of line 4, was struck out.

[4] A.E.H. canceled *very graves,* superscribing *graves tonight.* The rest of the line and its alternative were canceled when he produced in the right margin the line he wanted.

[5] Canc. *did battle.*

[*Piece 2*]⁶

Agued
Frustrate
Thwarted⁷ once like me were they,
But   find win
And⁸ I like them shall my my way⁹
Lastly   Only
        Safely
Takes us to the bed of mould
Where there's neither heat nor cold.

        But from my grave against my brow
            Blows¹⁰   stillness coolness
        Breathes no air of slumber now,   Blows no wind of healing now,
                        stand up to¹¹
        And fire and ice within me fight
        Beneath the suffocating night.

---

⁶ The open space left at the top of this piece suggests that A.E.H. at one time had in mind the substance of eight or nine intervening lines, but there is no evidence to show they were attempted here or on adjacent pages.

⁷ Canc. *Thwarted* and *Frustrate*.   ⁸ Canc. *And.*

⁹ After inadvertently repeating *my* after *shall*, he canceled the first *my* and set the needed verb *find* above it. The line now gave this reading with the next: . . . *I* . . . *shall find my way* / *Takes us to*. . . . He then substituted *But* for *And*, *win* for *find*, and *Safely* for *Takes us*, which made the sense . . . *shall win my way* / *Safely to*. . . . Later he balanced *Only* against *Safely*, lined it out after *Lastly* was chosen.

¹⁰ Canc. *Blows, slumber,* and *stillness.* The line at the right A.E.H. transcribed into printer's copy, perhaps unmindful that he had made a note on B 101 to change *Blows* to *Plays.* This change was made in the handling of proof.

¹¹ Canc. *stand up to.*

31

ON Wenlock Edge the wood's in trouble;
   His forest fleece the Wrekin heaves;
The gale, it plies the saplings double,
   And thick on Severn snow the leaves.

'Twould blow like this through holt and hanger
   When Uricon the city stood:
'Tis the old wind in the old anger,
   But then it threshed another wood.

Then, 'twas before my time, the Roman
   At yonder heaving hill would stare:
The blood that warms an English yeoman,
   The thoughts that hurt him, they were there.

There, like the wind through woods in riot,
   Through him the gale of life blew high;
The tree of man was never quiet:
   Then 'twas the Roman, now 'tis I.

The gale, it plies the saplings double,
   It blows so hard, 'twill soon be gone:
To-day the Roman and his trouble
   Are ashes under Uricon.

ASL 31 "On Wenlock Edge the wood's in trouble"

One entry: B [97]-98.

Laurence Housman's note in his Analysis for this poem names only one draft for it, on B 97-98: ". . . rough draft, many lines cancelled, dated Nov. 1895." The copy on B 98 cannot be this draft, for only six lines of it show alterations, and some of these are not significant. The page is not dated. It would seem that Laurence overlooked or failed to identify the B 98 holograph and made his notation concerning a page of the preceding sheet, which he eventually destroyed.

The five stanzas on B 98 have the appearance of a carefully made transcript. Housman's satisfaction with it is indicated by the fact that it shows no open alternatives. When the substitutes in the six challenged lines were written, the words they supplanted were lined out, leaving nothing to do in final copy but a verbatim reproduction of the revised draft.

G. M. Trevelyan testifies to the general high regard for this lyric and its author by recalling in his *A Layman's Love of Letters* (London: Longmans, 1954), p. 45, that "The MS [of the printer's copy] was placed on exhibition in the Library of his College during his lifetime, a rare honour."

ASL 31 "On Wenlock Edge the wood's in trouble"
Unique Draft

B 98, complete   Date: November, 1895
Pencil

On Wenlock[1] Edge the wood's in trouble;
    His forest fleece the Wrekin heaves;
The wind
It blows,[2] it plies the saplings double,
    And thick on Severn snow the leaves.

               through   holt
'Twould blow like this on hill[3] and hanger
    When Uricon the city stood;
   'Tis   old gale   old
'Twas[4] the same wind in the same anger,
             threshed
    But then it wreaked[5] another wood.

Then,
Once,[6] 'twas before my time, the Roman
    At yonder heaving hill would stare:
The blood that warms an English yeoman,
    The thoughts that hurt him, they were there.

There, like the wind through woods in riot,
    Through him the gale of life blew high,
The tree of man was never quiet:
    Then 'twas the Roman, now 'tis I.

The wind
It blows,[7] it plies the saplings double,
    It blows so hard, 'twill soon be gone:
Today the Roman and his trouble
    Are ashes under Uricon.

---

[1] The only inadvertence in the MS was the lower-case *w* here; the capital letter was written through it before the next letter of the word was formed.

[2] Canc. *It blows.*   [3] Canc. *on hill.*

[4] Canc. *'Twas, same, gale,* and *same.*   [5] Canc. *wreaked.*   [6] Canc. *Once.*

[7] Canc. *It blows.* Here, as in line 3 of the first quatrain, the printed texts have *The gale,* a substitution A.E.H. noted in the list of corrigenda on B 101 and carried into his poem during the reading of proof.

32

FROM far, from eve and morning
  And yon twelve-winded sky,
The stuff of life to knit me
  Blew hither: here am I.

Now—for a breath I tarry
  Nor yet disperse apart—
Take my hand quick and tell me,
  What have you in your heart.

Speak now, and I will answer;
  How shall I help you, say;
Ere to the wind's twelve quarters
  I take my endless way.

ASL 32 "From far, from eve and morning"

Two entries: A 144-45; A 158.

This poem is one of the few in Housman's first volume that are represented by as many as three notebook drafts. Unfortunately, only the last of these is complete and legible. The first was written out in full, in a small but clear penciled manuscript, on A 144 beneath the unique draft of the poem later published as *MP* 14 ("The farms of home lie lost in even"). Heavy erasure obliterated the upper half of A 144, and the pencil-black smeared over the first stanza of *ASL* 32 reduced the opening lines of the poem to almost complete illegibility. The first line was lost with a small strip taken from the middle of the page when a few lines from *ASL* 21 ("Bredon Hill"), on the page opposite, were cut away. Yet enough remains of this first version to indicate that it must have been very near the poem as we know it.

Of the second draft, on the facing page, only the last two stanzas have survived. Apparently the entire poem was written on the lower half of A 145, beneath an ink draft of the quatrain printed as *MP* 28 ("He, standing hushed, a pace or two apart"). The two stanzas of *ASL* 32 are also in ink, obviously a revised copy of the draft set down on the page opposite. An interesting feature of the second draft appears in the fate of the variants written into the lines and those interlined or set in the margins: before completing his session over A 145, Housman apparently rejected all of the new readings introduced into the last seven lines of his poem—the only lines that allow comparison with the first draft—and returned to the form of the version on A 144. (Some of these judgments were reversed or re-opened in the draft made on A 158.)

The revised ink draft on this page shows no variations from the text except that one alternative, carried over from A 145, was left open in line 10 *(serve—help)* and another *(dissolve)* was written beneath line 6. The small but significant change from *four* to *twelve* in the expression *the wind's four quarters* was one of the most fortunate strokes in the retouching of this draft. In some immeasurable way this new word expands the dimensions of the poem to infinity and declares the Lucretian concepts that so evidently entered into the making of it.

ASL 32 "From far, from eve and morning"
First Draft

A 144, lower half   Date: Between July, 1891,
Pencil   and February, 1893

                                    [?   ]¹
                                                windy
And yon four-winded sky   And [?   ] sky²
                                            to knit me
                                    The [?   ]
                                        Blew hither; here am I.
                                    [?   ]³
                                        [?   ]
                                                tarry
                                    Now, [?   ]
                                        Nor yet disperse apart,
                                    Take my hand quick and tell me
                                        What thought is in your heart.

                                    Speak now, and I will answer;
                                        How shall I serve you, say;
                                    Ere to the wind's four quarters
                                        I take my endless way.

¹ Above this cut-through line, on the upper section of the page, are the remains of another line, of which the first and last words may be *Far* and *morning*.
² Canc. this line and its alt., above.
³ Canc. the ending of this line.

ASL 32 "From far, from eve and morning"
Second Draft

A 145, portion from lower half
Ink, corrections in pencil

Now, for an hour I tarry   Now, for today I tarry
    Nor yet disperse apart,   An instant, and depart,
                Take my hand quick and tell me
                       thought
                 What thing[1] is in your heart.

               will
   Speak now, and I shall[2] answer; How would you have me help you,
         serve   Unlock
     How shall I help[3] you, say; Shew me[5] your soul and say,
         wind's
   Ere to the sky's[4] four quarters
     I take my endless way.

---

[1] Canc. *thing.*   [2] A.E.H. canceled *shall,* set *will* above a caret.
[3] Canc. *help.*   [4] Canc. *sky's.*   [5] Canc. *shew me.*

ASL 32 "From far, from eve and morning"
Third Draft

A 158, complete   Date: Early (probably
Ink, corrections in pencil   February) 1893

From far, from eve and morning
twelve
And yon four[1]-winded sky,
The stuff of life to knit me
Blew hither: here am I.

a breath
tonight
Now,—for an hour[2] I tarry
Nor yet disperse apart,—
dissolve
Take my hand quick and tell me
What thought is[3] in your heart.
have you

Speak now, and I will answer;
help
How shall I serve you, say;
twelve
Ere to the wind's four[4] quarters
I take my endless way.

---

[1] Canc. *four.*   [2] Canc. *an hour* and *tonight.*
[3] Canc. *thought is.*   [4] Canc. *four.*

33

If truth in hearts that perish
　　Could move the powers on high,
I think the love I bear you
　　Should make you not to die.

Sure, sure, if stedfast meaning,
　　If single thought could save,
The world might end to-morrow,
　　You should not see the grave.

This long and sure-set liking,
　　This boundless will to please,
—Oh, you should live for ever
　　If there were help in these.

But now, since all is idle,
　　To this lost heart be kind,
Ere to a town you journey
　　Where friends are ill to find.

ASL 33 "If truth in hearts that perish"

Two entries: A 148; A 164-65.

Both of these entries (called "rough drafts" in the Analysis) were extensively revised, but the revision left only four of the sixteen lines in the first draft unfinished, and three of these were brought to the reading of the text after Housman completed his rewriting of the second draft. The Analysis records that the page containing the later entry bore two canceled stanzas; these may have been on the lower third of the page, now lost. It appears that Housman may have projected at least one of them on A 148, where, after writing *There's none:* in the normal position of a new stanza opening below his third stanza, he dropped his pencil two or three lines' space and began his final quatrain.

Another small part of the manuscript of *ASL* 33 has survived on a fragment (1½" x 2¼") containing a beautifully penciled draft of stanza 3, the one that apparently proved most vexatious in the two drafts. The fragment may have been cut from a page adjacent to one or the other of the drafts, for it shows a brace enclosing the quatrain and a transfer-line running upward off the piece to the right. It is possible that the fragment belonged to the excised lower third of A 165, even though there is now no trace of the ending of the transfer-line on the surviving portion of this page. Of A 164, the facing page, only a minute portion has been preserved; it is not impossible that the stray fragment bearing the third quatrain of *ASL* 33 was once a part of that page, which Housman would have found convenient to use as a place to enter his nearly perfect version of his recalcitrant stanza.

This poem was originally number 24 in printer's copy. The lyric chosen to be number 33 was one of five pieces Housman withdrew after send-off his MS. The identification of the poem first copied under the numeral XXXIII is one of the minor problems of Housmanian scholarship.

ASL 33 "If truth in hearts that perish"
First Draft

A 148, nearly complete   Date: Between January, 1892,
Pencil   and February, 1893

If truth in hearts[1] that perish
                move   heavens[2]
        Could touch the powers on high,
                        cherish[3]
I think the love I bear you
        Should make you not to die.

        truth, if
If care or stedfast meaning single
                life poured out
        Or[4] strong [desire ?] could save,—
        sky   fall
The world might end tomorrow,
        You should not see the grave

    fears   thoughts   endless   longing   stedfast meaning[5] grieving
Long Vain care and [useless?] labour   sleepless care
            And fruitless hope to please,—   endless toil to please
Oh, you should live for ever,   hopeless pain(s)
        If there were help in these.

---

[1] This word is traced in heavy pencil as if it had been written over an earlier word.

[2] Canc. *heavens.*

[3] Canc. *cherish.* This alternative was probably set down to leave open the possibility of an *abab* rhyme pattern for the stanza.

[4] *If* is written through *Or.*

[5] Over *meaning* is a now undecipherable word. A.E.H. apparently wished to keep *stedfast meaning* in mind as an alternative ending here if the conclusion of line 5 as he had written it should eventually include *single,* above.

There's none:[6]

            that   laughter
But now, since all is idle,
    To this lost heart be kind,
Since you must house hereafter   town
Ere to a land you journey[7]
    Where friends are ill to find.

[6] Canc. *There's none:*.

[7] This line apparently developed thus: After writing *Ere to a land you journey,* A.E.H. superscribed the alternative line as shown, which would have carried out the rhyme scheme *abab* (once considered for stanza 1), *hereafter* rhyming with *laughter,* an alternative set over the end of the first line of this stanza. However, he lined out *hereafter,* intending apparently to abandon the whole line. He had jotted an alternative beneath *land* (it is now scarcely legible, may be *folk),* but this gave way to *town,* written out boldly at the end of the line. He drew a circle about this word and carried it back to a circle enclosing *land.*

ASL 33 "If truth in hearts that perish"
Second Draft

A 165, upper two thirds   Date: Between February, 1893,
Pencil   and August, 1894

If truth in hearts that perish
                    powers
        Could move the heavens on high
I think the love I bear you
        Should make you not to die.

                                        Sure, sure, if stedfast meaning,
            If truth, if stedfast meaning,   If single thought could save,
                        resolve
                If strong desire could save,—
                    world   end
            The sky might fall tomorrow,
                You should not see the grave

Hot hope
        fear   contriving   Fear and hot hope and thinking[1]
Long care and vain devising   Long fear and hope and striving
                    pains
        And hopeless toil[2] to please,—   And sick despair to please
Oh you should live for ever
        If there were help in these.

                    arc[3]
            But now, since all is idle,
                To this lost heart be kind,
            Ere to a town you journey
                Where friends[4] are ill to find.

[1] This accumulation of alternative phrases, all in the single vein of grief and despair, continued from the first draft, produces here an effect which is not paralleled elsewhere in Housman's notebooks.

[2] Canc. *toil*.   [3] Canc. *are*.

[4] Remains of some cut-through writing show between this word and the margin just below.

[*Stray Fragment*]

This long and [?   ][5] liking,
  This boundless[6] will to please,—
    endless thought
Oh you should live for ever
  If there were help in these.

---

[5] Above this now illegible word A.E.H. wrote an alternative (partly erased) that may have been intended to replace *and* also. It does not appear that either word was near the eventually chosen *sure-set*.

[6] Canc. *boundless;* above it an alternative has been erased.

34

THE NEW MISTRESS

"Oh, sick I am to see you, will you never let me be?
You may be good for something but you are not good for me.
Oh, go where you are wanted, for you are not wanted here.
And that was all the farewell when I parted from my dear.

"I will go where I am wanted, to a lady born and bred
Who will dress me free for nothing in a uniform of red;
She will not be sick to see me if I only keep it clean:
I will go where I am wanted for a soldier of the Queen.

"I will go where I am wanted, for the sergeant does not mind;
He may be sick to see me but he treats me very kind:
He gives me beer and breakfast and a ribbon for my cap,
And I never knew a sweetheart spend her money on a chap.

"I will go where I am wanted, where there's room for one or two,
And the men are none too many for the work there is to do;
Where the standing line wears thinner and the dropping dead lie thick;
And the enemies of England they shall see me and be sick."

ASL 34 "The New Mistress"

One entry: B 114-15.

This poem was one of three that Housman sent to his publisher after dispatching the complete sixty-five poems constituting the manuscript of *A Shropshire Lad*. It replaced "Yonder see the morning blink"[1] (later printed as number 11 of *Last Poems*), which must have been completed about the same time as its replacement, for two drafts of *LP* 11, dated "Dec. '95" were written on B 114, only two pages after the single entry of "The New Mistress."

The precise arrangement of the lines on B 114 indicates that the poem was not composed there but copied from a well-developed earlier draft, one perhaps never contained in the notebooks. Over half the lines of this version underwent still further revision varying from the substitution of a single word to recopying on the facing page, B 115. This shaping-up of the draft sent it verbatim into printer's copy except for the reinstatement of a canceled word in one line and the choice between open alternatives in another.

It may be worth mentioning that number 34 is one of four poems in *A Shropshire Lad* that Housman considered specifically as monologues and printed enclosed in quotation marks. The other three are *ASL* 8 ("Farewell to barn and stack and tree"), *ASL* 47 ("The Carpenter's Son"), and *ASL* 56 ("The Day of Battle"). The manuscripts of *ASL* 56, however, do not show the enclosing marks, which must have been added in proofreading; and only the printer's copy of *ASL* 8 and 47 show the sign of quotation at beginning and end. The draft of *ASL* 34 also bears evidence that Housman did not at one time consider his entire poem as an utterance viva voce, for only the first three lines of it are enclosed in quotation marks in the draft. It was during the composition of printer's copy that he set double quotation marks at the head of each stanza and at the end of the last and underscored the three opening lines. Above them appeared, for the first time, the title "The New Mistress." In a letter to Houston Martin, Housman explained his use of the underline in the text of *LP* 25 ("The Oracles"), where similar devices are employed. (See Laurence Housman's *Recollections,* p. 197.)

---

[1] The sheet of printer's copy bearing the poem, headed by the numeral XXXIV, was returned to A.E.H. and is now preserved among the foolscap sheets (number 146) in volume 6 of the Library of Congress collection. In the upper-left corner of the page A.E.H. wrote boldly "A Shropshire Lad"—a guide to the printer for the proper handling of the poem and the two others that went with it, probably *ASL* 37 ("As through the wild green hills of Wyre") and 41 ("In my own shire, if I was sad").

ASL 34 "The New Mistress"
Unique Draft

B 114, complete
Pencil

Date: Late (probably
December) 1895

'Oh sick I am to see you, will you never let me be?
　　　　　　　　　　　　you're little good to me[1]
You may be good for something but you are not good for me.
　Better
Oh[2] go where you are wanted, for you are not wanted here.'
And that was all the farewell when I parted from my dear.

I will go where I am wanted, to a lady born and bred
　　　　　　　　　　free
Who will dress me all[3] for nothing in a uniform of red;
She will not be sick to see me if I only keep it clean:
I will go where I am wanted for a soldier of the Queen.

I will go where I am wanted, for the sergeant does not mind;
　　may be[4]　　　　　　　but
　　　is not　　　　　　　and
He may be sick to see me but he treats me very kind:

　　　　　　　　　　　　　　　　　cap
He gives me beer and breakfast and a ribbon for my hat,[5]
　I'll　　　find　　　　　　　　will
And I never had[6] a sweetheart that would do as much as that.[7]
　　I never knew　　　　　spend her money on a chap.

---

[1] Canc. this alt. On the facing page, B 115, opposite this line A.E.H. wrote this tentative substitute: *If you're any good for anything, you're none at all for me,* later setting the alts. *to anyone* and *to* respectively over *for anything* and *for,* which he lined out. Eventually in composing his copy for the printer he went back to the line as he had first written it on B 114.

[2] Canc. *Oh.*　　　[3] Canc. *all.*

[4] Canc. *may be* and *is not, but* and *and.*　　　[5] Canc. *hat.*

[6] After canceling *I never had,* he superscribed *I'll* and *find,* rewriting *never* below the line. He then lined out *I'll* and *find,* beneath set *I* and *knew.*

[7] Canc. *that would do as much as that* and the alt., above, *will.*

work[8]

I will go where I am wanted, where there's room for one or two,

hands[9]   plenty   work

And the men are none too many for the job there is to do;

living   wears   dropping

Where the standing[10] line stands thinner and the falling dead lie thick;

stands

And the enemies of England they shall see me and be sick.

---

[8] Canc. *work*.   [9] Canc. *hands* and *job*.

[10] He canceled *standing*, wrote *-en* through the ending of *falling*, which gave way to *dropping; stands* and *wears,* above, were also struck out, then after the restoration of *stands* the reading was *Where the living line stands thinner and the dropping dead lie thick*. An untouched line written opposite on B 115 restored *standing* and *wears* and equates the text.

35

On the idle hill of summer,
  Sleepy with the flow of streams,
Far I hear the steady drummer
  Drumming like a noise in dreams.

Far and near and low and louder
  On the roads of earth go by,
Dear to friends and food for powder,
  Soldiers marching, all to die.

East and west on fields forgotten
  Bleach the bones of comrades slain,
Lovely lads and dead and rotten;
  None that go return again.

Far the calling bugles hollo,
  High the screaming fife replies,
Gay the files of scarlet follow:
  Woman bore me, I will rise.

ASL 35 "On the idle hill of summer"

Two entries: A 220; B 94.

The earliest entry of this poem consists of the remains of five or six lines scattered over the upper portion of A 220, three of them on an inch-wide piece constituting the marginal section of the page. Other lines belonging to *ASL* 35 may have been lost when a strip less than half the size of the section was excised to destroy some parts of *ASL* 4 ("Reveille"), written on the recto.

Since the lines heading A 220 do not have the appearance of a formal entry, they will not be displayed but will be described in their relation to the second entry of the lyric, on B 94. The first legible line on the section is *Soldiers marching, all to die,* written beneath an erased and canceled phrase, now illegible. This line passed unchanged into the fair copy as the conclusion of the second quatrain. To the right of this line on A 220 are the remains of two others, spaced as if they were meant to be the alternate lines of a stanza: *the* [?   ] *and* [?   ] *none alive.* No connection can be proved between the first and the language of *ASL* 35 as we know it, but the second may be an echo of the line at the top of the page or the genesis of the twelfth line of the poem: *None that go return again.* This line indeed seems definitely announced by one written near the top of the second piece of A 220: *Home for us there's no returning;* and the last of the five composing this entry (written less than an inch below the one just quoted), *Lovely lads and good to see,* became, with a difference, in the second entry: *Lovely lads and dead and rotten.*

This entry, made nine months later, is a fair copy which corresponds exactly to the text except for the next-to-final line, which on B 94 is *These are feet and they can follow.* Its substitute, *Gay the files of scarlet follow,* written on B 101 after printer's copy had gone off, was duly remembered and sent into the corrected proof. The awkward fifteenth line may have caused the destruction of Housman's final manuscript of *ASL* 35, which was not included in the bequest he made of the packet of printer's copy to the library of Trinity College, March 3, 1926. His letter to the curator simply states: "I enclose the MS. of *A Shropshire Lad.* XXXV is missing. . . . " I can find no record of a later handling of this sheet, and it is possible that Housman would have been moved to destroy this copy in order to suppress a line which displeased him.

ASL 35 "On the idle hill of summer"
Unique Draft

B 94, complete   Date: October, 1895
Pencil

On the idle hill of summer,
   Sleepy with the flow[1] of streams,
Far I hear the steady drummer
   Drumming like a noise in dreams.

Far and near and low and louder
   On the roads of earth go by,
Dear to friends and food for powder,
   Soldiers marching, all to die.

East and west on fields forgotten
   Bleach the bones of comrades slain,
Lovely lads and dead and rotten;
   None that go return again.

Far the calling bugles hollo,
   High the screaming fife replies.
These are feet and they can follow,[2]
   Woman bore me, I will rise.

---

[1] The word *flow* was written heavily through *noise*.

[2] If it is asked how such a banal line could have crept into this fair copy, an answer may be found on A 219, where A.E.H. had awkwardly used the word *feet* as an alternative in the last stanza of *ASL* 4 ("Reveille"). This verbal complex would naturally have been in his mind as he jotted down the adumbrations of *ASL* 35 on the verso of that page; perhaps some form of the troublesome fifteenth line resembling its successor on B 94 was composed on the now missing section of A 220. See the reprint of *ASL* 4, the last stanza.

36

WHITE in the moon the long road lies,
   The moon stands blank above;
White in the moon the long road lies
   That leads me from my love.

Still hangs the hedge without a gust,
   Still, still the shadows stay:
My feet upon the moonlit dust
   Pursue the ceaseless way.

The world is round, so travellers tell,
   And straight though reach the track,
Trudge on, trudge on, 'twill all be well,
   The way will guide one back.

But ere the circle homeward hies
   Far, far must it remove:
White in the moon the long road lies
   That leads me from my love.

ASL 36 "White in the moon the long road lies"

One entry: A 181.

This manuscript shows many corrections, all but two of which (in lines 5 and 6) were carried into the next, and final, copy, where two more lines (9 and 11) were altered from their readings in the draft.

The manuscript also shows that the determination of stanza sequence was something of a problem—a crux illustrated in a number of the drafts already examined. After composing the stanza we know as number 1, Housman wrote beneath it the quatrain eventually printed as number 3. Then, dropping his pencil an inch and a half, he ran off the final stanza. It turned out, however, that the space he had left open was not to be taken up with a new quatrain; but an intermediate one was written in the upper-right corner across from the one he had first set down. This latest written stanza went into printer's copy as number 2.

It appears that Housman intended to use the room above stanza 4 to compose a new draft of his second quatrain, but wrote out no more than the opening line of it, *The world, the world is round, they say,* perhaps dropping down to the bottom of his page to find easier room for the four lines. The lower third of A 181 has been destroyed, but that he continued his draft there is proved by the fact that the numeral 2 and a few truncated letters are clearly visible just above the cut margin of the page. Probably the final touch Housman gave to this draft was setting the numerals 1, 2, 3, and 4 carefully over his scattered stanzas, as had been his practice when closing his notebook cover on many of his revised drafts, some as early as those on A 64-65 and A 82-83. See the reprint of *ASL* 14 ("There pass the careless people").

ASL 36 "White in the moon the long road lies"
Unique Draft

A 181, upper two thirds   Date: Between February, 1893,
Pencil, much corrected   and August, 1894

1

Straight[1]
White in the moon the long road lies,

                    clear[2]
            stands   blank
    The moon swims bright above;

White in the moon the long road lies

    That leads me from my love.

2

            leaves
Still hangs[3] the hedge without a gust,

    Stone
    Still,[4] still the shadows stay:
            along[5]
    My feet upon the moonlit dust
            Tread [out ?] tireless
    Pursue the ceaseless way.

3

                            as I hear tell   as [strangers ?] tell
    reach
        stretch[7] The world is round, if truth they[6] tell:
    though seem   Though ne'er so straight the track,
And, straight [?] the track,   And if one needs must roam[8]
        Plod   long
        Trudge   Fare[9] far enough, 'twill all be well,
                            guide him back
                The way will lead one home.[10]
                    you

The world, the world is round, they say

---

[1] Canc. *straight.*   [2] Canc. *clear.*   [3] Canc. the *-s* of *hangs* and *hedge.*

[4] *Still* was lined out and *Stone* superscribed, but through it A.E.H. rewrote *Still.* A considerable part of the effect of this lyric lies in its repetitions, which began in the third line and reached their climax in the last two lines, which reiterate the third and fourth. The doublets *Still, still* in line 6, *Trudge on, trudge on* in line 11, and *Far, far* in line 14 carry on this effect—as does also the studied *The world, the world* in the single line below.

[5] Canc. *along.*   [6] Canc. *if truth they.*

[7] Canc. *stretch* and *seem.* Grant Richards in his *Memoir,* p. 192, quotes a letter from A.E.H. explaining his use of the subjunctive form of the word *reach.* It is obvious that his preference for this mood is also declared in the two alt. verbs.

[8] Canc. this line and the alt., above.   [9] Canc. *Fare* and *Trudge.*

[10] Canc. *him, you,* and *home,* the last after the second line, above, had been redrafted to give the rhyme *track—back.*

4

circuit backward[11]
But ere the circle homeward hies
it
Far, far must they[12] remove:
White in the moon the long road lies
That leads me from my love.

2

[11] Canc. *circuit backward.*
[12] Canc. *they.* Housman's use of *they* here is puzzling, as it lacks even a vaguely indicated antecedent nearby, unless *they* in the solitary line can qualify. Was it to have been written into the stanza intended to occupy the open space above? Or was it written in a quatrain on the lost lower section of the page?

37

As through the wild green hills of Wyre
The train ran, changing sky and shire,
And far behind, a fading crest,
Low in the forsaken west
Sank the high-reared head of Clee,
My hand lay empty on my knee.
Aching on my knee it lay:
That morning half a shire away
So many an honest fellow's fist
Had well-nigh wrung it from the wrist.
Hand, said I, since now we part
From fields and men we know by heart,
For strangers' faces, strangers' lands,—
Hand, you have held true fellows' hands.
Be clean then; rot before you do
A thing they'd not believe of you.
You and I must keep from shame
In London streets the Shropshire name;
On banks of Thames they must not say
Severn breeds worse men then they;
And friends abroad must bear in mind
Friends at home they leave behind.
Oh, I shall be stiff and cold
When I forget you, hearts of gold;
The land where I shall mind you not
Is the land where all's forgot.
And if my foot returns no more
To Teme nor Corve nor Severn shore,
Luck, my lads, be with you still
By falling stream and standing hill,
By chiming tower and whispering tree,
Men that made a man of me.
About your work in town and farm
Still you'll keep my head from harm,
Still you'll help me, hands that gave
A grasp to friend me to the grave.

ASL 37 "As through the wild green hills of Wyre"

Two entries: A 204; B 57.

This poem is another of several announced in the notebooks by scattered couplets and single lines. The first entry now consists of seven lines written on the upper half of A 204, of which the topmost inch has been cut away. Two more lines of the draft were destroyed with it, if Laurence's assignment of nine lines of *ASL* 37 to this page is correct. The seven surviving lines include three that were never retouched (numbers 6, 23, and 24); two versions of line 10; and lines 9 and 36 (the last). A high wavy line is drawn diagonally over the lower two thirds of the manuscript.

The second entry, written about one year later, shows that Housman must have sat down before this page of his notebook still without a clear prospectus of the shape of his poem. He left about twenty lines on B 57, but a fourth of these died on the page and as many more required considerable revision before they passed into final copy. It seems probable that the sheet torn out of Notebook B just in front of the one containing the second entry might have received other lines of the poem. The writing on B 57 begins near the top, so near that there was no room for Laurence to insert the numeral 57. His Analysis gives pages 57 and 58 to this draft, but this is clearly an error, for B 58, the verso of the page, is filled with the second draft of *ASL* 38. It is possible that Laurence may have intended to write "56" and "57" instead of "57" and "58"; at any rate, the crowded condition of B 57 strongly suggests that it was only a continuation page for a draft begun on the facing page, now missing.

ASL 37 is the second of two pieces Housman sent to his publisher after the main body of the manuscript had left his hands. The preparation of it, late in 1895, must have necessitated a thorough reshaping, of which no records have survived either in the Analysis or in the second notebook. Housman may have designed this poem to be the introduction of a series, 37-41, that expresses one of his main themes: the homesickness of one exiled in London. This theme, interrupted by numbers 42-49, resumes with *ASL* 50 and is continued in 51 and 52, again in 54 and 55.

The poem was not forwarded as a replacement of one already in the printer's copy; so when it arrived it was one of two carrying the numeral XXXVII, the first being the poem we now read as *ASL* 38 ("The winds out of the west land blow"). Housman made the necessary numerical adjustments in his table of contents, written after he had received his proof-sheets.

ASL 37 "As through the wild green hills of Wyre"
Fragments

A 204, nearly complete   Date: Between August
Pencil   and December, 1894

A grasp that friends me to the grave.[1]
          stiff
Oh I shall be [?   ][2] and cold
When
If I forget you, hearts of gold.[3]
That   you[4]
Had nearly wrung it from the wrist

My hand lay empty on my knee
Warm from many an honest fist
That nearly wrung it from the wrist

[1] Traces of writing above this line suggest that the opening line of the couplet was cut through. (See in the second entry the line *Souls to die for, hands that gave* and the line following.)

[2] Canc. this now illegible word.

[3] The last two or three words seem to have been lined out, but the cancel may be an eraser smear.

[4] The use of *you* here is puzzling until one discovers in the second entry this line: *Hands, you have held true fellows' hands.*

ASL 37 "As through the wild green hills of Wyre"
Unique Draft

B 57, complete   Date: August or September, 1895
Pencil, much corrected

And sure, the way's not hard to find:
             I need but keep[1] bear my friends in mind
               keep your friends in mind

And 'Don't[2] forget us, lad,' said they
    Oh, I shall be stiff and cold
    When I forget you, hearts of gold:

land
The place[3] where I   shall country[4]   mind you
    Is the land   The land where I remember not[5]
              Will be[6] the land where all's forgot.

    [   ] other lands
    Hand, you have held true fellows hands
    Today: be clean then; keep the touch

Men that made a man of me,
Hearts
Souls[7] to die for, hands that gave
A grasp to friend me to the grave.

---

[1] Canc. *keep*.

[2] The capital initial was written through *d* after *And* was tentatively dropped. This line, like two or three others below, was left without its complement.

[3] Canc. *place*.   [4] Canc. *country*.

[5] Canc. all of this line but *not*.   [6] Canc. *Will be*.

[7] Canc. *Souls*.

shop or farm
or in field or town
Rot before you Pen the fold and[8] mind the till
river[9]
By falling stream and standing hill   Ludlow
By Teme and Ony,[10] Corve and Clee
like my heart
on my knee
Aching on my knee[11] it lay:

That morning   In Ludlow twenty miles   half a shire
No wonder;   So many, when I came away,[12]
That morning   locked   fellow's
It clasped[13] so many an honest fist
That
Had Had[14] nearly wrung it from the wrist.

All from Wenlock Edge to Clee[15]
Under Wenlock, under Clee,

---

[8] Canc. *and*.   [9] Canc. *river.*

[10] A.E.H. lined out *Ony* after superscribing *Ludlow*.

[11] He canceled *on my knee* and wrote above it *like my heart,* which he also struck through, rewriting between them his original phrase.

[12] The line apparently evolved thus: After writing *So many, when I came away,* he lined out *when I came* and set above *twenty miles,* which later yielded to *half a shire,* set over a caret. *So many* gave way to *In Ludlow,* but, after trying *That morning* and *No wonder* at the head of the line and canceling them both, he finally restored *That morning*—leaving the line in the form it has (number 8) in the text.

[13] He struck through *It clasped* and the alternative *locked,* made the initial of *so* a capital, and set *fellow's* over a caret between *honest* and *fist.* These changes made line 9 of the text.

[14] Canc. *Had* and *That,* above.   [15] Canc. this line.

38

THE winds out of the west land blow,
    My friends have breathed them there;
Warm with the blood of lads I know
    Comes east the sighing air.

It fanned their temples, filled their lungs,
    Scattered their forelocks free;
My friends made words of it with tongues
    That talk no more to me.

Their voices, dying as they fly,
    Loose on the wind are sown;
The names of men blow soundless by,
    My fellows' and my own.

Oh lads, at home I heard you plain,
    But here your speech is still,
And down the sighing wind in vain
    You hollo from the hill.

The wind and I, we both were there,
    But neither long abode;
Now through the friendless world we fare
    And sigh upon the road.

ASL 38 "The winds out of the west land blow"

Two entries: A 233; B 58-59.

In addition to these entries Laurence's Analysis mentions A 231, where two lines of the poem were composed. Only the middle portion of this page has survived, and as it bears no trace of *ASL* 38 it may be assumed that the earliest sign of this poem perished beneath the scissors.

From the appearance of the writing on the upper half (all that has survived) of A 233, one would judge that the five-stanza poem at first consisted of three stanzas only, those we now read as numbers 1 (there are two drafts of it), 2, and 5. The first two stanzas received considerable revision, which left both in their final states, except for two unresolved alternatives in the second. The final quatrain was hardly retouched here and passed into the second draft with only two minor changes.

About six months later Housman produced his second draft, just overleaf from his second attempt at *ASL* 37 ("As through the wild green hills of Wyre"), which it so greatly resembles in sentiment. On B 58-59 he had little to change in the three quatrains already in being; but as if to have the advantage of a running start he copied stanzas 1 and 2 word-by-word at the top of B 58 and followed immediately with his first version of number 3, which after some second thought was brought to within one word of finality. This revision, however, probably had to wait for a later moment, as stanza 4 was pressing; so, dropping his pencil an inch, Housman wrote out the last two lines of it—both of which were abandoned. Only a little room remained now at the bottom of the page, and he filled it with a nearly exact copy of the final stanza written on A 233.

The history of the difficult fourth stanza is sadly incomplete; the sole relic of it exists on an inch-wide strip cut from B 59, which contains the quatrain, in fair copy, with just enough trace of writing on the upper and lower margins of the fragment to show there had been other matter on that notebook page.

ASL 38 "The winds out of the west land blow"
First Draft

A 233, upper half   Date: February or March, 1895
Pencil

                    The winds out of the west land blow,
                        My friends have breathed them there;
                    Warm with the blood of lads I know
                        Comes east the sighing air.

The wind out of the west land blows,[1]
                    them
    My friends have breathed it there,
And [?   ] I know[2]   And at my [ear the speech ?] it knows
        [sighing   ?   ]
    Fly silent on the air.   Is [?   ] on the air
                    fanned   temples
            It stroked[3] their faces, filled their lungs,
Scattered their forelocks free,   mouths
                    And from their lips flew free,[4]
            My friends
            And they made words of it with tongues
                    talk
            That say no more to me.

        The wind and I, we both were there,
            But neither long abode:
        Now through the friendless world we fare
                sigh
            And meet[5] upon the road.

        [1] Having written *The wind out of the west land blows,* A.E.H. decided he wanted the rhyme *blow—know* for lines 1 and 3; so he added a small *-s* to *wind* and struck the *-s* from *blows,* setting in line 2 the needed alternative *them* over it. However, the new version of line 3, ending . . . *it knows,* upset his plural forms in noun, verb, and pronoun; and he went back to undo his changes in line 1 and canceled *them* in line 2. All of these shifts were carefully reversed once more in the new reading of the stanza written in the upper-right corner.
        [2] Canc. this line.   [3] Canc. *stroked* and *faces.*
        [4] Having canceled all of this line but *And* and *free,* A.E.H. wrote the alternative as shown.
        [5] Canc. *meet.*

ASL 38 "The winds out of the west land blow"
Second Draft

B 58, complete   Date: August or September, 1895
Pencil

The winds out of the west land blow,
   My friends have breathed them there;
Warm with the blood of lads I know
   Comes east the sighing air.

     It fanned their temples, filled their lungs,
       Scattered their forelocks free:
     My friends made words of it with tongues
       That talk no more to me.

Their voices perished to a sigh[1]   dying as they fly
   Thick on   gale gusts
   Along[2] the wind are sown;
               soundless
The names of men go silent[3] by,
   My fellows' and my own.

So far the east is from the west
   The wind has lost the word.

The wind and I, we both were there,
   But neither long could stay;[4]
Now through the friendless world we fare
   And sigh upon the way.

[1] Canc. *perished to a sigh.*

[2] Canc. *Along.* The reading *Thick on the wind are sown* passed on into the text of the first edition and so remained until the 1923 reprint, where by Housman's direction *Thick* was replaced by *Loose.* (See Richards' *Memoir,* p. 264.) This change was accompanied by another minor substitution in *ASL* 52 ("Far in a western brookland").

[3] Canc. *silent.*

[4] Lines 2 and 4 went into printer's copy as shown here, but in handling proof A.E.H. changed the endings to conform with the reading of the first draft, on A 233.

ASL 38 "The winds out of the west land blow"
Second Draft continued

B 59, one-inch strip
Pencil

> My lads, at home I heard you plain,[1]
> But here your speech is still,
> And down the sighing wind in vain
> You holloa[2] from the hill.

---

[1] Having carried this line into his printer's copy A.E.H. penciled *Oh* above *My;* later he approved his alternative, carefully retraced it in ink, and canceled *My* thrice.

[2] In printer's copy the spelling was altered to *hollo.*

39

'Tis time, I think, by Wenlock town
    The golden broom should blow;
The hawthorn sprinkled up and down
    Should charge the land with snow.

Spring will not wait the loiterer's time
    Who keeps so long away;
So others wear the broom and climb
    The hedgerows heaped with may.

Oh tarnish late on Wenlock Edge,
    Gold that I never see;
Lie long, high snowdrifts in the hedge
    That will not shower on me.

ASL 39 " 'Tis time, I think, by Wenlock town"

Three entries: A 125; A 153; A 155.

Laurence's Analysis allows but two entries for this poem: A 124-25 and A 155. Of the former, nothing remains but the opening stanza, written on a 1½ inch strip cut from A 125 (or 126—the verso is blank). All of A 155 is extant. It contains a fair copy of *ASL* 39, written in ink and dated "Feb. 1893."

There remains one more piece of manuscript, inscribed with the same date, containing stanzas 2 and 3 of the poem. It is evident that several months separate this entry from the first, for an intervening page (A 135) bears the date "1891-2." The appearance of the page bearing the second entry indicates that no more than two quatrains were transcribed on it, for although a small strip has been sheared from the top, the page shows generous margins above and below the writing, and there are no signs of erasure. It would have been natural for the poet in moving from one entry to another to carry forward a new holograph not of his whole MS but only of stanzas left incomplete in an earlier entry; this, I believe, is what happened here.

I would locate this piece of manuscript two pages before the fair copy, even though the Analysis locates on A 153 an "unfinished poem of several verses." Laurence's tabulation of this portion of Notebook A is manifestly inaccurate—he locates *ASL* 54 ("With rue my heart is laden") on A 155-57; these three pages have survived uncut and show no trace of the poem— and he may have failed to identify the first of the two versions of the poem that bore the same date, "Feb. 1893."

The manuscript remains of the first and second entries are mounted together on the Library of Congress sheet number 152. This sheet, together with 151, 153, 154, 155, 156, and 157—containing twelve pieces of manuscript, all told—is now found in volume VII of the collection. It is to these pieces that Laurence referred in a letter to John Carter, dated August 31, 1939, written after the bulk of the notebook remains had been separated, cut and erased, and prepared for sale: "I find that my final haul is larger than I had expected. . . . Some of the fragments are, I think, duplicates of what I had already sent you either as fair copies or more complete drafts; and I had probably put them aside as not wanted and forgotten them." This bit of realism reveals all too plainly the harsh treatment to which the four notebooks were subjected.

ASL 39 " 'Tis time, I think, by Wenlock town"
Fragment

A 125, small strip only   Date: Between September,
Pencil   1890, and July, 1891

Stourbridge
'Tis time, I think, by— ‿¹ town
The golden broom should blow,
The hawthorn sprinkled up and down
Should charge the land with snow.

¹ Housman's fastidiousness with proper nouns appears in his hesitation in choosing this place name. After deciding in favor of *Stourbridge* he lined out the accent marks. A broad-arrow pointing toward them from the right margin shows that he wanted a reminder that the blank space was awaiting its word or that the word was still open to challenge, as the draft on A 155 proves it was. A similar debate between *Wenlock* and *Kinver,* in line 9 on A 153, was not resolved until the next draft of the poem.

ASL 39 " 'Tis time, I think, by Wenlock town"
First Draft

A 153, nearly complete   Date: February, 1893
Pencil

They will not wait the loiterer's time
Who keeps so long away;
So others wear the broom, and climb
The hedgerows heaped with May.[1]

       late   Kinver
O tarnish slow[2] on Wenlock Edge,
    Gold that I never see;
         high
Lie long, white[3] snowdrifts in the hedge
That hears no more of me.[4]
     shower[5]   on
That shall not shower on me.

                    Feb. 1893

---

[1] A.E.H. cut down the first stroke of the *M,* changing it to lower case. The word, of course, means "hawthorn."

[2] Canc. *slow* and *Wenlock.*   [3] Canc. *white.*   [4] Canc. this line.

[5] Canc. *shower* and the alt. *on.* These two words, standing midway between the two lines, suggest that A.E.H. may have intended them to combine with parts of both, to compose the reading *That shower no more on me.* This reading would have accounted for the restoration of the final *s* in *snowdrifts,* above; A.E.H. had written it thus but struck out the *-s* to make the word conform with the singular verb *hears* in the line following. His use of *shower* returned its subject to the plural form.

ASL 39 " 'Tis time, I think, by Wenlock town"
Second Draft

A 155, complete   Date: February, 1893
Ink; date and correction in pencil

May.
'Tis time,[1] I think, by Wenlock town
    The golden broom should blow;
The hawthorn sprinkled up and down
    Should charge the land with snow.

Spring
They[2] will not wait the loiterer's time
    Who keeps so long away;
So others wear the broom and climb
    The hedgerows heaped with may.

Oh tarnish late on Wenlock Edge,
    Gold that I never see;
Lie long, high snowdrifts in the hedge
    That shall not shower on me.[3]
                                    Feb. 1893

[1] These two words are struck through with a very light diagonal line, and there are faint remains of an alternative, above.

[2] Canc. *They*.

[3] Having taken this line into printer's copy, A.E.H. lined out *shall* and over it wrote *will*.

40

INTO my heart an air that kills
　From yon far country blows:
What are those blue remembered hills,
　What spires, what farms are those?

That is the land of lost content,
　I see it shining plain,
The happy highways where I went
　And cannot come again.

ASL 40 "Into my heart an air that kills"

One entry: A 63.

This is the earliest *Shropshire Lad* poem of which the notebooks show record. The Analysis describes the entry for A 63, " 'Into my heart an air that kills' (fair copy, slightly corrected.)" Housman inscribed this page only nine pages after his first notebook had ceased to be a medley of epigrams, classical notes, and nonsense verse and became the repository of his serious poetry. *ASL* 40 is preserved on the upper portion of A 63, of which a 1½ inch bottom strip has also survived.

This draft, which is in ink—as are nearly all the entries from A 57 to A 106—is undoubtedly a copy. If this is the poem which Housman had in mind when he spoke to Percy Withers about the composition of his earliest *Shropshire Lad* lyric, the draft from which it derived was, like the copy, probably written sometime during 1886.[1]

The fair copy on A 63 was subjected to considerable revision—when, it would be interesting to know: soon after transcription? when Housman was gathering his manuscripts for his first volume? The corrections, all in pencil, are most significant in line 3, the first form of which nevertheless survived in printer's copy. Experimentation in line 4 brought into conflict *fields, towns, farms, spires, paths,* and *shires,* some of which opposed each other again in lines of other poems. A decision made in another line (number 7) where a choice among *footpaths, wayside,* and *highways* presented itself and was finally settled in favor of the alliterative word, illustrates a process often followed in other revisions.

---

[1] *A Buried Life: Personal Recollections of A. E. Housman* (London: Cape, 1940), p. 67. The draft itself may have been written on one of the six now fragmentary pages just preceding A 63. The date 1886 accommodates itself to this area of the notebook, for A.E.H. sketched on A 66 a preliminary stanza of the poem, "1887" (*ASL* 1), describing events of June, 1887.

ASL 40 "Into my heart an air that kills"
Unique Draft

A 63, upper 2½ inches   Date: Between 1886 [?] and
Ink, corrections in pencil   September, 1890

Into my heart an air that kills
  From yon far country blows:
                    faint remembered   [?   ]
What are those blue remembered[1] hills,
       fields   paths
  What towns, what shires are those?
      farms   farms
    towns spires[2]

That is the land of lost content,
  I see it shining plain,
           wayside   highways
The happy footpaths[3] where I went
  And cannot come again.

---

[1] Canc. *blue remembered* and the alt., above. After it are traces of a substitute, no longer legible, that was in its turn rejected when A.E.H. composed his printer's copy.

[2] Of the alternatives written above and below this line, all but *spires* and the following *farms* are lined out.

[3] Canc. *footpaths* and *wayside*.

41

IN my own shire, if I was sad,
Homely comforters I had:
The earth, because my heart was sore,
Sorrowed for the son she bore;
And standing hills, long to remain,
Shared their short-lived comrade's pain.
And bound for the same bourn as I,
On every road I wandered by,
Trod beside me, close and dear,
The beautiful and death-struck year:
Whether in the woodland brown
I heard the beechnut rustle down,
And saw the purple crocus pale
Flower about the autumn dale;
Or littering far the fields of May
Lady-smocks a-bleaching lay,
And like a skylit water stood
The bluebells in the azured wood.

Yonder, lightening other loads,
The seasons range the country roads,
But here in London streets I ken
No such helpmates, only men;
And these are not in plight to bear,
If they would, another's care.
They have enough as 'tis: I see
In many an eye that measures me
The mortal sickness of a mind
Too unhappy to be kind.
Undone with misery, all they can
Is to hate their fellow man;
And till they drop they needs must still
Look at you and wish you ill.

ASL 41 "In my own shire, if I was sad"

One entry: [B 109-10].

The unique draft of this poem was destroyed by Laurence Housman in his removal of several consecutive pages (102-12) of the second book which Housman filled in November, 1895, just before and during the time he was assembling his final copy. Laurence describes the entry of *ASL* 41 as a "rough draft, many lines cancelled . . ."; it was written only four pages before "The New Mistress" (*ASL* 34), which accompanied it and "As through the wild green hills of Wyre" (*ASL* 37) to the printer after the main body of the manuscript had gone off.

The sheet of printer's copy is headed by the numeral XLI, but Housman's numbering of this late-sent copy must have been tentative and subject to correction in the handling of proof, as he knew that his manuscript already contained a poem under the numeral XLI. This was the one we now read as number 40. He made three other departures from copy during proof-reading: hyphens were placed in the compounds *shortlived* (line 6) and *deathstruck* (line 10), and in line 22 *comrades* was replaced by *helpmates*.

42

THE MERRY GUIDE

ONCE in the wind of morning
  I ranged the thymy wold;
The world-wide air was azure
  And all the brooks ran gold.

There through the dews beside me
  Behold a youth that trod,
With feathered cap on forehead,
  And poised a golden rod.

With mien to match the morning
  And gay delightful guise
And friendly brows and laughter
  He looked me in the eyes.

Oh whence, I asked, and whither?
  He smiled and would not say,
And looked at me and beckoned
  And laughed and led the way.

And with kind looks and laughter
  And nought to say beside
We two went on together,
  I and my happy guide.

Across the glittering pastures
  And empty upland still
And solitude of shepherds
  High in the folded hill,

By hanging woods and hamlets
  That gaze through orchards down
On many a windmill turning
  And far-discovered town,

With gay regards of promise
  And sure unslackened stride
And smiles and nothing spoken
  Led on my merry guide.

By blowing realms of woodland
  With sunstruck vanes afield
And cloud-led shadows sailing
  About the windy weald,

By valley-guarded granges
    And silver waters wide,
Content at heart I followed
    With my delightful guide.

And like the cloudy shadows
    Across the country blown
We two fare on for ever,
    But not we two alone.

With the great gale we journey
    That breathes from gardens thinned,
Borne in the drift of blossoms
    Whose petals throng the wind;

Buoyed on the heaven-heard whisper
    Of dancing leaflets whirled
From all the woods that autumn
    Bereaves in all the world.

And midst the fluttering legion
    Of all that ever died
I follow, and before us
    Goes the delightful guide,

With lips that brim with laughter
    But never once respond,
And feet that fly on feathers,
    And serpent-circled wand.

ASL 42 "The Merry Guide"

Three entries: A 106-7; A 108-9; A 114-15.

The most casual observer turning the early pages of Housman's first note-book could hardly fail to notice the differences between A 106-7 and the pages immediately preceding: he moves from the storeroom to the work-shop. At page 106 Notebook A becomes a composition book, and the first entry produced one of the longest manuscripts devoted to a single *Shrop-shire Lad* poem. The first draft is dated "Sept. 1890."

In his initial draft of "The Merry Guide," as we now have it, Housman composed the first five stanzas (two versions of stanzas 2 and 3) and the last five (the next-to-final quatrain thrice rewritten). There are no traces here of the middle third of the poem. (Did this portion perish with an in-tervening page not counted in the Analysis?) The revision of A 106-7, partly in ink and probably the work of another day, is abundant: of the completed quatrains—the first on A 107 lacks the opening line—only one, the last, escaped retouching here or in later drafts. What we now read as the fourth quatrain was revised to the form of its final copy, and in two others—numbers 2 and 13—only one word made the difference between their corrected versions and the copy seen by the printer.

Page 108 preserves a holograph of the first five stanzas. It is beautifully written in ink, in a very small hand that found room for two uncrowded columns on the four-inch width of the page. This spacing is continued on what remains of A 109; only the lower two thirds of the page has survived, containing the last four quatrains of the lyric. The first page of this entry exhibits a number of alterations penciled into stanzas 1, 3, and 5, the first and last of these stanzas attaining thereby the reading of the text. Here also, to the right of and beneath stanza 1, appear penciled versions of quatrains 9 and 10, the latter so heavily erased as to defy all efforts at decipherment beyond a very few words; the first and last words of the fourth line of 10 are certainly *With* and *guide*. Housman threw a double loop about these two late-arrived stanzas and extended it into a transfer-line, evidently in-tending to carry them across to the upper part (now missing) of the facing page, A 109. In the lower-right corner of A 108 he penciled one more stanza, only the remains of which are now legible but clear enough to identify the quatrain as number 6. Thus page 1 of the second draft of "The Merry Guide" received eight of the fifteen stanzas of the poem.

Of the four quatrains surviving on the lower two thirds of A 109, the first (printed as number 12) was brought over from A 107 verbatim except for a difference in one line, altered in the third draft to the reading now shown in the text; the next quatrain also was transcribed verbatim and the change on this page of one word eventually gave the stanza its final form. The fourteenth stanza, thrice rewritten on A 107 without a decisive shaping of the first line, was brought over with a new opening, which after some experimental revision was left for the next draft to perfect. The final quatrain was copied on A 109 in its original form, which it carried on into printer's copy.

The third draft, also dated "Sept. 1890," preserves in their final order all fifteen stanzas of the poem—the first ten in two columns on A 114 and the last five in the left column on the following recto page. The other column of this page is partly filled with two revisions of stanza 9. Housman's dissatisfaction with this stanza was evident in his heavy correction of it on A 114, and it further appears (from the fact that his first penciled revision of it on A 115 is fronted with a brace extended into a transfer-line drawn toward the interval between stanzas 14 and 15) that he at one time may have considered changing the position of the quatrain. Whatever unfulfilled plans he may have had for it, his revision here brought the stanza to the status of printer's copy. The third draft of "The Merry Guide," incorporating the hard-won improvements wrought out in the preceding entries, was in its turn subjected to further experimentation. The reading of ten stanzas was challenged, and three—6, 8, and 9—were substantially rewritten, some alternatives in these and others being left open to await the decision of another day.

ASL 42 "The Merry Guide"
First Draft

A 106, complete   Date: September, 1890
Pencil, one stanza in ink

Sept. 1890.

The Merry Guide.
Ἑρμῆς ψυχοπομπός[1] ψυχαγωγός.

Once in the wind of morning
   I ranged the highland wold;
The world-wide
When the sharp[2] air was azure
   And all the brooks ran gold.

There in the windy moorland
   A youth before me trod
That wore a cap with feathers
       twisted
   And twirled a wreathen rod.

     With level brows of friendship
       And gay delightful guise
     Amidst the azure morning
       He looked me in the eyes.

There thro' the dews beside me
   Behold a youth that trod,
With feathered cap on forehead,
   And twirled a golden rod.

All in the azure morning
   With gay delightful guise
       gaze
And level brows of friendship
   He looked me in the eyes.[3]

O whence, I asked, and whither?
I asked him whence and whither,[4]
       smiled
He laughed[5] and would not say,
But[6]
And looked at me and beckoned,
   And laughed and led the way.

And with kind looks and laughter
   And naught to say beside
We two went on together,
   I and my merry guide.

[1] Canc. this word. The Greek subtitle ("Hermes, guide of souls") does not appear elsewhere in the MSS of this poem. A phrase from Euripides is usually regarded as the source, but there the name refers to Charon. Perhaps to avoid this allusion, A.E.H. dropped the Greek subtitle.
  [2] Canc. *When the sharp.*   [3] This stanza is in ink.
  [4] Canc. this line.   [5] Canc. *laughed.*   [6] Canc. *But.*

ASL 42 "The Merry Guide"
First Draft continued

A 107, complete
Pencil, two stanzas in ink

> Along the breezes blown
> We two fare always onward,
>   But not we two alone.

With   On
> Down[1] the great gale we journey
>   By withering gardens thinned,
> Borne in the drift of blossoms
> [?   ][2]
>   Whose petals throng the wind.

> Buoyed on the heaven-heard whisper
>   Of dancing leaflets whirled
> From all the woods that autumn
>   Deflowers
>   Despoils in all the world.

And on with leaf and blossom   And gay unslackened stride[3]   And [?   ][6]
  And all that ever died   By path and pool and hamlet   With all that ever died
I follow, and before us   And laughing lips before me   us
  Goes the delightful guide,[5]   on   happy   I follow, and before me
                                 Goes my delightful guide,[4]
                                                                       Goes the delightful guide.

---

[1] *Down* is heavily inked over by an undula; it may also have been canceled by A.E.H.

[2] Canc. this line.

[3] Above this line are traces of two attempts at line 1 of the stanza.

[4] After writing *Goes my delightful guide,* A.E.H. canceled *delightful,* set over it the alt. *happy,* and wrote *on* above a caret between *Goes* and *my. Goes* was later struck through and two now illegible words were subscribed. The line and its rhyming complement *And gay unslackened stride* became, with minor changes, the fourth and second lines of stanza 8.

[5] This stanza was written in ink on an upward slope.

[6] The last two or three words of this line were struck through. Above it are the remains of three other lines.

With lips that brim with laughter
But never once respond,
And feet that fly on feathers,
And serpent-circled wand.

                    one wind
And down the gale together
With all that ever died
I follow, and before us
Goes the delightful guide,[7]

            leaf and blossom
And [?   ][8]
And all that ever died,
We follow, and before us
Goes the delightful guide,

[7] This quatrain was written in ink through a pencil draft of the same; lines 1 and 2 of the first version may be read in part:

And [?   ] *with the legion*
Of all that ever died.

[8] The phrase *leaf and blossom* connects this revised stanza with the ink copy of it that A.E.H. crowded into the left margin. (See p. 209.)

ASL 42 "The Merry Guide"
Second Draft

A 108, complete   Date: September, 1890
Ink, corrections in pencil

Once in the wind of morning   By² [?   ]
           thymy   With³ [?   ] revealed
   I ranged the woodland¹ wold;   And cloudy shadows sailing
The world-wide air was azure   endless
   And all the brooks ran gold.   On all the windy weald;

By [?   ]   There thro' the dews beside me
   And [?   ]   Behold a youth that trod,
[?   ]   With feathered cap on forehead,⁴
   With [?   ] guide.   And twirled a golden rod.

      radiant
   With gallant mien of morning⁵
Amid
All in the azure morning
   And
   With⁶ gay delightful guise
   friendly brows and laughter⁷
And level gaze of friendship
   He looked me in the eyes.

      O whence, I asked, and whither?
      He smiled and would not say,
   And looked at me and beckoned
      And laughed and led the way.

---

¹ Canc. *woodland.*   ² Above *By* are traces of three or four erased words.
³ Canc. a word after *With.*
⁴ At this point the transfer-line leaves the page.
⁵ This alt. is in ink.   ⁶ Canc. *With.*   ⁷ This alt. is in ink.

And with kind looks and laughter
    And naught to say beside
We two went on together,
        happy
    I and my merry[8] guide.

                                         pastures
                Amid the [?   ]
                    And [?   ] still,
By And[9] [?   ] shepherds
              Amid the folded hill;
              High in [   ]

[8] Canc. *merry*.   [9] Canc. *And*.

ASL 42 "The Merry Guide"
Second Draft continued

A 109, lower two thirds
Ink, corrections in pencil

Down
With[1] the great gale we journey
    That blows from
      By withering[2] gardens thinned,
Borne in the drift of blossoms
    Whose petals throng the wind;

                Buoyed on the heaven-heard whisper
                    Of dancing leaflets whirled
            From all the woods that autumn
                Bereaves
                    Despoils in all the world.

        rustling
     mid the marching
And whirling with the[3] legion
    Of all that ever died
I follow, and before us
    Goes the delightful guide,

                With lips that brim with laughter
                    But never once respond,
            And feel that fly on feathers,
                  And serpent-circled wand.

[1] Canc. *With.* Just above this line show traces of a cut-through line. If the small script and the stanza spacing shown in this portion of the page were characteristic of the missing upper section, it could easily have contained the five intermediate stanzas of the poem.

[2] Canc. *By withering.*

[3] Canc. *whirling with the.* A later hand has partly obscured *marching,* which A.E.H. may also have canceled.

ASL 42 "The Merry Guide"
Third Draft

A 114, complete   Date: September, 1890
Ink, corrections in pencil

Once in the wind of morning
        highland
  I ranged the thymy[1] wold;
The world-wide air was azure
  And all the brooks ran gold.

There thro' the dews beside me
  Behold a youth that trod,
With feathered cap on forehead,
       poised
  And twirled[2] a golden rod.

    mien to match the morning
    radiant
With gallant mien of[3] morning
  And gay delightful guise
And friendly brows and laughter
He looked me in the eyes.

            glistening[4]
Across the glittering pastures
      empty
  And idle[5] upland still
And solitudes
  By heathy bourns of shepherds
    High in the folded hill,

        crofts[6]
By hanging woods and hamlets
  That gaze thro' orchards down
On many a windmill turning
  And far-discovered town;

        of promise
    gay regards reverted[7]
With friendly look reverted
    light unswerving
  And gay unslackened[8] stride
    sure unslackened
And smiles and nothing spoken
  Led on my merry guide.

[1] Canc. *thymy*. A.E.H. may have written another alt. beside *highland*.

[2] A heavy ink undula over *twirled* may have also obscured a cancel-line by A.E.H.

[3] The comment in note 2 also applies to *gallant mien of*.

[4] Canc. *glistening*.

[5] The comment in note 2 applies to *idle* and to *By heathy bourns* in the next line.

[6] Canc. *crofts*.

[7] Canc. *reverted*. A heavy undula has obscured all but the first word of the line as originally written.

[8] Having superscribed *light unswerving*, A.E.H. lined out *gay unslackened*, later writing the other alt., below.

               billowy
          murmuring realms
           surging plains
O whence, I asked, and whither?   By windy shires of woodland
              sunlit roofs afield
He smiled and would not say,   With steeples dim-revealed
     cloudland cloud-cast flakes of shadow
And looked at me and beckoned   And cloudy shadows sailing[9]
           About   windy
And laughed and led the way.   On all[10] the endless weald,

           poplar
And with kind looks and laughter   By valley-guarded granges
    And naught to say beside   And silver waters wide,
We two went on together,   Content at heart I followed
    I and my happy guide.   With my delightful guide.

---

[9] This line seems to have developed thus: After writing *cloud-cast* over *cloudy*, he lined out both words with a single pencil stroke and wrote *cloudland* above the head of the line. Over the end of it he set *flakes of shadow*. This left the two readings *And cloudland shadows sailing* and *And cloudland flakes of shadow*. After the line, A.E.H. wrote parallel with the margin a combination of the two: *And cloud and shadow sailing.*

[10] Canc. *On all.*

ASL 42 "The Merry Guide"
Third Draft continued

A 115, complete

And like the cloudy shadows
            country
    Across the champaign blown
We two fare on for ever,
    But not we two alone.

With
Down[1] the great gale we journey
        breathes
    That blows[2] from gardens thinned,
Borne in the drift of blossoms
    Whose petals throng the wind;

                                blowing
Buoyed on the heaven-heard whisper   By heaving[4] realms of woodland
    Of dancing leaflets whirled   With sun-struck vanes afield
From all the woods that autumn   And cloud-led shadows sailing
    Bereaves in all the world.   About
                                       Broad on[5] the windy weald,

        midst   fluttering
And mid[3] the rustling legion   By billowy [?   ] land
    Of all that ever died   With [?   ] afield
I follow, and before us   cloud[6]
    Goes the delightful guide,   And [?   ] sailing
                                          About [?   ] weald,

With lips that brim with laughter
    But never once respond,
And feet that fly on feathers,
    And serpent-circled wand.

                                                    Sept. 1890.

    [1] Canc. *Down.*
    [2] A heavy ink undula has obscured *blows* and any cancel A.E.H. may have used
on it.
        [3] Canc. *mid.* The word *rustling* is in the same case as *blows,* noted above.
        [4] Canc. *heaving.* This stanza and the one below are in pencil.
        [5] Canc. *Broad on.*   [6] Canc. the now illegible word below *cloud.*

43

THE IMMORTAL PART

WHEN I meet the morning beam
Or lay me down at night to dream,
I hear my bones within me say,
"Another night, another day.

"When shall this slough of sense be cast,
This dust of thoughts be laid at last,
The man of flesh and soul be slain
And the man of bone remain?

"This tongue that talks, these lungs that shout,
These thews that hustle us about,
This brain that fills the skull with schemes,
And its humming hive of dreams,—

"These to-day are proud in power
And lord it in their little hour:
The immortal bones obey control
Of dying flesh and dying soul.

" 'Tis long till eve and morn are gone:
Slow the endless night comes on,
And late to fulness grows the birth
That shall last as long as earth.

"Wanderers eastward, wanderers west,
Know you why you cannot rest?
'Tis that every mother's son
Travails with a skeleton.

"Lie down in the bed of dust;
Bear the fruit that bear you must;
Bring the eternal seed to light,
And morn is all the same as night.

"Rest you so from trouble sore,
Fear the heat o' the sun no more,
Nor the snowing winter wild,
Now you labour not with child.

"Empty vessel, garment cast,
We that wore you long shall last.
—Another night, another day."
So my bones within me say.

Therefore they shall do my will
To-day while I am master still,
And flesh and soul, now both are strong,
Shall hale the sullen slaves along,

Before this fire of sense decay,
This smoke of thought blow clean away,
And leave with ancient night alone
The stedfast and enduring bone.

ASL 43 "The Immortal Part"

Two entries: A 228-29; B 72-73.

The first draft of this poem is one of the most revealing illustrations in the notebooks of Housman's description of the working of his poetic imagination. The ideas of this afternoon stroll literally burst their bounds as he sat down to write, running pell-mell over a full recto page and spilling over onto a blank verso, which also received nearly full measure. Crowding thoughts were captured and immediately put down as they came within the net of language: here a complete stanza, there a quatrain later to be divided and its couplets better paired, separate couplets, single lines. Perhaps the best way to show here the pristine form—or formlessness—of this poem is to number the elements of it in the order in which they were put on paper. The first page (A 229)—which was headed with the title—contained stanza 1, couplet 1 of stanza 2, couplet 2 of stanza 4, couplet 1 of stanza 3, a mixed quatrain consisting of couplet 1 of stanza 5 and couplet 2 of stanza 9, stanza 10, and stanza 11. On the second page of this draft (A 228) were couplet 2 of stanza 6, stanza 8, stanza 7, another version of stanza 8, and a quatrain later to be divided into couplet 2 of stanza 5 and couplet 2 of the second stanza. Many of these units underwent radical revision *in situ,* and for others, as will be shown in the transcripts, alternative stanzas and couplets were written in the right margins. These alternatives have suffered heavy erasure; in some cases hardly more than enough writing remains to declare the parts of the poem they represent.

It is important, however, to note that, despite the large amount of revision still to be done, Housman put down the substance of his poem in this draft; every stanza is accounted for, and just twenty-two lines of the eleven quatrains were left on these pages exactly in the form in which we now read them. But after he had done with this draft Housman must have realized that much work of a different kind remained for another day, work which he often found as arduous as the reshaping of language—the determination of the proper sequence of his scattered quatrains.

This task was only partly accomplished six months later. In the second draft, on B 72-73, the bloc consisting of stanzas 1 and 2 was carried over from the first version; stanzas 9, 10, and 11 were also transcribed in this order, the first couplet of stanza 9 now appearing for the first time; and stanzas 7 and 8 were kept together and preceded by number 6, which in the first draft had been represented by only its second couplet. This rearrangement produced the following stanza order: 1, 2, 6, 7, 8, 5, 3, 4, 9, 10, 11. Here three stanzas form a group that conflicts with the sequence of the poem and is in need of shifting within itself. These stanzas—5, 3, and 4 —belong to the first part of the poem, which is the *protest* of the rebellious bones. The misplaced trio injects an awkward repetition of protest that conflicts with the *command* of the bones, which begins with the stanza we read as number 6. All that was needed was to put last the first member of this group and move the whole to follow stanza 2. A heavy caret at the end of this stanza, on B 72, proves that Housman recognized the need of some transitional stanzas at this point.

As to the language of the second draft, after revision only seven lines were left short of their final reading and some of these only by a word or two—further evidence that Housman's verbal creativeness usually outran his sense of organization. Of these seven lines, however, four[1] had to be modified after printer's copy was written, and two of them were not definitely phrased until the handling of proof.

[1] Line 11—canc. *mind,* and *brain* set above, reversing a decision in the second draft.

Line 15—*bones must brook control,* as in first and second drafts; but printed *bones obey control,* once rejected in first draft.

Line 17—*'Tis time that eves and morns were gone,* approximately as in second draft; printed *'Tis long till eve and morn are gone.*

Line 25—Canc. *To bed, to bed; lie down in dust,* as in first and second drafts; but altered in printer's copy to *Lie down in the bed of dust.*

ASL 43 "The Immortal Part"
First Draft

A 229, complete   Date: February or March, 1895
Pencil

The immortal part

Eve and morning, every day[1]   clinging slave of us
I hear my bones within me say   This smothering cloak[4] of life be torn
     night   day,
'Another eve,[2] another morn,   And you be dead and we be born
It is long till we be born.[3]   Till you are dead and we are born,[5]

     When shall this slough of flesh be cast,
               life
   This dust of thought be laid at last[6]
               life
   This tyranny be overpast[7]

                   bear
               must brook
     The immortal bones obey[8] control
     Of dying flesh and dying soul

This tongue that talks, these lungs that shout,
These thews that hustle us about

         morn   eve
   When will nights and days be gone
   And the endless night come on?
   Another night, another day.'
   So my bones within me say.

     they shall do
Therefore I will have[9] my will
Today while I am master still,
And flesh and soul, now both are strong,
   haul
Shall lug the sullen slaves along,

---

  [1] Canc. this line.   [2] Canc. *eve* and *morn*.   [3] Canc. this line.
  [4] Canc. *smothering cloak*.   [5] Canc. this line.
  [6] This line, an alt., crowded the one above; so *life* was first set below *thought*. This alt. was itself canceled but rewritten above.
  [7] Canc. this line.   [8] Canc. *obey*.   [9] Canc. *I will have.*

                              sense
        Before these fires[10] of flesh decay,
                        thoughts
        This smoke of soul[11] blow clean away,
        And leave with ancient night alone
        The thoughtless[12] and enduring bone.
                    senseless
                    stedfast

---

[10] In this line A.E.H. wrote *this* through *these,* struck off the -*s* of *fires,* and canceled *flesh.*

[11] Canc. soul.   [12] Canc. *thoughtless* and *senseless.*

ASL 43 "The Immortal Part"
First Draft continued

A 228, complete
Pencil

When shall [?   ]¹

           We [?   ] rest²

      'Tis that every mother's son
       Travails with a skeleton.   To bed, to bed: the throe of birth
Lie down, wanderers, jaded sore,   [   ]
     after   wearying   Heals [?   ]
Rest you now from³ travail sore,   Cures you of the ill of [?]
    so from   [?] will sleep [?]

Fear the heat o' the sun no more,
    Nor the snowing
Shrink no more at winter wild,   When we are born and you are dead,
    Now you labour not with
Once [?   ] your child⁴ [?] no more: to bed, to bed.

To bed, to bed; lie down in dust,   Once the [?   ] born
                       Eve is all [?   ]
Bear the fruit that bear you must;
Bring the man of bone to light
And morn is all the same as night.

        so, [?   ]
     Rest you, wanderer,⁵ jaded sore,
     Fear the heat o' the sun no more
     Nor the snowing winter wild
     Now you labour not with child.

         Bring the man of bone to birth
         He shall last as long as earth
         How long till
         When will flesh and soul be slain
         And the man of bone remain?

¹ This line may be a part of the evolving second stanza.

² It is possible that this line adumbrates *Know you why you cannot rest?*—the second line of stanza 6. If so, the lines just to the left below compose with it the last three lines of that stanza. The remaining lines in the right-hand column apparently forecast stanza 7; some portions are line-canceled.

³ Canc. *now from*. The line above is the alternative.

⁴ Canc. all but the word *child*.   ⁵ Canc. *wanderer*.

ASL 43 "The Immortal Part"
Second Draft

B 72, complete   Date: August or September, 1895
Pencil

When I meet the morning beam
                    eve
Or lay me down at night[1] to dream
                         night
                    lift
When at morn I heave my head[2]
Or lay me down at eve to bed,
I hear my bones within me say
'Another night, another day.

                         sense
  'When shall this slough of flesh[3] be cast,
  This dust of thoughts be laid at last,[4]
                    web   How long till   The man of
  This fluttering veil of life be torn   When shall flesh & soul be slain
  And you be dead and we be born?[5]   And the man of bone remain?

    Men go   men go
'Journeyers eastward, journeyers west, Wanderers[6]
          they
    men   they
Know you why you cannot rest?
'Tis that every mother's son
Travails with a skeleton.

    [1] Having canceled *night* and superscribed *eve,* A.E.H. canceled *eve* and rewrote
night below.
    [2] After writing the couplet at the top of the page, he struck out this and the follow-
ing line, not touching *lift.*
    [3] Canc. *flesh.*
    [4] Having run his interrogation over into the next couplet, A.E.H. stroked out a
question mark here.
    [5] This couplet developed in these stages: After writing the two lines as shown
A.E.H. set down their alternatives to the right and canceled the original couplet together with the superscribed *web.* In the first of the two alternative lines he canceled
When shall and wrote above *How long till,* but this substitute was in its turn struck
out and *The man of* written after it.
    [6] Over *Wanderers* there is a large caret pointing to the left, indicating that A.E.H.
purposed to add or transpose one or more stanzas here. This was accomplished by
bringing up and rearranging the last stanza on this page and the first two on the next.

'To bed, to bed; lie down in dust,
Bear the fruit that bear you must;
eternal
destined seed
Bring the man of bone[7] to light
And morn is all the same as night.

so   trouble
dead from sorrow sore,
'Rest you so, lad, jaded sore,[8]
Fear the heat o' the sun no more
Nor the snowing winter wild
Now you labour not with child.

were
'Tis time that[9] 'Tis long till eve and morn be[10] gone,
Slow the endless night comes on;
ripeness grows
And late to fulness comes[11] the birth
That shall last as long as earth.

[7] Canc. *man of bone*. He probably did this after he found he needed the phrase in the couplet above, right. (See p. 224.) Canc. *destined*.

[8] Housman's use of *lad* here is another example of his curious infatuation for this word. Fortunately, it disappeared beneath the cancel-line that struck out the last four words. The substitute first considered was *dead from sorrow*. It is hard to believe that his ear would have allowed him to let *sore* follow immediately; rather, he probably struck out *sorrow* and superscribed *trouble*. This permitted him to bring back the rhyming word *sore*, which he rewrote; *so* was likewise restored, after *dead* was canceled.

[9] These three words are the substitute for *'Tis long till,* canceled.

[10] Canc. *be*.   [11] Canc. *fulness comes*.

ASL 43 "The Immortal Part"
Second Draft continued

B 73, complete
Pencil

This tongue that talks, these lungs that shout,
These thews that hustle us about,
       mind   holds   fills the skull with
This brain[1] that [?] a thousand schemes,
And all[2] its humming hive of dreams:

    These today are proud in power
    And lord it in their little hour:
    The immortal bones must brook control
    Of dying flesh and dying soul.
          Empty vessel, garment cast
      Flesh and soul are garments cast;
                you
But We The bone that wore them long shall last.
      But soon shall 'Tis not long till day be gone
    'When will morn and eve be gone
    And the endless night come on?
    Another night, another day.'
    So my bones within me say.[3]

   [1] Canc. *brain* and the words between *that* and *schemes*. The alt. first written produced the ending *holds a thousand schemes.* Then A.E.H. extended his cancel-line to cover *a thousand,* struck out *holds,* and wrote out after it *fills the skull with.*

   [2] Canc. *all.*

   [3] In these six lines, although the ninth stanza was eventually extracted from them, it appears that A.E.H. was at first intent on merely composing couplets from recollections of the earlier three pages of this poem. The first line (later canceled), *Flesh and soul . . . ,* was an echo of phrases written at the top of A 229. The second line of this couplet began with *The bone,* which gave way to *We.* He tried out *But* as the opening word of the line, then struck it out. The word *them* was rejected in favor of *you* when *garments* gave way to *garment* in the substitute for the preceding line.

Therefore they shall do my will
Today while I am master still,
And flesh and soul, now both are strong,
Shall hale the sullen slaves along,

Before this fire of sense decay,
This smoke of thought blow clean away,
And leave with ancient night alone
The stedfast and enduring bone.

44

SHOT? so quick, so clean an ending?
    Oh that was right, lad, that was brave:
Yours was not an ill for mending,
    'Twas best to take it to the grave.

Oh you had forethought, you could reason,
    And saw your road and where it led,
And early wise and brave in season
    Put the pistol to your head.

Oh soon, and better so than later
    After long disgrace and scorn,
You shot dead the household traitor,
    The soul that should not have been born.

Right you guessed the rising morrow
    And scorned to tread the mire you must:
Dust's your wages, son of sorrow,
    But men may come to worse than dust.

Souls undone, undoing others,—
    Long time since the tale began.
You would not live to wrong your brothers:
    Oh lad, you died as fits a man.

Now to your grave shall friend and stranger
    With ruth and some with envy come:
Undishonoured, clear of danger,
    Clean of guilt, pass hence and home.

Turn safe to rest, no dreams, no waking;
    And here, man, here's the wreath I've made:
'Tis not a gift that's worth the taking,
    But wear it and it will not fade.

ASL 44 "Shot? so quick, so clean an ending?"

One entry: B 60-65.

Housman's absorption in this poem, the subject of which was contained in a news clipping found among his papers after his death (*Recollections,* pp. 103-5), is attested by the fact that after his first draft he directly composed another, very heavily revised, and after that produced a third, which he corrected until he had brought to finality every line but four of the twenty-eight-line poem.

It seems probable that he began his first draft on B 61 and wrote perhaps five stanzas there, using the facing page 60 for experimental sketching—a method he sometimes practiced in getting his stanzas down in order. However, the scantiness of what remains of B 60 balks conjecture: all we have is a narrow strip containing six scattered lines, unrhymed. None of them entered intact into the poem being wrought out on B 61, but all anticipate turns of thought or language that took shape there or in the four following pages.

Presumably, the opening quatrain has been lost with a strip cut from the top of B 61; the remainder of the page contains numbers 2, 3, 4, and 5. The draft shows no hesitation in deciding the order of sequence. The stanza we now know as number 3 was composed here in the exact form in which it is now read but the other three underwent extensive reshaping, which for stanzas 4 and 5 was not completed even in the third draft, on B 64-65.

The second draft contains the seven stanzas of the poem—the first four on B 62 (the last two lines of the fourth quatrain lost with a strip cut from the bottom); numbers 5, 6, and 7 on the facing page, at the bottom of which Housman wrote a redraft of stanza 4, the latter lines of which have been cut away. The writing on B 61-63 was subjected to heavy revision; and in an effort to obscure the many alternative phrases, some struck through only lightly, Laurence Housman erased large portions of the manuscript. B 63 presents special difficulties; nearly every line now appears lined out wholly or in part; it is indeed possible that Housman intended to cancel the entire draft, and every word that seems not to have been lined out has escaped only by accident. Some of the cancel-strokes may have been the work of another hand. My notes to the drafts of "The Merry Guide" called attention to the problem of describing accurately several heavily canceled passages, and the same difficulty of interpreting between one cancel-line and another that covers it frequently presents itself on B 63. The writing on this page has been further dimmed by the effects of a soft eraser over pencil and by the layer of mucilage applied to this side of the notebook sheet.

The two pages preserving the third draft have been trimmed at the bottom but no more than a few lines of the total manuscript seem to have been destroyed. B 64 lost an inch when the sheet was cut to take out a few alternative lines of the second draft, on the opposite side, but the scissors-stroke passed just below stanza 4 on B 64, leaving all intact there. A strip about the same size was removed from the bottom of B 65, probably to destroy a redraft of the opening couplet of stanza 4, of which one alternative version can just be deciphered amid the cancellation and erasure above the cut margin. From the first draft on, this couplet proved intractable and the surviving versions of it—all eventually rejected—are a study in Housman's search for the language appropriate to the pressing theme of this lyric.

There is one more relic of the manuscript of this poem, which Housman wrote on B 101 while preparing copy for the printer or after it had gone off. It consists of the brief notation: *Shot?*] *Today? Last night?*—tentative substitutes for the opening phrase of line 1. The sheet of copy itself shows no sign that either alternative was taken up.

ASL 44 "Shot? so quick, so clean an ending?"
Fragment

B 60, one-inch strip   Date: August or September, 1895
Pencil

Oh you fell down as fits a man.[1]
Found the road too foul to tread
And died a man and not a slave
Sigh for the lad they[2] never saw
Oh boy, lie dear and envied down.
You struck straight [?   ][3]

[1] This line was cut through.
[2] *they* anticipates *friend and stranger* of the second draft.
[3] This line was cut through.

ASL 44 "Shot? so quick, so clean an ending?"
First Draft

B 61, nearly complete
Pencil

<pre>
                You¹ had eyes
      Oh you had forethought and your reason
                 found your
      And judged the² road too foul to tread,
                wise   brave
      And early³ brave and wise in season
          Put the pistol to your head.

          Oh soon, and better so than later
            After long disgrace and scorn,
        You shot dead the household traitor,
            The soul that should not have been born.

                     you
      You [?   ] and⁴ guessed the morrow
          And took [?   ] end on trust:
      Dust's your wages, son of sorrow;
          But men may come to worse than dust.

          Self undone, undoing others,—
            It has been since the world began.
          You would not live to wrong your brothers:
            Oh lad, you died as fits a man.
</pre>

¹ Canc. *You.* Just below this alt. phrase are traces of another, in part canceled.
² Canc. *judged the.*
³ This word seems to have been written through another beginning with *t*, perhaps *timely.*
⁴ Canc. this line through *and.* Portions of an erased alt. line, above, show cancel-strokes.

ASL 44 "Shot? so quick, so clean an ending?"
Second Draft

B 62, nearly complete   Date: August or September, 1895
Pencil

    Shot? Dead?   and
    Nineteen![1] so quick, so clean an ending?
          Shot? so quick, so clean an ending?
      young
    So soon? so quick and clean an ending?[2]
        that was   that was
      Oh you did[3] right, lad, you were brave:
    Yours was not an ill for mending,
      'Twas   hide   in
      'Tis[4] best to take it to the grave.

            eyes and use of
             sense
    Oh you had eyes[5] and used your reason,
     And   You
      And[6] found your road too foul to tread,
               prompt[8]
    And timely[7] wise and brave in season
               shrewd
      Put the pistol to your head.

---

  [1] Canc. *Nineteen!* and *so.*

  [2] This line, the second version on this page of the opening line, was canceled by an undula in pencil.

  [3] Canc. *you did* and *you were.*

  [4] Canc. *'Tis* and the alts. *hide* and *in,* above.

  [5] Canc. *eyes* and another alt., immediately above, now illegible.

  [6] Canc. *And* and the alt. *You,* above.

  [7] As on B 61, an earlier word—here *timely*—was written through by the word *early.*

  [8] Canc. the alts. *prompt* and *shrewd.*

Oh soon, and better so than later
  After long disgrace and scorn,[9]
  struck   shot
You shot[10] dead the household traitor,
  The soul that should not have been born.

                              Right you guessed the[11]
  Far before   Before the noon
Before 'twas high you guessed the morrow[12]
  And took the ruinous end on trust,

[9] The suicide note quoted in the newspaper clipping contained the phrase, "...
better than a long series of sorrows and disgraces." (*Recollections,* p. 104.)
  [10] Canc. *shot* and the alt. *struck,* above.
  [11] Canc. two or three illegible words after *the.*
  [12] Canc. this line down to *morrow* and the alts. *Far before* and *Before the noon,*
above.

ASL 44 "Shot? so quick, so clean an ending?"
Second Draft continued

B 63, nearly complete   Date: August or September, 1895
Pencil, much corrected

> Souls undone
> Self undone,[1] undoing others,—
> > There have been such since time began.
> > It has been since the world began.[2]
> > It has been since the world began.
>
> You would[3] not live to wrong your brothers:
> > Oh lad, you died as fits a man.[4]
>
> > > > shall
> > To deck   Here to [?   ] will   let
> > Here to your grave should friend and stranger[5]
> > > but
> > > Few friends and many a stranger come.[6]
> > > Undishonoured
> > And with the saved and clear of danger,[7]
> > > Undishonoured, housed at home.[8]
> > > Clean of guilt, pass hence and home.

---

[1] Canc. *Self undone.*   [2] Canc. this line and its alt. lines, above and below.
[3] Canc. *You would.*   [4] Canc. this line.
[5] Canc. this line. Other cancel-strokes above the line were probably meant to strike out all the alt. phrases. Remains of a now illegible word show after the alt. *Here to; will, shall,* and *let* were tentative substitutes for *should.*
[6] Canc. this line. To replace it, A.E.H. wrote the line below beginning *With grief.* ... He set a square bracket in front of the line and drew a transfer-line upward to the word *Few.*
[7] Canc. this line and the alt. *Undishonoured.*
[8] Canc. this line. It was not set in as an interlined alternative, but was composed before the one beginning *Clean of guilt.* ... The writing of the third line of this stanza compares with the experimentation on B 60.

soft
Lie down   Sleep you well Lie down to sleep Turn safe to sleep
Oh lad, sleep well, no dreams, no waking:[9]
here, man, take   of verse
And take to wear the wreath I've made:[10]
'Tis not a gift that's worth the taking,[11]
But wear it and it will not fade.[12]

ruth   awe
With grief and ruth and envy come[13]

sullying blackening morrows
fate-sent
You would not brook the fate-fouled morrows[14]
wade   mud
Nor tread the leagues of mire you must[15]

[9] Canc. this line. All of the alt. openings above, with the possible exception of the last, *Turn safe to sleep,* were also lined out.

[10] Canc. this line, together with the alts. above except *here, man.* The alt. *of verse* (set above a caret) was intended to enter into a line reading *And take the wreath of verse I've made.*

[11] Canc. this line.

[12] A long cancel-stroke running through this line does not cover *fade.*

[13] Canc. this line and the alt. *awe,* above.

[14] Canc. this line and all the alts., above. The final *-s* of *morrows* is struck off. This and the following line are the remains of a revision of stanza 4, of which the last two lines have been cut away. A brace-and-transfer carried the stanza over to the bottom of the preceding page, where the second version of it had been composed.

[15] Canc. this line and the alts., above.

ASL 44 "Shot? so quick, so clean an ending?"
Third Draft

B 64, nearly complete   Date: August or September, 1895
Pencil

Shot? so quick, so clean an ending?
 Oh that was right, lad, that was brave:
Yours was not an ill for mending,
                    The place to hide was the grave.[1]
 'Twas best to take it to the grave.

                forethought, you could reason,
Oh you had eyes and use of reason[2]
        saw   and where it led,
 And found[3] your road too foul to tread,
And early wise and brave in season
 Put the pistol to your head.

Oh soon, and better so than later
 After long disgrace and scorn,
You shot dead the household traitor,
 The soul that should not have been born.

                clouding
                sullying ruinous
You would not breast the blackening morrow[4]
        tread the leagues of mire
 Nor do and bear the wrong you must.[5]
Dust's your wages, son of sorrow,
 But men may come to worse than dust.

---

[1] Canc. this alt. line.
[2] Canc. *eyes and use of reason*. The substitute, which went into print, is near the reading of the first form of the line, on B 61.
[3] Canc. *found* and *too foul to tread*.
[4] Canc. all of this line but *morrow;* canc. also the alts. above.
[5] Canc. all of this line but *you must* and all of the alts. but *mire*.

ASL 44 "Shot? so quick, so clean an ending?"
Third Draft continued

B 65, nearly complete
Pencil

> Souls undone, undoing others,—
>   Long time[1] since the world began.
> You would not live to wrong your brothers:
>   Oh lad, you died as fits a man.
>
> Now to your grave shall friend and stranger
>   With ruth and awe and envy come:
> Undishonoured, clear of danger,
>   Clean of guilt, pass hence and home.
>
> Turn safe to rest, no dreams, no waking;
>   the
> And here, man,—here's a[2] wreath I've made:
> 'Tis not a gift that's worth the taking,
>   But wear it and it will not fade.
>
> Before it [dawned ?] you [sensed ?] the morrow[3]
>   And would not tread the mire you must.

---

[1] *Long time* was heavily penciled over *It has been.*   [2] Canc. *a.*

[3] A.E.H. penciled a light undula over these lines, which represent his final effort in the notebooks to produce a satisfactory reading for the opening couplet of the fourth quatrain of this lyric.

45

IF it chance your eye offend you,
  Pluck it out, lad, and be sound:
'Twill hurt, but here are salves to friend you,
  And many a balsam grows on ground.

And if your hand or foot offend you,
  Cut it off, lad, and be whole;
But play the man, stand up and end you,
  When your sickness is your soul.

ASL 45 "If it chance your eye offend you"

One entry: B 66.

The eight lines of this poem were written in the form of two quatrains (the one we now read as number 2 drafted at the top of the page) separated by four other unrelated lines. A little more than an inch of B 66 has been cut away, but there is no evidence that any writing has been lost.

The draft occurs on the verso of the page containing the final stanzas of the third draft of *ASL* 44. The content of the quatrain first written on B 66 links it still more closely with the poem that filled the six preceding pages, for the issue debated and settled in the three drafts of *ASL* 44 is taken up anew on B 66—and brought about to a different conclusion.

Without the complementary stanza at the bottom of the page, the one at the top might have survived only as another of the many gnomic fragments Housman scattered throughout his four notebooks. When did he recognize his two stanzas as two halves of a whole? Was the second one held in thought while the first was being written? In order to show the manuscript context, the twelve lines of B 66 are reproduced here.

ASL 45 "If it chance your eye offend you"
Unique Draft

B 66, nearly complete   Date: August or September, 1895
Pencil

<blockquote>

If your hand or foot offend you
   Cut it off, lad, and be whole;
But play the man, stand up and end you
   When your sickness is your soul

But I shall go and come no more
And two and two will still be four.[1]

They would not but they must

I would not but I shall

     If it chance your
Sinner, if your[2] eye offend you
         man,
        lad, and
   Pluck it out, and,[3] so be sound;
       here are salves
'Twill hurt, but earth has balms[4] to friend you
       balsam
   And many a simple[5] grows on ground

</blockquote>

[1] This germinal line may have been in Housman's mind when he wrote in his second entry (B 160) of *LP* 35 ("When first my way to fair I took") the opening line of the concluding stanza:

<blockquote>

To think that two and two are four
   And neither five nor three
The heart of man has been long been sore
   And long 'tis like to be.

</blockquote>

[2] Canc. *Sinner, if your.*

[3] A.E.H. struck out *and,* then superscribed *lad* and put a comma before *so;* he then canceled *so,* setting over it the alt. *and;* lastly he struck out *lad* and wrote above it *man.*

[4] Canc. *earth has balms.*   [5] Canc. *simple.*

46

BRING, in this timeless grave to throw,
No cypress, sombre on the snow;
Snap not from the bitter yew
His leaves that live December through;
Break no rosemary, bright with rime
And sparkling to the cruel clime;
Nor plod the winter land to look
For willows in the icy brook
To cast them leafless round him: bring
No spray that ever buds in spring.

But if the Christmas field has kept
Awns the last gleaner overstept,
Or shrivelled flax, whose flower is blue
A single season, never two;
Or if one haulm whose year is o'er
Shivers on the upland frore,
—Oh, bring from hill and stream and plain
Whatever will not flower again,
To give him comfort: he and those
Shall bide eternal bedfellows
Where low upon the couch he lies
Whence he never shall arise.

ASL 46 "Bring, in this timeless grave to throw"

Two entries: A 84; A 116-17.

Of the first entry of this poem only the opening stanza (ten lines) has survived, the remaining twelve having perished when the lower half of the sheet was cut away. The surviving manuscript, closely written in pencil, is difficult to read beneath the undulating pencil strokes that cover most of the lines. It shows further signs of deterioration, resulting probably from the effects of the mucilage used to affix page 84 to the mounting sheet. Added to these casualties, heavy ink showing through from A 83 unhappily coincides with the endings of the first four lines of the draft, making their obliteration virtually complete.

This entry is of unusual extrinsic interest, as it preserves one of the three *Shropshire Lad* poems entered in Housman's first notebook before the memorable appearance of "The Merry Guide" in September, 1890. This interest is heightened by the fact that Housman wrote his second version of *ASL* 46 on the reverse of the sheet containing the final stanzas of his third draft of "The Merry Guide." His prompt transcription of this early lyric—something he did not do for the other two "pre-1890" pieces—indicates his high regard for it and his intention to bring it into the main stream of his new poetry that had just burst forth with "The Merry Guide."

The copy on A 116 occupies the full page and, according to Laurence Housman's Analysis, extended into A 117, which has not survived. The second draft, however, is complete as it stands: it is in ink, with corrections in ink and pencil, and headed by the penciled title "A winter funeral." The title was not carried into the copy seen by the printer.

The numeral XXXV was originally set over this poem, but it was changed to XLVI before the copy was sent off. The numeral XXXV was, apparently, given to "On the idle hill of summer," which carries that heading in the text. The sheet containing this lyric was missing from the MS of *A Shropshire Lad* when Housman gave it to the library of his College.

ASL 46 "Bring, in this timeless grave to throw"
First Draft

A 84, upper half   Date: Before September, 1890
Pencil

    in
Bring on[1] this [?   ]
No cypress, sombre in the [?];
  Break not
Nor[2] [?] from [?   ]   break not from the yew
The [?   ]   The [?] that lives the winter thro'
T [?   ]   For him that did not, no nor look
Proffers dark sprays all seasons, leave; For willows leafless in the brook[3]
            winter land
Nor plod the frozen fields to look
For willows in the icy brook
  bring   to
To strew[4] them on his funeral: bring
No branch that ever buds in spring.

[1] Canc. *on.*   [2] Canc. *Nor* and the following word.

[3] After *brook* a transfer-line running back to the left column leads to the space above the second line from the bottom. The sequence indicated thus was followed in the second draft.

[4] Canc. *strew* and *on.*

ASL 46 "Bring, in this timeless grave to throw"
Second Draft

A 116, complete   Date: Between September, 1890,
Ink, corrections in pencil   and July, 1891

A winter funeral.

Bring, in this timeless grave to throw,
No cypress, sombre on the snow;
  Snap   frosted
Break[1] not from the bitter yew
       leaf   live lasts
His Its[2] leaves that thrive December through;
Rosemary   brave
  Ivy[3] bring not, bright with rime
      brighter   killing clime   sparkling to
  And braver for the cruel time;   And glistering in the cruel clime
  Nor plod the winter land to look
  For willows in the icy brook
cast strew
  To lay them leafless round him: bring
  No spray that ever buds in spring.

[1] Canc. *Break.*

[2] Canc. *Its.* The alts. *leaf* and *lasts* were intended to be read together.

[3] Canc. *Ivy.* Having superscribed the alt. *Rosemary,* A.E.H. drew a loop around it, brought it down in front of *bright,* and struck the *-t* from *not.* This left the line *Bring no rosemary bright with rime.* Although *bright* was struck out later and replaced by *brave,* it was restored in printer's copy.

has

But if the Christmas fields have[4] kept
Haulms[5]
Straws the last gleaner overstept,
flower is
Or shrivelled flax, whose eye of[6] blue
A single season
Beholds one summer,[7] never two;
Or if one haulm
If any[8] weed whose year is o'er   Or bring some weed whose year is o'er
Shivers on the upland frore,—
hill   hedge
Oh[9] bring from hedge and hill and plain
stream
Whatever will not flower again,
To give him comfort; he and those
Shall bide eternal bedfellows
Where low upon the couch he lies
Whence he never shall arise.

---

[4] Canc. *have* and the *-s* in *fields*.

[5] *Haulms* is lined out, and *Straws* is underlined—a sign of preference rarely found later in the notebooks. A.E.H. wrote *Straws* into his printer's copy, lined it out in favor of *Awns*.

[6] Canc. *eye of*. Toward the right margin he wrote two now illegible alts. for this line and the one following, later canceled them with an undula.

[7] Canc. *Beholds one summer*.

[8] After lining out *If any*, A.E.H. set above a caret its penciled alt., through which he later wrote heavily, in ink, *Or if one*. He struck out *weed* and over a caret following it wrote, in ink, *haulm*. The penciled line at the right, apparently an intermediate alternative, was canceled with an undula.

[9] The spelling was changed to *O*. In printer's copy this line is prefaced with a dash.

47

THE CARPENTER'S SON

"HERE the hangman stops his cart:
Now the best of friends must part.
Fare you well, for ill fare I:
Live, lads, and I will die.

"Oh, at home had I but stayed
'Prenticed to my father's trade,
Had I stuck to plane and adze,
I had not been lost, my lads.

"Then I might have built perhaps
Gallows-trees for other chaps,
Never dangled on my own,
Had I but left ill alone.

"Now, you see, they hang me high,
And the people passing by
Stop to shake their fists and curse;
So 'tis come from ill to worse.

"Here hang I, and right and left
Two poor fellows hang for theft:
All the same's the luck we prove,
Though the midmost hangs for love.

"Comrades all, that stand and gaze,
Walk henceforth in other ways;
See my neck and save your own:
Comrades all, leave ill alone.

"Make some day a decent end,
Shrewder fellows than your friend.
Fare you well, for ill fare I:
Live, lads, and I will die."

ASL 47 "The Carpenter's Son"

Two entries: B 49; B 53-54.

Laurence Housman's Analysis ascribes to B 49 only the last two lines of "The Carpenter's Son." They have survived on a narrow strip cut from the lower half of the page:

> *Fare you well, for ill fare I:*
> *Live, lads, and I will die.*

The date is July or August, 1895. The space, small though it is, remaining above and below the couplet would indicate that it was not composed in context.

The second entry preserves all but one couplet (the first of stanza 6) of the twenty-eight-line poem. The full page B 53 received stanzas 2, 3, 4, and 5 headed by the title the poem carried into print. A narrow strip cut from the top of the facing page bears the opening quatrain; and the last two lines of what we now read as number 6, followed by the final stanza, are on another closely trimmed piece taken from the lower half of the page.

There is a deliberateness in the manuscript, in its carefully formed letters and the regular spacing of the stanzas, that would belong to the product of an afternoon walk that had come near finality before the notebook page was laid open. The draft shows not a little revision, but that was concerned with comparatively minor readjustments. The only noteworthy aberration in the first version of the draft was a false start in the stanza following the one written on B 53 as number 3, where Housman wrote a couplet that was later abandoned.

It may be assumed that while writing the stanza at the head of the second page of the draft, he was consciously composing the opening quatrain of his lyric. The one below the title on the preceding page does not create a satisfactory opening; it is a protest lacking an object; but he did not stop for that until he had filled the remainder of the page with the first fruits of inspiration and needed only two more stanzas to make the protest complete.

In his printer's copy Housman placed quotation marks at the head of the first line and at the end of the last line. Those appearing in the text at the head of the other stanzas were added in the reading of proofsheets. At this time he also set an apostrophe before *Prenticed,* line 6.

ASL 47 "The Carpenter's Son"
Unique Draft

B 53, complete   Date: August, 1895
Pencil

August 1895

The carpenter's son.

Oh, at home had I but stayed
Prenticed to my father's trade,
    Had I stuck to
Shaping planks with[1] plane and adze,
                lost
I had not been here,[2] my lads.

I might then[3]
Then I might have built perhaps
Gallows-trees for other chaps,
Never dangled on my own,
                let
Had I but left[4] ill alone.

    Now, you see, they hang me high,
    And the
     So that[5] people passing by
     Halt upon
    Stand beside[6] the road to curse;
    So 'tis come from bad to worse.

Lock your heart and sink the key[7]
With the millstone in the sea

    Here hang I, and right and left
    Two poor fellows hang for theft;
    They the fruit of stealing prove,—[8]
    Here the midmost hangs for love.
        All the same's the luck we prove,
        Though the midmost hangs for love.

---

[1] Canc. *Shaping planks with.*   [2] Canc. *here.*

[3] These three words were abandoned as soon as written and the new line begun immediately.

[4] Canc. *left.*   [5] Canc. *So that.*   [6] Canc. *Stand beside.*

[7] This couplet was lined out with a high wavy pencil stroke.

[8] Canc. this line and the one following.

ASL 47 "The Carpenter's Son"
Unique Draft continued

B 54, two 1½ inch strips
Pencil

[*Piece 1*]
Now the hangman stops his cart,
And the best of friends must part.
Fare you well, for ill fare I:
      and   shall will
Live, lads, for[1] I must die.

[*Piece 2*]
See my neck and save your own:[2]
      let[3]
Comrades all, leave ill alone.   make a cleaner
                        Then you'll find a decent[4] end,
Have a less unhappy end,   Make some day a decent end,
Wiser fellows than your friend.
Fare you well, for ill fare I:
Live, lads, and I will die.

---

[1] Canc. *for, must,* and *shall.*

[2] Traces of a cut-through line show above this couplet.

[3] A.E.H. here made the same choice in favor of *let* as in the second stanza on B 53—a choice that was reversed in printer's copy.

[4] Having written this line, he struck out *find a decent,* superscribing *make a cleaner;* then after writing the full line below, he canceled all the experimental sketching above it and drew a long pencil stroke through his original line, *Have a less unhappy end. Shrewder,* opening line 2 of the stanza, appeared for the first time in printer's copy.

48

BE still, my soul, be still; the arms you bear are brittle,
  Earth and high heaven are fixt of old and founded strong.
Think rather,—call to thought, if now you grieve a little,
  The days when we had rest, O soul, for they were long.

Men loved unkindness then, but lightless in the quarry
  I slept and saw not; tears fell down, I did not mourn;
Sweat ran and blood sprang out and I was never sorry:
  Then it was well with me, in days ere I was born.

Now, and I muse for why and never find the reason,
  I pace the earth, and drink the air, and feel the sun.
Be still, be still, my soul; it is but for a season:
  Let us endure an hour and see injustice done.

Ay, look: high heaven and earth ail from the prime foundation;
  All thoughts to rive the heart are here, and all are vain:
Horror and scorn and hate and fear and indignation—
  Oh why did I awake? when shall I sleep again?

ASL 48 "Be still, my soul, be still . . ."

Two entries: A 146-47; A 159.

About all we can with certainty say of the shape of the first entry of *ASL* 48 is that the second stanza and part of the third were written on A 146, the first and fourth on the facing page. The writing on both pages is small and crowded, and the destroyed portions of A 146, amounting to one third of the page, could have provided enough room for two stanzas. A strip missing from the top of the page probably contained the opening quatrain; the remainder has survived in two pieces, the upper of which shows stanza 2, standing beneath its numeral, and the numeral 3 just a line's space above a cut-through line. The other piece is blank except for the significant broad-arrow pointing toward a large X. This symbol Housman usually employed at the end of finished poems that had not turned out well—evidence here that the draft on A 146, though not finished, was substantially complete.

Of A 147 a one-inch strip has been cut from the top, and with it one stanza may have been destroyed. The writing on this piece shows every sign of inspiration crowding the pencil: numerous open alternatives, some-times as many as three vying for one position, are ranged above each other, and the space between stanzas was so filled with substitutions that Housman was forced to rewrite his jostled numeral 4 in order to adjust it to the head-ing of the last quatrain.

A 159 preserves a complete, firmly written ink draft of the poem, with several corrections in pencil. Portions of seven lines have been heavily inked over by a later hand. Stanza 3, making here its sole appearance in the drafts, is the only one of the four showing no revision—suggesting that it may have been brought to finality or near it in the first draft, on A 146 or A 147. Of the twelve other lines here, only three show variation from printer's copy, but among these is the often quoted opening line; the third line, linked to it by rhyme, had also to undergo revision during the prepara-tion of the final holograph.

ASL 48 "Be still, my soul, be still . . ."
Fragments

A 146, about one third missing
Pencil

Date: Between January, 1892,
and February, 1893

    unkindness   heartless
      not kindness 2^1 thoughtless
Men loved injustice then, but shapeless in the quarry
    I slept and saw not;[2]
[?   ] in the quarry,

I never [?   ];[3] I did not hate him: might was right;
[   ]; injustice [?   ] I did not mourn:
I recked of naught[4]

Sweat ran and blood sprang out and I was never sorry:
Tears
    Then it was well with me, in days ere I was born.

       3[5]

---

[1] The numeral 2 is in the manuscript.

[2] This is an alt. for the opening of a canceled and now illegible line below.

[3] Canc. this line from *never* to this point.

[4] *I recked of naught* appears to be an alt. which, with some phrases in the right margin, may have been intended to compose the line *I recked of naught, I did not hate him, did not mourn.* Above *I recked of naught* appear two canceled phrases.

[5] Traces of a cut-through line beginning *Now and I* show beneath this numeral. The broad-arrow pointing to the X (perhaps a double X is intended) appears on the second piece of this page approximately at the same distance from the left margin as the position of the numeral 3 shown here.

ASL 48 "Be still, my soul, be still . . ."
First Draft

A 147, nearly complete
Pencil

no help will come of[1]
no profit is in hating
will not mend with grieving
Be still, my soul, be still, it never can be mended:
Earth and high heaven
This heaven and earth were fixt of old and founded strong.
Rather recall   to while the hour of waiting
Be still and call to thought   [?   ]
Think and recall to mind, to speed the while of waiting
The days when we had rest, O soul, for they were long.

Think and tell o'er in thought   4
Think rather, and recall
4
rives
I cannot look; it[2] tears the heart, it sears the brain:
Horror and scorn and hate and fear and indignation,—
Oh why did I awake? when shall I sleep again?
rest

Look forth
But look: high heaven
Look on[3] [?   ] and earth ail from the first creation;
All thoughts[4] [?   ] are vain;
come thick
Horror and scorn and hate and fear and indignation;
Oh why did I awake? when shall I sleep again?

---

[1] This and the two phrases below were written slanting toward the top margin.
[2] *it* was heavily written through *I*.   [3] Canc. *Look on*.
[4] After *thoughts* there is an illegible alt. above the line. Two or three words at the end of this line may have been struck through.
   Laurence remarks of this line (*Recollections,* p. 253) that in one draft of it A.E.H. wrote the following alternatives for *rive* (here erased): *vex, plague, tear, wrench, rend, wring, break, pierce.* Since this collection of words is not extant on any of the surviving manuscripts of the poem, it may be assumed that A.E.H. wrote them on a clipping that has been destroyed—the strip from the head of this page or the one preceding, or (more likely) the section cut from the mid-portion of that page, A 146.

ASL 48 "Be still, my soul, be still . . ."
Second Draft

A 159, complete   Date: Spring of 1893
Ink, corrections in ink and pencil

Be still, my soul, be still; no help will come of hating:
    Earth and high heaven are fixt of old and founded strong.
               'twill
Think rather, and recall, to[1] speed the while of waiting,
Think rather, call to thought—'twill ease the while of waiting—
    The days when we had rest, O soul, for they were long.

                  lightless
Men loved unkindness then, but shapeless[2] in the quarry
            tears fell down
    I slept and saw not; might was right, I did not mourn;
Sweat
    Tears[3] ran and blood sprang out and I was never sorry:
    Then it was well with me, in days ere I was born.

Now, and I muse for why and never find the reason,
    I pace the earth, and drink the air, and feel the sun.
Be still, be still, my soul; it is but for a season:
    Let us endure an hour and see injustice done.

                  High heaven and earth and man
An hour; but   Look how high   prime foundation
Look forth: high[4] heaven and earth ail from the first creation:
      thoughts   wrench
    All pains[5] to rive the heart are here, and all are vain,—
Horror and scorn and hate and fear and indignation:
    Oh why did I awake? when shall I sleep again?

---

[1] A.E.H. penciled *'twill* above *to* and added a comma after *recall;* eventually he struck out the entire line after *rather,* writing the substitute, below, in pencil.

[2] He may have lined out *shapeless.* The same is true of the correction in the following line.

[3] Canc. *Tears. Sweat* is in pencil above a caret.

[4] A.E.H. struck out the first three words of this line and set their alternative above a caret, thus making the line echo the last line of stanza 3. He then canceled *An hour; but* and wrote the substitute *Look how high,* which in turn gave way to *High heaven and earth and man.* Going back to the first form of the line, he extended his cancel-stroke to cover *heaven and earth* and also lined out the last word, writing over the last two the alternative *prime foundation.* Thus only the phrase *ail from the* survived, but it, joined with others chosen from the alternatives above the line, composed the line except for the difference of one word, *Ay,* which was added in printer's copy.

[5] Canc. *pains* and *wrench.*

49

THINK no more, lad; laugh, be jolly:
   Why should men make haste to die?
Empty heads and tongues a-talking
Make the rough road easy walking,
And the feather pate of folly
   Bears the falling sky.

Oh, 'tis jesting, dancing, drinking
   Spins the heavy world around.
If young hearts were not so clever,
Oh, they would be young for ever:
Think no more; 'tis only thinking
   Lays lads underground.

ASL 49 "Think no more, lad; laugh, be jolly"

Two entries: B 12; B 90.

Some two dozen lines arranged in two columns fill the twelfth page of Housman's second notebook. The general air of lighthearted satire which most of them express may have been the reflex of feeling arising from the composition of the full draft of *ASL* 19 ("To an Athlete Dying Young"), which he had just written on the two preceding pages. About one half of the lines on B 12, most of them grouped in couplets or triplets, clearly announce the theme of *ASL* 49, and some contain phrases that went unchanged into the text, e.g., *feather pate of folly* and ... *'tis only thinking / Lays lads under ground.*

The scattered groups of lines on this workshop page afford an opportunity of watching Housman's inventiveness at work; here we may recognize more than one expression that later engendered or became a part of one or another of three poems. Thus *Strip to bathe on Severn shore,* written near the top of the page, entered intact into *ASL* 55 ("Westward on the high-hilled plains"); and in two other entries on B 12 occur phrases that, curiously, echo or foretell parts of two different poems. These are pointed out in the footnotes to the reprint.

The draft on B 90 produced the two full stanzas of the poem. Several lines of it were heavily corrected but, even so, much revising lay between it and the copy forwarded to the printer; for Housman closed his notebook on page 90 with the rhyme pattern of stanza 1 incomplete and two lines in the second stanza canceled and abandoned without alternatives.

ASL 49 "Think no more, lad; laugh, be jolly"
Fragments

B 12, complete   Date: April or May, 1895
Pencil

'Tis because it thinks of nought[1]
That the giddy world goes round

Beer is good, and good are skittles[2]
[   ] 'tis only thinking   'Tis the feather pate of folly
Lays lads under ground   Keeps the head from earth[3]

   the singing   head
'Tis a lightsome heart alone   'Tis the laughing heart alone

Sets   Keeps afoot the sullen bone[4]
Drills to march the sullen bone   lie
That longs to lie in earth   That longs to rot[5] in earth

---

[1] This is the first line in the right column.

[2] Above this line are eleven others, some unfinished. For a complete transcription of this page, see my *Manuscript Poems of A. E. Housman*, pp. 57-58.

[3] A few days later, on B 26, this line and those in the triplet below were echoed in the conclusion of *ASL* 17:

> *Wonder 'tis how little mirth*
> *Keeps the bones of man from lying*
> *On the bed of earth.*

[4] The phrase *sullen bone* and the general significance of these lines and their alternatives to the left may have been recalled from the first draft of *ASL* 43 ("The Immortal Part"), written on A 228-29 in February or March of 1895: ... *flesh and soul, now both are strong, / Shall haul the sullen slaves along.*

[5] Canc. *rot.*

ASL 49 "Think no more, lad; laugh, be jolly"
Unique Draft

B 90, upper two thirds   Date: September or
Pencil   October, 1895

       lad; cheer, be jolly;[1]
Think no more; sit down, be jolly;
    Why should men make haste to die?
Empty heads and tongues a-talking
Make the rough road easy walking,
And   feather pate
'Tis[2] the feathered [mop ?] of folly
    Keeps the head from earth.[3]   Bears the falling sky.

Oh, 'tis laughing, dancing, drinking
    Spins the heavy world around.
  If young fellows would be gay   hearts were always gay,
If young heads were not so clever[4]
Oh, they would be young for aye:
Oh, they would be young for ever:[5]
Think no more; 'tis only thinking
    Lays lads under ground.

[1] Having superscribed the alt., A.E.H. changed the semicolon after *more* to a comma.

[2] Canc. *'Tis* and *feathered* and the word following.   [3] Canc. this line.

[4] A.E.H. struck out this line and superscribed *If young fellows would be gay;* then, leaving *If young* intact, he changed the ending to *hearts were always gay,* but later canceled everything except *hearts,* leaving the line unresolved.

[5] He also canceled this line and mechanically copied it above, only substituting *aye* for *ever,* to accommodate the new rhyme-word *gay* in the line just preceding. Finally *aye* was canceled, and the ending of the line left to the decision of another day.

50

Clunton and Clunbury,
  Clungunford and Clun,
Are the quietest places
  Under the sun.

IN valleys of springs of rivers,
  By Ony and Teme and Clun,
The country for easy livers,
  The quietest under the sun,

We still had sorrows to lighten,
  One could not be always glad,
And lads knew trouble at Knighton
  When I was a Knighton lad.

By bridges that Thames runs under,
  In London, the town built ill,
'Tis sure small matter for wonder
  If sorrow is with one still.

And if as a lad grows older
  The troubles he bears are more,
He carries his griefs on a shoulder
  That handselled them long before.

Where shall one halt to deliver
  This luggage I'd lief set down?
Not Thames, not Teme is the river,
  Nor London nor Knighton the town:

'Tis a long way further than Knighton,
  A quieter place than Clun,
Where doomsday may thunder and lighten
  And little 'twill matter to one.

ASL 50 "In valleys of springs of rivers"

One entry: B 40-41.

The entry consists of two facing pages, the first containing three stanzas, the second, four, of the six-stanza poem. It would seem that Housman, having written the first two quatrains on B 40, humored himself by interposing the four traditional lines (probably in his mind when he put pencil to the page) that make the headpiece of the lyric in the printed text.[1] The well-known stanza, which is not present in the printer's copy, was carefully set down in Housman's smallest hand and duly enclosed in quotation marks. Below it came stanza 3, and the fourth was probably composed at the very bottom of the page, of which an inch-wide strip has been cut away.

Writing his second draft of the lyric, some days or even months afterwards, Housman brought across from B 40 stanzas 1 and 2, making some changes as he did so; then he went on to compose two new quatrains that eventually became 5 and 6 of the text. He did not take the trouble to transcribe stanza 3, nor is there any trace on B 41 of the missing fourth stanza. This page, like the one preceding, has been trimmed at the bottom and there is a strong likelihood, since the lower part of the verso was almost certainly blank, that the missing section of B 41 carried a variant draft of the fourth quatrain.

Housman expended considerable revision on the two drafts of this lyric, and when all was over he had brought it very near its final shape. The fourth stanza aside, only one word makes the difference between printer's copy and the reading of the corrected stanzas on B 40 and 41, although it must be added that in assembling this copy Housman restored one line he had canceled in his second draft and one word from the first.

---

[1] Although A.E.H. declared that the opening quatrain belonged to traditional verse (see Laurence's *Recollections,* p. 195), it was, oddly enough, ascribed to him in the comprehensive editions, including the Penguin reprint (1956) edited by John Sparrow. The indexes generally cited *ASL* 50 not by its first line but by the line *Clunton and Clunbury.* The error was corrected in the Centennial edition (1959).

ASL 50 "In valleys of springs of rivers"
First Draft

B 40, nearly complete   Date: June or July, 1895
Pencil

In valleys of springs of rivers,
    By Oney[1] and Teme and Clun,
The country of[2] quiet livers,
In hamlets of [old ?] long livers,[3]
    The quietest under the sun,

There still were
The [most ?] had[4] troubles to lighten,
    We still had
    One could not be always glad:
            would be   had sorrows   knew sorrow
            were
And lads could be sorry at Knighton[5]
When I was a Knighton lad.[6]

"Clunton and Clunbury
    Clungunford and Clun
Are the quietest places
    Under the sun."

---

[1] So spelled in the two drafts but changed to *Ony* in printer's copy.
[2] *for* was written heavily through *of*.   [3] Canc. this line.
[4] A.E.H. struck out the first three words of this line, writing over a caret *There still were;* then, canceling this, he wrote below the line *We still had.*
[5] Having written the line as shown, A.E.H. canceled *could be* in favor of *were,* which in turn gave way to *would be.* This substitute was also struck out and a different sense made with *had sorrows,* set in over a caret; then this was canceled to allow *knew sorrow* to complete the line, leaving the reading *And lads knew sorrow at Knighton.* At this time, or possibly earlier, the initial *And* was lined out and a capital *L* overwritten on the first letter of *lads.*
[6] Carl J. Weber in a note to this poem in his admirable edition of *A Shropshire Lad* (1946) asks if this line originally read "When I was a Shropshire lad" (p. 119). The answer is no: The title of Housman's first book of poetry was suggested to him by his old college friend, A. W. Pollard; it does not occur in the notebooks.

By bridges that Thames runs under,
  In London, the town built ill,
'Tis sure small matter for wonder
    sorrow[7]   with one
  If trouble is on me still.

                        [?   ] is more[8]

---

[7] Canc. *sorrow* and *on me.*

[8] The ending of this cut-through line, evidently intended as an alternative for something written on the missing strip, is an unmistakable link with line 2 of stanza 4, printed *The troubles he bears are more.*

ASL 50 "In valleys of springs of rivers"
Second Draft

B 41, nearly complete
Pencil

In valleys of springs of rivers,
  By Oney and Teme and Clun,
        easy
The country for quiet[1] livers,
  The quietest under the sun,

                     Still we had loads to lighten,
        trouble[2] burdens
  We still had sorrows to lighten
        for ever
    One could not be always glad,
And lads   sorrow
  Lads[3] knew trouble at Knighton
  When I was a Knighton lad.

           to
     can one halt and[4]   does
Where should the porter deliver   Where can one halt to deliver
        loads   one   The luggage I'd lief set down?
  The luggage that wearies him down?
Not Thames, not Teme is the river,
  Nor London nor Knighton the town.

---

  [1] Canc. *quiet.*

  [2] A.E.H. wrote *trouble* as an alt. for *sorrows,* then wrote *burdens.* After approving the substitute written out toward the margin, he lined out the original line and its alts. In printer's copy the line was restored.

  [3] Canc. *Lads* and *sorrow.*

  [4] Having written this alt., A.E.H. lined out *and,* replacing it with *to.* He then wrote the two lines at the right, in the first canceling *can* in favor of *does* and writing *This* through the first word in the second. Approving these, he struck through the two lines they supplanted, together with their alts., although the words *to* and *one* in the first and second, respectively, by chance escaped.

'Tis long leagues
and[5]   A long way further than Knighton,
'Tis Further than Teme or Knighton,
'Tis a long way further than Knighton,
A quieter place than Clun,
Where doomsday may thunder and lighten
And little 'twill matter to one.

---

[5] After exchanging *and* for *or,* A.E.H. wrote the alt. *A long way* . . . ; then he tested *'Tis long leagues* as a possible opening. All these trials were canceled after he wrote the line below his original (which he finally struck through), where *'Tis* had been set at the head of the line and the *F* of *Further* changed to *f.*

51

LOITERING with a vacant eye
Along the Grecian gallery,
And brooding on my heavy ill,
I met a statue standing still.
Still in marble stone stood he,
And stedfastly he looked at me.
"Well met," I thought the look would say,
"We both were fashioned far away;
We neither knew, when we were young,
These Londoners we live among."

   Still he stood and eyed me hard,
An earnest and a grave regard:
"What, lad, drooping with your lot?
I too would be where I am not.
I too survey that endless line
Of men whose thoughts are not as mine.
Years, ere you stood up from rest,
On my neck the collar prest;
Years, when you lay down your ill,
I shall stand and bear it still.
Courage, lad, 'tis not for long:
Stand, quit you like stone, be strong."
So I thought his look would say;
And light on me my trouble lay,
And I stept out in flesh and bone
Manful like the man of stone.

ASL 51 "Loitering with a vacant eye"

One entry: B 8-9.

The manuscript of this poem filled the larger part of page 8 of the second notebook and the lower two thirds of page 9. The first page now exists in two pieces, the upper containing the opening six lines of the poem, with line 14 set off beneath them—its final word, *not,* tentatively surmounted by *lot,* the rhyming word of line 13.

A half inch of open space remains between this inset and the lower cut margin and suggests that Housman may at one time have considered the first six lines as a stanza in themselves. This question undoubtedly was answered on the section (one and one-half inches) cut from the middle of the page. It probably was taken up with the matter of both stanzas of the printed poem (one line, number 20, exists just below the cut margin of the second piece); but whatever experiments were made on the lost middle section of B 8, Housman produced on the very bottom of the page only the last four lines of what we now read as stanza 1 of the lyric.

The blank upper third of B 9 leads one to believe that the poet in continuing this part of his draft must have had in mind a piece of considerably larger dimensions than the one he produced. A little above the middle of the page he wrote *Still he stood and eyed me hard* and went on to compose the remaining lines of the poem. Of these, 17 and 18 were carefully inscribed parallel to the right margin and headed by a large caret pointing to their proper location.

Whatever slips there may have been between Housman's conception of the poem and its execution, he expressed his dissatisfaction with it by striking two large X's over the lines on B 8 and crossing out in the same manner the contents of the following page. Apparently abandoned (like many other pieces Laurence found in the notebooks and destroyed or erased), this lyric was taken in hand again; and extensive revision, done possibly seven or eight months later when the material of *A Shropshire Lad* was being chosen, reshaped it nearer the form it carried into print.

ASL 51 "Loitering with a vacant eye"
Unique Draft

B 8, middle strip missing   Date: April or May, 1895
Pencil

[*Piece 1*]

Loitering[1]
Moving[2] with a vacant eye
   Along the Grecian
In the Graeco-Roman gallery   brooding
                              thinking on
Moving through the rooms at will[3]   And [   ] my heavy ill
I met a statue standing still.
Still in marble stone stood he
    steadfastly he
And he stood and[4] looked at me.
                  [   ] lot
                 I too would be where I am not

[*Piece 2*]

                          I shall stand and bear it still
                 the look would
'Well met', I thought he meant to[5] say,
'Comrade, well met!' he seemed to say,
                 that meant to say

'We both were fashioned far away;
We neither knew, when we were young,
These Londoners we live among.'

---

[1] An uncharacteristic laxity appears in an undotted *i* in *Loitering;* also in *thinking,*
below, right.

[2] Canc. *Moving.* A now illegible alt. was written above *vacant.*

[3] Canc. this line.   [4] Canc. *he stood and.*

[5] Canc. *he meant to.*

ASL 51 "Loitering with a vacant eye"
Unique Draft continued

B 9, complete
Pencil

> Still he stood and eyed me hard,
> An earnest and a grave regard:
>   drooping
> 'What, lad, fainting[1] with your lot?
> I too would be where I am not.
> I too survey that endless line
> Of men whose thoughts are not as mine.
> Years After when
> Long, when you[2] lay down your ill,
> I shall stand and bear it still.
>   Cheer, my[3]
> Courage, lad, 'tis not for long;
>   Stand
> Stand fast, quit you like stone, be strong'.[4]
> So I thought his look would say;
> And light on me my trouble lay,
>   stepped[5] out
> And I went forth in flesh and bone
> Manful like the man of stone.

Years, ere you stood up from rest,
collar
On my neck the burden[6] prest,

---

[1] Canc. *fainting*.

[2] The opening of the line first read *Long, when you*. . . . Then A.E.H. experimented with substitutes for *Long*, first trying *Years*, then *After*. He finally canceled *After*, leaving *Years when* as the opening; he also canceled the original *Long, when*.

[3] Canc. *Cheer, my*.

[4] The original reading was *Stand fast, quit you*. . . . Having struck out *Stand fast*, he capitalized the first letter of *quit* and lengthened *you* to *yourself*. Not satisfied with this, he rewrote *Stand* above the opening of the line and lined out *self*, leaving the line as we read it now.

[5] *stept* was written through *stepped*.   [6] Canc. *burden*.

52

FAR in a western brookland
That bred me long ago
The poplars stand and tremble
By pools I used to know.

There, in the windless night-time,
The wanderer, marvelling why,
Halts on the bridge to hearken
How soft the poplars sigh.

He hears: no more remembered
In fields where I was known,
Here I lie down in London
And turn to rest alone.

There, by the starlit fences,
The wanderer halts and hears
My soul that lingers sighing
About the glimmering weirs.

ASL 52 "Far in a western brookland"

One entry: A 134-35.

The holograph of *ASL* 52 occupies two complete facing pages, each containing a full draft of the four stanzas of the poem. The earlier draft, written in pencil and much corrected, has suffered heavy erasure and several words of it are no longer legible. Housman wrote it on the verso of the page containing his first draft of "Bredon Hill" (*ASL* 21), and although the two poems are separated in time by six months or more, they are at one in their sense of melancholy and their nostalgic invocation of the *genii loci* in earth and air. It may have been Housman's recommitment to these influences during his absorption in the two drafts of "Far in a western brookland" that turned him to the composition of the second draft of "Bredon Hill" only six pages later, on A 142-43.

The later draft of *ASL* 52 was written in ink and, despite efforts to obliterate portions of lines 1 and 13, every word of the manuscript has survived. It shows several corrections in pencil and bears the penciled date "1891-2."

ASL 52 "Far in a western brookland"
First Draft

A 134, complete   Date: Late 1891 or early 1892
Pencil, much corrected

<pre>
                    cloven
      Far   distant
      Deep in a [?   ] brookland
      Far in a patterned ploughland¹
                loved² long
      That bred me years ago
      The poplars stand and tremble³
        By pools I used to know.
</pre>

<pre>
              when the night is windless,   night-time
      There, in the windless midnight,⁴   in the windless midnight
                        wandering
        The traveller[s?] passing by⁵ The wanderer marvelling why
      Halts
      Pause[s]⁶ on the bridge to hearken
          How soft the poplars sigh.
</pre>

<pre>
              long
              clean
      He hearkens; long⁷ forgotten
        In all that⁸ country [round ?]   Here I lie down in London
      I lay me down in slumber⁹ to slumber With [?   ] leagues around.
          With [?   ]¹⁰ [?   round.]
</pre>

¹ Canc. this line and the one above, together with the other alts., except *Far* and *brookland*. The first syllable of this latter word was heavily written through *plough*.

² Canc. *loved* and *years*. Another alt., now illegible, was added over a caret in front of *ago*.

³ The first letter of this word, *tremble*, is written through the initial—*s*—of a word A.E.H. originally intended here.

⁴ After deleting *in the windless midnight* and the alt. he had written above, he rewrote at the end his original phrase, finally canceling *midnight* in favor of *night-time*.

⁵ Canc. this line and the alt., above. The ending of the second word cannot be certainly read, but the form was probably plural as the first word of the next line must have been *Pause* rather than *Pauses,* which would have marred the rhythm.

⁶ Canc. *Pause[s?]* A.E.H. wrote the alt. *Halts* to read with *wanderer,* in the alt. line to the right, above.

⁷ Canc. *long* and *clean*.   ⁸ Canc. *In all that.*

⁹ Canc. this line and a now illegible alt., above the middle.

¹⁰ Above this line A.E.H. wrote a now illegible alt. and another at the end of the line; all three were deleted.

There, by the starlit palings,
      wanderer
  The traveller halts and hears
      lingers
My soul that wanders sighing
  About the glimmering meres.

ASL 52 "Far in a western brookland"
Second Draft

A 135, complete
Ink, corrections in pencil

western brookland
Far in a cloven ploughland[1]
That bred me long ago
The poplars stand and tremble
streams[2]
By pools I used to know.

There, in the windless night-time,
The wanderer marvelling why
Halts on the bridge to hearken
How soft the poplars sigh.

He hears: long since forgotten[3]
In fields where I was known,
Here I lie down
I lay me down in London[4]
dreams
And turn to rest alone.[5]

There, by the starlit palings,[6] fences,
The wanderer halts and hears
My soul that lingers sighing
About the glimmering weirs.

1891-2.

[1] Canc. *cloven ploughland.*

[2] Canc. *streams* and a now illegible alt. below *pools.*

[3] The last three words of this line went into print as shown here and stood unchanged through a number of reprintings until 1922, when A.E.H. substituted *no more remembered.* (See Grant Richards, *Memoir,* pp. 264-65.)

[4] A light pencil stroke was drawn through this line. After *London* there are some erased pencil traces.

[5] This line was struck through like the one just preceding. One or two penciled alts. below *rest* have been obliterated.

[6] Canc. *palings.*

53

THE TRUE LOVER

THE lad came to the door at night,
When lovers crown their vows,
And whistled soft and out of sight
In shadow of the boughs.

"I shall not vex you with my face
Henceforth, my love, for aye;
So take me in your arms a space
Before the east is grey.

"When I from hence away am past
I shall not find a bride,
And you shall be the first and last
I ever lay beside."

She heard and went and knew not why;
Her heart to his she laid;
Light was the air beneath the sky
But dark under the shade.

"Oh do you breathe, lad, that your breast
Seems not to rise and fall,
And here upon my bosom prest
There beats no heart at all?"

"Oh loud, my girl, it once would knock,
You should have felt it then;
But since for you I stopped the clock
It never goes again."

"Oh lad, what is it, lad, that drips
Wet from your neck on mine?
What is it falling on my lips,
My lad, that tastes of brine?"

"Oh like enough 'tis blood, my dear,
For when the knife has slit
The throat across from ear to ear
'Twill bleed because of it."

Under the stars the air was light
But dark below the boughs,
The still air of the speechless night,
When lovers crown their vows.

ASL 53 "The True Lover"

One entry: A 210-13.

This single entry contains two drafts of the poem, each on two facing pages. In composing the first, on A 210-11, Housman may have turned back and forth between the two pages, using the verso as a trial field for stanzas that crystallized too rapidly for their proper sequence to be immediately determined and for others that he knew would require considerable revision if accepted. Remains of a severed line at the top of A 210 indicate that one or two quatrains may have been lost with a missing strip. Four stanzas (1, 6, 7, and 8) are preserved on this page; the first is intact and passed on into print without the change of a word, although a second version of it was written on A 212.

The holograph of the second page consists of two closely written columns: the first contains stanzas 1, 2, 4, 5, and 9 (Housman left after stanza 5 a two- or three-stanza space, probably intending to bring quatrains 6, 7, and 8 across from A 210, but having used part of the room for a version of the ninth stanza, he did not transfer the three earlier stanzas); the second column received a stanza later abandoned, then number 3 and the last two lines of 5, followed by two versions of the ninth, with the date "December 1894" crowding the margin.

Except for some doubt as to the position intended for the stanza we now read as the third, it is clear that the sequence of the nine quatrains was settled on A 211. The same is not true of the language of the poem, for only stanza 3 reached finality there. Many signs of uncertainty appear in the others; some show two lines canceled with no alternatives in view, others with open alternatives in two or more lines.

However, when Housman began his second draft a few days later, most of the irresolutions carrying over from the first had disappeared or were overcome during the writing of the near fair copy he produced on A 212-13. Only one quatrain, the fourth, required extensive reshaping; when that was done, the lyric was within a few words of the copy received by the printer.

ASL 53 "The True Lover"
First Draft

A 210, nearly complete   Date: December, 1894
Pencil

The lad came to the door at night,[1]
When lovers crown their vows,
And whistled soft and out of sight
In shadow of the boughs

[?   ] loud 'twould knock;
Last night, love, loud enough 'twould knock;   Oh loud, my love, it once would knock
          My girl, last night I [?   ] Last night you might have heard it knock
[?   ] we heard it knock;[2]
Oh loud enough it used to knock   My girl, last night I felt it knock,
          You should have felt it then.   You could have heard it then.
          But since for you I stopped the clock
          It never goes again."

                                        "Oh lad, what is it, lad, that drips
                                              Wet
                                          Down[3] from your neck on mine?
Oh lad, what is it [?   ] neck[4]   What is it falling on my lips,
[?   ] so soft on mine?"   My lad, that tastes of brine?"

          'Tis
"Why, "Why,[5] like enough 'tis blood, my dear;
          For when the knife has slit
          The throat across from ear to ear
          It [bleeds because ?] of it."[6]
          It [?   ]
          'Twill bleed because of it.

---

[1] Remains of a heavily erased line appear between this line and the margin.
[2] Of this line and its many alts. (most, heavily erased) A.E.H. apparently deleted nothing but this line through *we* and possibly two or three words above *last night* in the last alt., to the right, below.
[3] Canc. *Down.*   [4] Canc. this line and the next one, below.
[5] After deleting *Why* and *'Tis,* he rewrote *Why* at the head of the line.
[6] Canc. this line, together with an alt. above the second word. The second alt. line, below, was also deleted.

ASL 53 "The True Lover"
First Draft continued

A 211, complete
Pencil

He whistled soft and out of sight	his She rose, she followed at the call,
	And
In shadow of the boughs.	She knew not why nor how.
	boy
"Come down, my girl, for now is night,	"I never loved the man at all:
And lovers crown their vows."[1]	What takes me to him now?"[2]

"I shall not vex you with my face
       love
Again, my girl, for aye:
So take me in your arms a space
    Before the east is grey.

She came, she knew not how nor why;	When I from hence away am past
head to	
Her hand in his she laid;	I shall not find a bride;
lips to	
And it under	
The air was light beneath[3] the sky	And you shall be the first and last
And	
But dark beneath the shade	I ever lay beside."

breast	
"Oh do you breathe, lad, that your chest[4]	
Seems not to rise and fall,	
with my head against	here my
And at my ear beneath your breast[5]	And close[6] upon your bosom prest
I hear	There beats
There beats no heart at all."	I feel no heart[7] at all?"

---

[1] Having struck through every line of this stanza, A.E.H. drew a high undula over it.

[2] This stanza, seemingly written immediately after the one to the left, contained the germ of the third quatrain in the left column—later, stanza 4. A.E.H. deleted this stanza as he had the one opposite it.

[3] Canc. *beneath*.   [4] Canc. *chest*.

[5] Canc. this line and the one below, together with their alts., above and right.

[6] Canc. *close* and *your*.   [7] *heart* was penciled heavily over another word.

Under the stars
Beyond the tree the air
The air beyond the tree was light[8]
below
But dark beneath[9] the boughs,
The still air of the speechless night,
When lovers crown their vows.

Beyond the tree the moon made light,
But none beneath the boughs,
And all was in the whispering night,
When lovers crown their vows.

Beyond the tree the air was light,
But night beneath the boughs,
The season of the whispering night,[10]
When lovers crown their vows.

December 1894.

[8] After writing this line, A.E.H. struck through all but *was light,* writing above the opening of the line the substitute *Beyond the tree the air,* of which he deleted all but *the air.* The replacement *Under the stars,* followed stairwise down through the un-canceled endings, making the line that went into print.

[9] Canc. *beneath.*

[10] Canc. this line and the one following. A.E.H. also struck two diagonal lines through the stanza and similarly deleted the one to the left, besides striking through each line of it.

ASL 53 "The True Lover"
Second Draft

A 212, complete   Date: December, 1894
Pencil

> The lad came to the door at night,
>   When lovers crown their vows,
> And whistled soft and out of sight
>   In shadow of the boughs.
>
> "I shall not vex you with my face
>   Henceforth, my love, for aye;
> So take me in your arms a space
>   Before the east is grey.
>
> "When I from hence away am past
>   I shall not find a bride,
> And you shall be the first and last
>   I ever lay beside."

```
                                   and      and
                      She heard, she went, she knew not why;
            and       and
She heard, she went, she knew not why;¹
      His face she could not see
Her eyes [          ?          ]²   Her heart to his she laid.
The air was light beneath the sky³   within
          beneath the tree         beneath the shade.
But dark within the shade.⁴        under
```

> "Oh do you breathe, lad, that your breast
>   Seems not to rise and fall,
> And here upon my bosom prest
>   There beats no heart at all?"

¹ Having written this line, A.E.H. lined out all of it but *went* and later the alternative *and*'s above *she . . . she.* The alts. were left open in the line rewritten to the right, above.

² Canc. this line and its alt., above.

³ This line was carried into printer's copy as shown, but, probably to vary the rhythm, A.E.H. there deleted *The air was light* in favor of *Light was the air.*

⁴ Canc. *within the shade* and the alt., above. In the alt. ending, to the right, *beneath* and *within* were lined out.

ASL 53 "The True Lover"
Second Draft continued

A 213, complete
Pencil

> Oh loud, my girl, it once would knock;
> 　You should have felt it then.
> But since for you I stopped the clock
> 　It never goes again."
>
> "Oh lad, what is it, lad, that drips
> 　Wet from your neck on mine?
> What is it falling on my lips,
> 　My lad, that tastes of brine?"
>
> Oh like enough 'tis blood, my dear,
> 　For when the knife has slit
> The throat across from ear to ear
> 　'Twill bleed because of it."
>
> Under
> Beneath
> Under[1] the stars the air was light
> 　But dark below the boughs,
> The still air of the speechless night,
> 　When lovers crown their vows.

[1] A.E.H. canceled *Under,* superscribing *Beneath,* but this was in turn deleted and *Under* restored.

54

WITH rue my heart is laden
    For golden friends I had,
For many a rose-lipt maiden
    And many a lightfoot lad.

By brooks too broad for leaping
    The lightfoot boys are laid;
The rose-lipt girls are sleeping
    In fields where roses fade.

ASL 54 "With rue my heart is laden"

Laurence's Analysis records for A 155-57 " 'With rue my heart is laden' (dated Aug. 1893) and fragments." He seems to be in error here, however, for all of these pages have survived complete, and they do not contain the poem or any traces of it. A 155 carries an ink draft of *ASL* 39 dated February, 1893; A 156, two dissociated quatrains, the lower half of the page blank; A 157 was headed with some metric signs and a partly canceled couplet, the rest of the page blank; and A 158 was filled with an ink draft of *ASL* 32. The Library of Congress index of the notebooks carries under the entry for "With rue my heart is laden" the comment "No manuscript found." It is probable that the eight-line lyric was overlooked on a crowded page of fragments and destroyed, or it may have been abstracted from the notebook remains between the time they were being prepared for sale and the date of their arrival at the Library of Congress.

In preparing copy for the printer Housman spelled *roselipt* as a solid word in lines 3 and 7 but later carefully inserted a hyphen between the two syllables.

55

WESTWARD on the high-hilled plains
　　Where for me the world began,
Still, I think, in newer veins
　　Frets the changeless blood of man.

Now that other lads than I
　　Strip to bathe on Severn shore,
They, no help, for all they try,
　　Tread the mill I trod before.

There, when hueless is the west
　　And the darkness hushes wide,
Where the lad lies down to rest
　　Stands the troubled dream beside.

There, on thoughts that once were mine,
　　Day looks down the eastern steep,
And the youth at morning shine
　　Makes the vow he will not keep.

ASL 55 "Westward on the high-hilled plains"

Three entries: A 221; B 12; B 20-21.

The first entries of this poem are two faint adumbrations which, although written amid dissociated fragments jotted down weeks before the poem was seriously taken in hand, embodied three lines that were carried into print unchanged.

The earlier of the two occurs at the top of A 221, written in January or February, 1895:

> *And the youth at morning shine*
> *Makes the vow he will not keep*

These two lines became the conclusion of the lyric.

The second entry, written three or four months later, is on B 12, which is a remarkable page of fragments that must have been long remembered, for Housman returned to them in the making of at least four completed poems. Here occurs the line *Strip to bathe on Severn shore,* which became number 6 of *ASL* 55.

Only a few days after filling in B 12, he came to grips with his poem on B 20, which still preserves the last three stanzas, complete but for the second line of the third. A missing strip from the top of the page probably contained the opening quatrain. At the same sitting or a few days later— Notebook B shows signs of rapid composition in these opening pages— Housman wrote the first stanza at the top of B 21, copying with corrections, it is likely, from B 20; then, leaving a blank space for stanza 2, which had been brought to finality in the first draft, he set down a full revision of the third quatrain. As for the final stanza, he had before him on B 20 an intact draft except for an open alternative in the first line, which he had written *There to clearer eyes than mine.* But could he admit that there would be clearer eyes than his? He had set *later* over that invidious adjective, which nevertheless found its way into an alternative for the first revise of the line on B 21, but which was superseded by *There on thoughts that once were mine,* leaving the poem within one word of the printed version.

In the printer's copy the opening line of stanza 3 was taken from the second draft but, questioning *ashen,* A.E.H. penciled above it *hueless*— used, I believe, in his first draft—then canceled *ashen* and retraced his alt. in ink.

ASL 55 "Westward on the high-hilled plains"
First Draft

B 20, lower three fourths   Date: May or June, 1895

Pencil

[?]
lads
Now that other men¹ than I
    Strip to bathe on Severn shore
They, I [?   ] think,   no help,
    Other men, for all they try²   They must needs, for all they try
                mill
                round
    Tread the [road ?]³ I trod before.

There when [hueless ?] down the west⁴

Still above the sleeping breast
    Bends the troubled dream beside.
                later
        There to clearer eyes than mine
            Day looks down the eastern steep,
        And the youth at morning shine
            Makes the vow he will not keep.

---

¹ *lads* was heavily penciled through *men*. Canc. two alts. above *men*.

² A.E.H. first wrote *Other men, for all they try*, which would have carried an unfortunate echo from line 1. He canceled *Other men* and set above it the alt. as shown; then *think* was substituted for the now illegible verb. At last, having struck out *I*, he moved over to the right and wrote the new version of the line. After *must needs* was replaced by the phrase *no help*, the line required only a comma after *They*.

³ Canc. [*road?*] and *round*.   ⁴ The line is struck through.

ASL 55 "Westward on the high-hilled plains"
Second Draft

B 21, complete   Date: May or June, 1895
Pencil

high-hilled

Westward on the hills and[1] plains
   Where for me the world began
      be sure,   for sure,
Still, I think,[2] in newer veins   , I think,
      changeless
   Frets the ancient[3] blood of man.

There, when ashen is the west
      darkness
   And the twilight hushes wide,   silence settles
   Still where
Sure as lads lie down to rest[4]   Where the lad lies down to rest
   Stands the troubled dream beside.
        clearer [?] than mine
   There to eyes that wake like mine
There on thoughts that once were mine

---

[1] Canc. *hills and.*   [2] Canc. *I think* and *for sure.*   [3] Canc. *ancient.*
  [4] After experimenting with the alt. *Still where,* A.E.H. wrote out the alt. line to the right and canceled all of the other matter in the line.

56

THE DAY OF BATTLE

"FAR I hear the bugle blow
To call me where I would not go,
And the guns begin the song,
'Soldier, fly or stay for long.'

"Comrade, if to turn and fly
Made a soldier never die,
Fly I would, for who would not?
'Tis sure no pleasure to be shot.

"But since the man that runs away
Lives to die another day,
And cowards' funerals, when they come,
Are not wept so well at home,

"Therefore, though the best is bad,
Stand and do the best, my lad;
Stand and fight and see your slain,
And take the bullet in your brain."

ASL 56 "The Day of Battle"

One entry: A 236-37.

This entry consists of a rough draft in pencil and an ink copy, dated March, 1895, which but for minor differences in four lines presents the four quatrains of the poem as we now read them. Neither draft is complete. Of the first, the second stanza was destroyed when the middle third of the page was cut out; of the second, the first version of the fourth line of stanza 2 disappeared when a similar operation was performed on A 237.

The concluding couplet of quatrain 1 of the earlier draft has been heavily erased, but enough of one alternative remains to show that the poem was intended to be read as a conversation between the poet-soldier and his heart, or his second self. It is unfortunate that the remainder of the poem was not in its later stages kept in line with this original dialogue pattern, which was also clearly written into the third stanza of the first draft. In the text, the meaning of the word *Comrade* (line 5) is confused; it seems to address the voice that pronounces *"Soldier, fly or stay for long."*[1] And that is the message not of the speaker's heart but of the guns (line 3). Housman in his second draft copied from the first the saving phrase *in my heart,* but —tempted by alliteration?—altered it to read *the guns,* which carried into his final transcription. While handling proof he enclosed the entire poem in quotation marks, thus steering farther away from his original dialogue pattern, and leaving *Comrade* quite unintelligible, or at the least ambiguous.

---

[1] Cf. the ending of *MP* 13:

> My kind and foolish comrade
> That breathes all night for me.

ASL 56 "The Day of Battle"
First Draft

A 236, middle third missing   Date: March, 1895
Pencil

[*Piece 1*]

Far I hear the bugle blow
    us
To call me[1] where I would not go,
And the [?   ] begin   in my heart
Forth [.]   And the drums[2] begin the song
                      'Soldier, fly or stay for long'.

[*Piece 2*]

But since the man that runs away
Lives to die another day,
And cowards' funerals, when they come,
Are not wept so well at home,

      Therefore, though the best is bad,
We'll Stand fast and
      We both must[3] do the best, my lad:
So charge   fast[4]   tread
      Stand, and kill and see your slain
      And take the bullet in your brain.

[1] Canc. *me*. The *us* A.E.H. preferred here fits (like *We* in stanza 3) with the two-part nature of the poem as he first conceived it.

[2] Canc. *the drums*. The letter *-s* was added to *begin* after the alt. was written above.

[3] After canceling *We both must*, A.E.H. wrote above it *Stand fast and*. Later he deleted *fast* and left the alt. *We'll stand and*, with the first letter of *Stand* reduced to lower case. At one time the removal of *fast* made way for *Stand fast and* in the following line.

[4] Over a caret he added *fast* to follow *stand*, but canceled both words when he opened the line with *So charge; see* was lined out.

ASL 56 "The Day of Battle"
Second Draft

A 237, nearly complete
Ink; title, date, and corrections in pencil

[*Piece 1*]

March 1895

The day of battle.

Far I hear the bugle blow
         me
To call us[1] where I would not go,
       the guns
And in my heart[2] begins the song
'Soldier, fly or stay for long.'

Comrade, if for once to fly
Would make a soldier never die,
          you, I guess,   and who would not?
Fly I would, and I can tell[3]

[*Piece 2*]

'Tis sure no pleasure to be shot.

But since the man that runs away
Lives to die another day,
And cowards' funerals, when they come,
Are not wept so well at home,

Therefore, though the best is bad,
Stand   We'll stand[4] and do the best, my lad;
                see
Charge So charge[5] and kill and tread your slain
And take the bullet in your brain.

---

[1] Canc. *us.*   [2] Canc. *in my heart* and the *-s* in *begins.*
[3] Canc. *I can tell* and its alt.   [4] Canc. *We'll stand.*
[5] Canc. *So charge* and *tread.*

57

YOU smile upon your friend to-day,
    To-day his ills are over;
You hearken to the lover's say,
    And happy is the lover.

'Tis late to hearken, late to smile,
    But better late than never:
I shall have lived a little while
    Before I die for ever.

ASL 57 "You smile upon your friend to-day"

Two entries: A 164; B 51-52.

The Analysis describes A 164 as containing a rough draft of this poem, "all but the last verse cancelled." The concluding quatrain is the only portion of the draft that has survived; it is on a fragment only slightly larger than the tiny bloc of manuscript it preserves. The language of the stanza is identical with that of the text.

When Housman returned to the poem, perhaps all of two years later, he apparently began his second draft with the indecision that had caused him to abandon it on A 164. The manuscript on the top section of B 51 (the lower half has been destroyed) shows a fair copy of the second quatrain, but the first, overscored with many cancel-lines and alternatives, is still short of completeness. The poet's effort to get the stanza he wanted was continued as far as the top of B 52, where he made a final but still inconclusive essay at the opening two lines of the poem. Not until the preparation of his final copy, apparently, was the second line determined.

ASL 57 "You smile upon your friend to-day"
First Draft

A 164, fragment   Date: Between February, 1893,
Pencil   and August, 1894

'Tis late to hearken, late to smile,[1]
But better late than never:
I shall have lived a little while
Before I die for ever.

---

[1] The upper margin shows traces of a cut-through line.

Second Draft

B 51, upper half   Date: July or August, 1895
Pencil

July 1895

upon your friend today,
You smile, your words are kind[1] today,
You smile today, you hearken now[2]   So now his ills are over
    all   his ills   So all his trouble's over
So sighs[3] and griefs are over;
    hearken to   say
You [give again ?][4] the lover's vow,   You listen now the lover's say[5]
And happy is the lover.

listen
'Tis late to hearken, late to smile,
But better late than never:
I shall have lived a little while
Before I die for ever.

---

[1] Canc. *your words are kind.*   [2] Canc. this line.
[3] Canc. *sighs.*   [4] Canc. the two words in the bracketed space and *vow.*
[5] The use of *listen* and *say* in this line will serve as a reminder that A.E.H. wrote into his drafts many more archaisms than he sent into print. (He may have recalled *listen* from Tennyson.)

ASL 57 "You smile upon your friend to-day"
Fragment

B 52, complete
Pencil

    Your looks are kind,
      Oh
    Now you look kind,[1] you smile today,
      So now my ills are over;

[1] Canc. *Now you look kind* and the alt. *Oh,* above.

58

WHEN I came last to Ludlow
    Amidst the moonlight pale,
Two friends kept step beside me,
    Two honest lads and hale.

Now Dick lies long in the churchyard,
    And Ned lies long in jail,
And I come home to Ludlow
    Amidst the moonlight pale.

ASL 58 "When I came last to Ludlow"

One entry: B 45.

The two stanzas of this poem, dated "July 1895," occupy the upper half (all that has survived) of B 45. The first stanza, like the corresponding stanza of *ASL* 57, exhibits many signs of revision, suggesting that still further versions may have been attempted on the missing lower section of the page. Line 3 proved to be the greatest stumbling block: seldom—in fact, only on the following page, where line 7 of *ASL* 16 shows nine different versions—does one find a single line so often rewritten. When he closed his notebook on B 45, Housman had among a patchwork of alternatives and interlineations at least three surviving readings of the third line to arbitrate. The second stanza apparently flowed without hesitation and in this unique holograph equates the text.

In composing printer's copy he tentatively penciled above the poem the title "The Return of the Native," liked it, and traced it over in ink. However, the title was abandoned during the handling of proof.

ASL 58 "When I came last to Ludlow"
Unique Draft

B 45, upper half   Date: July, 1895
Pencil

                                                                July 1895

                    I came last
            When last I came[1] to Ludlow
                Amidst the moonlight pale,   stepped out
        There trod   alongside   kept step
            I had two friends to talk to,[2]   walk with   beside me,
                Two honest lads   A pair of friends
                And both free men[3] and hale.   Two friends of mine beside me
                                                  Kept step, clean lads and hale.

            Now Dick lies long in the churchyard
                And Ned lies long in jail
            And I come home to Ludlow
                Amidst the moonlight pale.

---

[1] Canc. *last I came*

[2] This line seems to have developed thus: After writing the line as shown, A.E.H. tried out two alts. for the ending of the line, *alongside* and *walk with*. Going back to the head of the line, he set *There trod* above *I had,* and lined out *to talk to* and *walk with.* After *walk with* he wrote *beside me* and canceled *alongside,* leaving the readings *There trod two friends beside me* and *I had two friends beside me.* He struck out *I had* and *There trod,* made the initial of *two* a capital, and wrote *kept step* above *walk with.* Now the line read *Two friends kept step beside me*—the reading of the text. Above *kept step* he wrote the alt. *stepped out,* which was eventually deleted. At the end of the fourth line he wrote *Two friends of mine beside me,* which with an alt. opening was left uncanceled.

[3] Canc. *And both free men.*

59

THE ISLE OF PORTLAND

THE star-filled seas are smooth to-night
   From France to England strown;
Black towers above the Portland light
   The felon-quarried stone.

On yonder island, not to rise,
   Never to stir forth free,
Far from his folk a dead lad lies
   That once was friends with me.

Lie you easy, dream you light,
   And sleep you fast for aye;
And luckier may you find the night
   Than ever you found the day.

ASL 59 "The Isle of Portland"

One entry: A 192.

Like the unique draft of *ASL* 45 ("If it chance your eye offend you"), on B 66, the single entry of this poem was composed on a page that now exhibits a large proportion of random jottings. After inscribing the three stanzas of his poem on the upper portion of A 192, Housman filled the remainder of the page with a couplet later incorporated into *ASL* 26 as lines 9 and 10 of that poem, followed by the quatrain "When Adam first the apple ate,"[1] and three or four other scattered lines. The title, "The Isle of Portland," squeezed between the upper margin and an alternative line, seems to have been a last-minute addition to the holograph. The first two quatrains required extensive revision, but the third shows no reshaping and passed unchanged into print.

The fact that this poem was composed on the reverse of the page bearing *ASL* 8 ("Farewell to barn and stack and tree") is a reminder that the story of the fratricide must have been in the poet's mind as he described the felon's burial of the lad *That once was friends with me.* It was with a more deliberate gesture that, while selecting and putting in order the lyrics that would make up *A Shropshire Lad,* he put *ASL* 59 immediately after "When I came last to Ludlow," as a supplement to the poem it so closely resembles in mood and allusion—one of his few concessions to thematic design.

[1] Published in my *Manuscript Poems of A. E. Housman,* p. 48.

ASL 59 "The Isle of Portland"
Unique Draft

A 192, complete
Pencil

Date: Between August and
December, 1894

The Isle of Portland.

      star-filled
     The heaven-filled² seas are smooth tonight,
The wind at sea from France tonight¹ From France to England strown;
  Is soft to England blown;
Black towers above
  High juts behind³ the Portland light
   The felon-quarried stone.

     On
     In⁴ yonder Island, not to rise,
       step
     Never to go forth free,   Never to stir forth free,
    Before his time set free⁵
      folk
   Far from his home⁶ a dead lad lies
    That once was⁷ friends with me.

Lie you easy, dream you light,
  And sleep you fast for aye;
And luckier may you find the night
  Than ever you found the day.

---

¹ Canc. this line and the one following.   ² Canc. *heaven-filled*.
³ Canc. *High juts behind*.
⁴ Canc. *In*. The capital *I* in *island* was reduced to lower case.
⁵ Canc. this line and *go* in the alt. line.   ⁶ Canc. *home*.
  ⁷ Housman's rapid pencil—crowded by the already perfected final stanza?—began after *once* the first letter of *friends*. He brushed off the top and bottom of the perpendicular and wrote *was* without loss of space.

60

Now hollow fires burn out to black,
    And lights are guttering low:
Square your shoulders, lift your pack,
    And leave your friends and go.

Oh never fear, man, nought's to dread,
    Look not left nor right:
In all the endless road you tread
    There's nothing but the night.

ASL 60 "Now hollow fires burn out to black"

One entry: A 207.

Like the page containing "The Isle of Portland," A 207 is a crowded and diversified page, the first third of it containing a much-corrected draft of *ASL* 60 and the remainder filled with three of the four stanzas of *MP* 31 ("Because I liked you better"). These stanzas are accompanied with the X-and-trail that Housman used to designate pieces he had rejected in making the collection of materials for *A Shropshire Lad*.

The legibility of the eight lines of *ASL* 60, left sufficiently difficult by the poet's cancellations, has been further impaired by later erasures, and the restoration of parts of three lines is conjectural. It appears that Housman abandoned the poem without reaching a satisfactory version of the opening line, but all save one of the remaining lines, in their original or corrected reading, show in this holograph the forms they carried into print.

The sheet bearing this poem in printer's copy was once headed by the numeral LXIV, indicating that Housman at one time meant it to be the next-to-last number in his book. (The MSS of *A Shropshire Lad,* it should be remembered, originally numbered sixty-five pieces.) This arrangement would have put two poems of leave-taking at the end, and it may be assumed that he would not have disturbed this arrangement but for the desirability of finding a place near the end for his longest poem, "Terence, this is stupid stuff." So it and another piece for which no location had been designated—"Hughley Steeple"—were put in between "Now hollow fires burn out to black" and the poem that had probably been long since elected to be the last, "I hoed and trenched and weeded."

Having interposed "Hughley Steeple" and "Terence . . . ," each now headed with its proper numeral, Housman went back to alter LXIV over "Now hollow fires . . ." to XLII. The fact that the two inserted pieces had not up to this moment been numbered indicates that Housman had been seeking places for them as the sheets of his printer's copy accumulated and that the near-terminal location of the two pieces we now read as 61 and 62 was a last-minute decision—the result of necessity, not of design.

ASL 60 "Now hollow fires burn out to black"
Unique Draft

A 207, complete   Date: Between August and
Pencil   December, 1894

[faded ?]
Now hollow fires are [fallen ?] to black[1]
grow[2]
Now is the time when fires [?   ] black
  And lights are burning low:
Square your shoulders, lift your pack,
            leave your friends   take my hand
  And here's my hand,[3] and go.   And say goodbye, and go.
                                           [night ?]

Oh, never fear, man;
            Never fear, man; nought's to dread;
            Step out, man; [?   ] dread;[4]
            nor
  Look not left or[5] right:
            to
In all the endless road you'll[6] tread
There's nothing but the night.

---

[1] The position of this line, crowded against the margin, suggests that it was written as the alternative. There are other pencil traces in the right corner, some apparently lined out. The word *to* was deleted, together with the alt. above the preceding word.

[2] In front of *grow* A.E.H. wrote another now illegible alt.

[3] Canc. *here's my hand* and probably all the alts. at the end of the line.

[4] Having begun the line *Step out, man,* he superscribed *Never fear, man,* but lined this out. Going into the left margin, he penciled *Oh, never fear, man;* then, passing over to the end of the line, he wrote the alt. *nought's to dread.* The original opening of the line may have been left uncanceled, but the last two or three words of it were struck through.

[5] Canc. *or.*

[6] A.E.H. struck off the *'ll* of this word and canceled the alt. *to.*

61

HUGHLEY STEEPLE

THE vane on Hughley steeple
   Veers bright, a far-known sign,
And there lie Hughley people,
   And there lie friends of mine.
Tall in their midst the tower
   Divides the shade and sun,
And the clock strikes the hour
   And tells the time to none.

To south the headstones cluster,
   The sunny mounds lie thick;
The dead are more in muster
   At Hughley than the quick.
North, for a soon-told number,
   Chill graves the sexton delves,
And steeple-shadowed slumber
   The slayers of themselves.

To north, to south, lie parted,
   With Hughley tower above,
The kind, the single-hearted,
   The lads I used to love.
And, south or north, 'tis only
   A choice of friends one knows,
And I shall ne'er be lonely
   Asleep with these or those.

ASL 61 "Hughley Steeple"

One entry: A 193.

The unique draft of "Hughley Steeple" just fills the notebook page, with some crowding of the lower margin, where the last four lines of the poem were rewritten. Stanza 1 was evidently written *currente calamo* and not a word of it was ever retouched. Of the two other stanzas, all but three lines of the second were revised and all but two of the third; but when Housman laid down his pencil on this notebook page he had brought the poem to the status of printer's copy except for the difference of one word and a resolution of one open alternative. The draft shows no trace of the title beneath which the poem was inscribed on the sheet of final copy.

In writing this poem Housman was describing a place he had never seen, a church in a tiny Shropshire village he looked down upon from Wenlock Edge two years later, several months after the publication of his book. Then he discovered, as others had, that a number of details in his lyric did not fit the scene. He confessed in a letter to Laurence that the place that was actually in his mind had an unpleasing name and, further, he did not "apprehend that the faithful would be making pilgrimages to these holy places." (*Recollections,* pp. 82, 165.)

ASL 61 "Hughley Steeple"
Unique Draft

A 193, complete
Pencil

Date: Between August and
December, 1894

The vane on Hughley S[1] steeple
    Veers bright, a far-known sign,
And there lie Hughley people,
    And there lie friends of mine.
Tall in their midst the tower
    Divides the shade and sun,
And the clock strikes the hour
    And tells the time to none.

To south the headstones cluster,
           lie
    The sunny mounds stand[2] thick;
The dead at Hughley muster[3]   The dead are more in muster
    Much [denser ?] than the quick.   At Hughley than the quick.
      North, for a soon-told number,
        Their
   Dark Few[4] graves the sexton delves,
         -shadowed
And steeple-shaded[5] slumber
    The slayers of themselves.

          lie
   To   to   sleep
So, north and south, lie parted,[6]
    With Hughley tower above,
        single-[7]
The kind, the constant-hearted,
    The lads I used to love.

---

[1] Canc. this initial.   [2] Canc. *stand*.   [3] Canc. this line and the one following.
[4] Canc. *Few* and *Their*.   [5] Canc. *-shaded*.
  [6] The line began originally *So, north and south*. . . . When *So,* . . . *and* was replaced by *To* . . . *to,* a comma was inserted after *north*. A.E.H. deleted *lie* in favor of *sleep,* which in turn gave way to *lie*.
  [7] Canc. *constant-*.

ne'er
scarce
'Twill not be lonesome, truly,[8]
sleep with friends
To lie by lads one knows,
tower
When underground at Hughley
rest   by
I sleep with these or those.

south or north
And, north or south,[9] 'tis only

A choice of friends one knows,

And I shall ne'er be lonely

Asleep with
At rest by these or those

[8] This line and the three following he deleted, together with some of the alts.; one or two of these escaped the cancel-stroke, perhaps by chance, and as many more seem to have been obliterated by a later hand.

[9] Canc. *north or south.*

62

"TERENCE, this is stupid stuff:
You eat your victuals fast enough;
There can't be much amiss, 'tis clear,
To see the rate you drink your beer.
But oh, good Lord, the verse you make,
It gives a chap the belly-ache.
The cow, the old cow, she is dead;
It sleeps well, the horned head:
We poor lads, 'tis our turn now
To hear such tunes as killed the cow.
Pretty friendship 'tis to rhyme
Your friends to death before their time
Moping melancholy mad:
Come, pipe a tune to dance to, lad."

Why, if 'tis dancing you would be,
There's brisker pipes than poetry.
Say, for what were hop-yards meant,
Or why was Burton built on Trent?
Oh many a peer of England brews
Livelier liquor than the Muse,
And malt does more than Milton can
To justify God's ways to man.
Ale, man, ale's the stuff to drink
For fellows whom it hurts to think:
Look into the pewter pot
To see the world as the world's not.
And faith, 'tis pleasant till 'tis past:
The mischief is that 'twill not last.
Oh I have been to Ludlow fair
And left my necktie God knows where,
And carried half-way home, or near,
Pints and quarts of Ludlow beer:
Then the world seemed none so bad,
And I myself a sterling lad;
And down in lovely muck I've lain,
Happy till I woke again.
Then I saw the morning sky:
Heigho, the tale was all a lie;
The world, it was the old world yet,
I was I, my things were wet,

And nothing now remained to do
But begin the game anew.

Therefore, since the world has still
Much good, but much less good than ill,
And while the sun and moon endure
Luck's a chance, but trouble's sure,
I'd face it as a wise man would,
And train for ill and not for good.
'Tis true, the stuff I bring for sale
Is not so brisk a brew as ale:
Out of a stem that scored the hand
I wrung it in a weary land.
But take it: if the smack is sour,
The better for the embittered hour;
It should do good to heart and head
When your soul is in my soul's stead;
And I will friend you, if I may,
In the dark and cloudy day.

There was a king reigned in the East:
There, when kings will sit to feast,
They get their fill before they think
With poisoned meat and poisoned drink.
He gathered all that springs to birth
From the many-venomed earth;
First a little, thence to more,
He sampled all her killing store;
And easy, smiling, seasoned sound,
Sate the king when healths went round.
They put arsenic in his meat
And stared aghast to watch him eat;
They poured strychnine in his cup
And shook to see him drink it up:
They shook, they stared as white's their shirt:
Them it was their poison hurt.
—I tell the tale that I heard told.
Mithridates, he died old.

ASL 62 "Terence, this is stupid stuff"

Two entries: [A 187-89]; B 84-87.

Laurence's Analysis describes the contents of A 187-89 as "An unfinished poem, fragments, and a few couplets from 'Terence, this is stupid stuff.' " The sheet containing A 189-90 he destroyed, and of A 187-88 only the upper halves remain; they contain nothing of *ASL* 62.

Of the second entry, only one page, B 84, has survived uncut. In the Library of Congress collection the lower inch of it is covered by a slip cut from B 85 but the covered portion is blank. This page contains lines 28 to 42, and lines 47 and 48. The contents of the fragments may be catalogued as follows:

B 85 (three pieces). 1. An abandoned line and lines 57, 58, and 56. 2. Lines 55, 56, 43, 44, and an abandoned line. 3. Three abandoned lines, 55 to 58, and 51 and 52.

B 86 (three pieces). 1. Lines 59 to 62. 2. Lines 63 to 66. 3. Lines 67 to 76. The final stanza was completed on this page.

B 87 (two pieces). 1. Lines 5 and 6, 13 to 18, 1 and 2, and 7 and 8. 2. Lines 19 to 22, and 49 to 54.

In sum, the intact page B 84 and the five fragments of the two following sheets preserve sixty-three lines of the poem; thirteen—all but two of these from the first two stanzas—have been lost with the excisions of B 85-87.

It is significant to note that in the lines that remain only a half dozen appear twice. This would lead to the conclusion that in these four pages Housman was not dealing with two different drafts. It also seems clear, since B 84 opens with line 28 and runs on with a sequence, very lightly corrected, of the next thirteen lines of the poem, that he was revising a copy of an early draft not preserved in his notebooks. Having completed his revision of the second stanza on B 84, he took up again his third on B 85, the fourth on B 86; and on B 87 he went back to the beginning of his poem, mending couplets of stanzas 1 and 2 and rewriting (or composing) three couplets of the third stanza.

The diplomatic reprints of this material will indicate that the poem Housman left on B 84-87 must have undergone much more revision before printer's copy was written—revision worked out in a draft not contained in Notebook B. Though long passages of the holograph have the look of completeness, being written without gaps, many familiar lines are missing, and often those in the manuscript vary from the reading in the text.

ASL 62 "Terence, this is stupid stuff"
Unique Draft

B 84, complete   Date: September or
Pencil   October, 1895

      misery
   The mischief is that 'twill not last.
   Oh I have been to Ludlow fair,
   And left my necktie God knows where,
   And carried halfway home, or near,
   Pints and quarts of Ludlow beer:
   Then the world seemed none so bad
         sterling
   And I myself a decent[1] lad;
   And down in lovely muck I've lain
   And liked it till I woke again.
   Then I saw the morning sky:
   Heigho, the tale was all a lie,
         more was
   And there was[2] nothing left to do
   But begin the game anew.[3]
     The world, it was the old world yet,
     I was I, my things were wet,
   I'd take it as a wise man would;
   Dress for ill and not for good.

---

[1] Canc. *decent.* [2] Canc. *there was; more was* above a caret.
[3] This couplet was faced with a transfer-line and led down to follow the couplet
below it.

ASL 62 "Terence, this is stupid stuff"
Unique Draft continued

B 85, nearly complete
Pencil

[*Piece 1*]

When
Against you stand where I have stood;
And I will friend you, if I may,
In the dark and cloudy day.
    When your soul is in my soul's stead[1]

[*Piece 2*]

        may
This will[2] be good for heart and head
When your soul is in my soul's stead;
    Well, then   earth
    Therefore, since the world has still[3]
Much good, but much less good than ill,
And heaven and earth, as all can see,

---

[1] Canc. this line and one just below, cut through. Between them show some traces of erased writing.

[2] Canc. *will*.

[3] A.E.H. drew a curved stroke out from the first letter of this line to *Much*, in the next, making equal the margins of the two lines.

[*Piece 3*]

How well his vaccination took,—[4]
I think   bits of rime [?]
So these [?   ] that I glean[5]
         should[6]
If you come where I have been,   Against you come where I
    do   some to   have been[7]
May be[8] good for heart and head
When your soul is in my soul's stead;
And I will friend you, if I may,
In the dark and cloudy day.
                              scored
And from a stalk that scratched[9] the hand
I wrung it in a weary land.

---

[4] The excised lines just above this piece, introducing the idea of vaccination, led on to the allusion to Mithridates and the substance of the last stanza of the poem.

[5] After deleting *So* and *that* and the last word in the brackets, and choosing *I think* to open the line, A.E.H. threw an enclosure about it and its alts. and drew it down to follow the line below. The passage was intended to read thus:

> *If you should come where I have been,*
> *I think these bits of rime*[?] *I glean*
> *May do some good to heart and head....*

[6] The alt. *should* was set over a caret.

[7] This line is also an alt. to the line shown at the top of piece 1.

[8] A.E.H. lined out *be* and wrote *do some* above a caret; canc. *for*.

[9] Canc. *scratched*.

ASL 62 "Terence, this is stupid stuff"
Unique Draft continued

B 86, nearly complete

[Piece 1]

There was a king reigned in the east:
    That feared   I hear
There, when kings will sit to feast,[1]
They get their fill before they think
I hear,[2] With poison in their meat and drink
[?]

[Piece 2]

He gathered all that springs to birth[3]
       venomed
From the many-poisoned earth;
First a little, so to more,

                    her
He tasted all that Asia bore[4] the killing store
                              she ever bore;

[1] After writing the line as shown, A.E.H. superscribed the alt. opening *That feared*. He must have rejected at once the closer connection this change made with the preceding line for he made no move to strike out the colon after *east*. Instead he wrote *I hear,* encircled it and drew it back to follow *There,* and lined out *sit to*. This left the reading *There, I hear, when kings will feast.* This did not please; he deleted *I hear* and restored *sit to* with a wavy underscore—leaving the line as he had first written it. *That feared* had also been lined out.

[2] Canc. *I hear* and the other now illegible alt., below. The full line is an alt. to another, cut through at the bottom of this piece.

[3] Remains of a cut-through line show on the margin above.

[4] Canc. *that Asia bore* and *she ever bore;* also *the,* above.

[*Piece 3*]

Easy, smiling,[5] seasoned sound,
            healths
Sat the king when wine[6] went round.
 His   foes They
They[7] put arsenic in his meat
And stared aghast to watch him eat;
      poured
They put[8] strychnine in his cup
And shook to see him drink it up;
They shook, they stared as white's their shirt;
Them it was their[9] poison hurt.
—[10]I tell the tale that I heard told.
Mithradates,[11] he died old.

---

[5] Canc. *Easy, smiling.* Traces of an alt. for *smiling* show near the margin.
[6] Canc. *wine.*   [7] Canc. *They* and *His foes.*   [8] Canc. *put.*
[9] First-written *the* was extended to *their.*
[10] The dash, an afterthought, was correctly aligned in printer's copy.
[11] In printer's copy this word was spelled *Mithridates;* so in the text.

ASL 62 "Terence, this is stupid stuff"
Unique Draft continued

B 87, nearly complete
Pencil

[*Piece 1*]

[   ] the pains you poets take   But meant 'twas not, and no
                                                          mistake
To give a chap the belly-ache.   To give your friends the
                                                    belly-ache
To drive one melancholy mad;   And drive them melancholy mad,
Do pipe a tune to dance to, lad.'   Pipe a tune to dance to, lad.

Oh if 'tis dancing you would be
   There's brisker pipes than
You need not wait for poetry.[1]
   Lad   poles
My man Say,[2] for what were hopyards meant,
   And why was Burton built on Trent?
Oh, Terence, this is stupid stuff:
You eat your victuals fast enough
   The cow, the old cow, she is dead;
   It sleeps well the horned head[3]

[*Piece 2*]

Oh many a peer of England brews
A livelier liquor than the Muse,
And malt does more than Milton can
To justify God's ways to man.
   'Tis true, the stuff I bring for sale
   Is not so brisk a brew as ale:
   Out of a stalk that scored the hand
   I wrung it in a weary land.
   But take it: if the taste is sour,
   I think that in[4] The better for the embittered hour?

---

[1] Canc. all of this line but *poetry*.

[2] Canc. *Say* and *My man;* also *yards.*

[3] The scissors-cut trimmed this line, removing probably a comma after *well* and a colon at the end. It is probable that some lines from stanzas 1 and 2 now missing from the manuscript were lost with the excised section of this page.

[4] Canc. *I think that in.*

63

I HOED and trenched and weeded,
    And took the flowers to fair:
I brought them home unheeded;
    The hue was not the wear.

So up and down I sow them
    For lads like me to find,
When I shall lie below them,
    A dead man out of mind.

Some seed the birds devour,
    And some the season mars,
But here and there will flower
    The solitary stars,

And fields will yearly bear them
    As light-leaved spring comes on,
And luckless lads will wear them
    When I am dead and gone.

ASL 63 "I hoed and trenched and weeded"

The Library of Congress collection does not contain a manuscript of this poem, and it is Laurence's opinion (*Recollections*, p. 255) that it may have perished with a page torn from the notebooks. He surmises further that his brother destroyed the draft to prevent the solution of the conundrum he set his hearers at the Leslie Stephen lecture, May 9, 1933.

Having mentioned the two stanzas first set down, Housman spoke of the one that came with "a little coaxing" and another that took more than a year in the making. He added, "I do not say which" and it was this tantalizing challenge that set off—as he probably intended—a widening ripple of speculation as to the order in which the four quatrains of the lyric had actually been put down on paper. It was one of his dearest prerogatives to foil inquiry when it pleased him to do so, and it pleased him in this case to turn a stony ear to all who asked him if their guesses were correct. It would have been thoroughly characteristic of him to put solution forever out of reach by destroying the relevant notebook material.[1]

---

[1] In the *London Times* for Nov. 4, 1936, p. 10, Archibald Y. Campbell ("Housman's Poser") makes the suggestion that stanzas 1 and 2 were done on the walk, the fourth came with tea and coaxing, and 3 was the difficult one. Laurence Housman, in the Nov. 9, 1936, number of the *Times,* under the same heading, p. 13, agrees with Campbell; and, according to Maude M. Hawkins—*A. E. Housman: Man Behind a Mask* (Chicago: Regnery, 1958), p. 279—twenty years later Laurence confirmed to her his earlier opinion. No one knows: A.E.H., like his youthful athlete, has taken this small trophy safely with him beyond the low lintel.

Selected Bibliography

The manuscript sources used in the preparation of this variorum are the following:

Housman, Alfred Edward. Manuscript Poems (MSS in the Library of Congress, Washington, D.C.). 8 vols.
———. Printer's copy of *A Shropshire Lad* (MS in the library of Trinity College, Cambridge, England).

The principal published sources include:

Gow, A. S. F. *A. E. Housman, A Sketch.* Cambridge: at the University Press, 1933. Personalia by a colleague of Trinity College, Cambridge.

Haber, Tom Burns (ed.). *The Complete Poems of A. E. Housman.* Introduction by Basil Davenport. (Centennial edition.) New York: Holt, 1959. The author published the first two sections: *A Shropshire Lad* (*ASL*) in 1896; *Last Poems* (*LP*) in 1922. *More Poems* (*MP*), edited by Laurence Housman, appeared in 1936. Eighteen pieces of the twenty-three *Additional Poems* (*AP*), first added to the *Collected Poems* in 1939, were originally published in Laurence Housman's *My Brother, A. E. Housman.*

———(ed.). *The Manuscript Poems of A. E. Housman.* Minneapolis: University of Minnesota Press, 1955. Eight hundred lines of hitherto uncollected verse.

Housman, A. E. *The Name and Nature of Poetry.* Cambridge: at the University Press, 1933. The Leslie Stephen lecture, delivered at Cambridge May 9, 1933.

Housman, Laurence. *My Brother, A. E. Housman: Personal Recollections together with Thirty Hitherto Unpublished Poems.* New York: Scribner's, 1938. Also includes several letters and an Analysis of the notebooks. (Abbreviated *Recollections.*)

Richards, Grant. *Housman: 1897-1936*. New York: Oxford University Press, 1942. Records in detail Housman's relations with his publisher; valuable also for its letters and appendices. (Abbreviated *Memoir*.)

[Wallace-Hadrill, F. (ed.).] *Alfred Edward Housman, Recollections by Katharine E. Symons* [and Others]. New York: Holt, 1937.

Watson, George L. *A. E. Housman: A Divided Life*. London: Rupert Hart-Davis, 1957. The best critical biography.

Withers, Percy. *A Buried Life, Personal Recollections of A. E. Housman*. London: Cape, 1940. Close-range observations over the last twenty years of Housman's life.